Additional Praise for
The Family Council Handbook

"Thanks to the principles outlined in McClure and Eckrich's *The Family Council Handbook*, our family business has smoothly transitioned from an entrepreneurial company built by two brothers to a third-generation global leader in the wine industry. We raise a glass of wine in honor of their guidance and wisdom. Salute!"

—James Mariani and Cristina Mariani-May,
co-CEOs, Banfi Vintners

"*The Family Council Handbook* persuasively sets out the benefits to be gained when family and business are brought together in a well-managed structure. Business families will recognize themselves in the examples and case studies, and will find this detailed, practical, step-by-step guide indispensable in achieving the optimal outcome: maximizing business gains while building family strength and harmony."

—Marcia Sauder, chair, Sauder Family Council

"A good step to achieve success in your family business and family council is to have this book on your night stand."

—Cristina Porres, chair, Grupo
Porres Family Council

The Family Council Handbook

A FAMILY
BUSINESS
PUBLICATION

Family Business Publications are the combined efforts of the Family Business Consulting Group and Palgrave Macmillan. These books provide useful information on a broad range of topics that concern the family business enterprise, including succession planning, communication, strategy and growth, family leadership, and more. The books are written by experts with combined experiences of over a century in the field of family enterprise and who have consulted with thousands of enterprising families the world over, giving the reader practical, effective, and time-tested insights to everyone involved in a family business.

The Family Business Consulting Group, Inc., founded in 1994, is the leading business consultancy exclusively devoted to helping family enterprises prosper across generations.

The Family Council Handbook

How to Create, Run, and Maintain a Successful Family Business Council

Christopher J. Eckrich and
Stephen L. McClure

THE FAMILY COUNCIL HANDBOOK
Copyright © Christopher J. Eckrich and Stephen L. McClure, 2012.

All rights reserved.

First published in 2012 by
PALGRAVE MACMILLAN®
in the United States—a division of St. Martin's Press LLC,
175 Fifth Avenue, New York, NY 10010.

Where this book is distributed in the UK, Europe and the rest of the world,
this is by Palgrave Macmillan, a division of Macmillan Publishers Limited,
registered in England, company number 785998, of Houndmills,
Basingstoke, Hampshire RG21 6XS.

Palgrave Macmillan is the global academic imprint of the above companies
and has companies and representatives throughout the world.

Palgrave® and Macmillan® are registered trademarks in the United States,
the United Kingdom, Europe and other countries.

ISBN: 978–0–230–11219–3

Library of Congress Cataloging-in-Publication Data is available from the
Library of Congress.

A catalogue record of the book is available from the British Library.

Design by Newgen Imaging Systems (P) Ltd., Chennai, India.

First edition: June 2012

10 9 8 7 6 5 4 3 2 1

This book is dedicated to the thousands of business owners who have worked with us, the Family Business Consulting Group, Inc. We thank you for believing in an enterprising family life, your courage to try new things and overcome challenges, and your passion to become better versions of yourselves. You have taught us much about what it means to believe in the power of an enterprising family and the power of family itself.

Contents

Figures

Preface

This handbook is an owner's manual for family councils. It is meant to be used as a reference by business families wanting to find the answer to a specific question about how to start and maintain a family council or how to enhance the performance of an existing one. Strong family councils engage the entire family, allow important voices to be heard, contribute to family unity, increase effective family communication, and concentrate the influence of a family on its enterprise. We have been honored to witness these results in many business families.

We have been fortunate to consult with diverse business families and their family councils, including entrepreneurial founders and their children as well as multinational family enterprises owned by active and engaged cousins. Furthermore, we are surrounded with dedicated colleagues whose natural curiosity and desire to serve their clients produces a continuous flow of new ideas and practical solutions for family governance. The members of the Family Business Consulting Group have been learning from our experience, collaborating with one another, and have catalogued tools and resources for this book for fifteen years. This is our attempt to make all this information available to business families.

The book contains examples, guides, and tools to be applied when they fit. There is no one best way that works for all. We believe that while there are common structures and tools to organize families, the individual values, beliefs, skills, cultures, and experiences of a family will determine what works best for that family. Many of the ideas, structural guidelines, and practical tools presented are the ones we have used and adapted to help business families reach the next step in their development. It is our sincere hope that many more families will benefit by finding what they need in these pages to better organize themselves and more effectively work together as a business family.

Acknowledgments

We wish to thank several people for their contributions to this work. First and foremost, we thank family business consulting field pioneers Craig E. Aronoff and John L. Ward for their tremendous influence on us as friends, mentors, teachers, leaders, and partners. We also wish to thank the Family Business Consulting Group consultants who have helped us develop and hone our thinking through years of sharing information, tools, case conceptualizations, and challenging philosophical discussions in our regular meetings, shared consulting engagements, and countless phone calls.

We are grateful for the initial work of Jane Aronoff, who helped us organize our initial thoughts, and for the work of our excellent staff at FBCG. We thank Drew Mendoza and Carol Ryan for developing the relationship with Palgrave and for expecting much from us, Ken Bosshart for encouraging us to stay on track and for finding information no matter how obscure the request, Paige Gomez for helping us free up writing time by assisting us with other professional obligations, and Janna Renner for her help in scheduling, getting us needed information and for the artwork.

We are forever indebted to our clients, who have taught us much about how to best meet their families' needs and have exposed us to new ways of thinking about the celebration and management of family enterprising activities. Much of what we have learned, we have learned in the field by collaborating with our clients as they explored and discovered a better way to do things.

Some of what we present in this book is field knowledge, accumulated over time in small bits and pieces. We heartily thank all those who have dedicated their research and their work to helping families work and function more effectively. Your work has inspired us.

A special thank you to Laurie Harting of Palgrave, who kept us moving when our schedules were full of writing distractions and gave us valuable input on how to write a more useful field manual.

We also thank our families: Chris's wife Carol Ann and his children—Andrew, Karen, and Julia—who endured his absence during the writing process. Steve is forever grateful to his parents, Norma and Charles, who taught him that if you want to know about something, read a book. We hope that some of what our readers want to know is in this one.

I

Family Organization and Governance for Sustaining the Family Business: A Field Manual

"It was decided that a family council will be established for the purpose of conducting regular family business meetings. The family council will involve all family members above the age of 15. The purpose of
family council meetings will be to educate and facilitate communication between family members and to provide a forum for constructive
discussion, problem solving and decisions about the family as it relates
to Sullivan Industrial Products as well as the business as it relates to
the family. The forum is being established now as it will be vital to our
preparation and implementation of the handoff of the business from the
brothers' generation to their children, the cousins. We will refer to these
meetings as the Sullivan Family Council, and it will meet quarterly;
each meeting will begin promptly at 2:00 p.m. on the third Thursday of
the month that begins a new quarter. The meetings will end promptly
at 5:00 p.m., unless it is agreed to extend them to finish discussing an
agenda item. Each meeting will be followed by dinner or some other
family event that will allow us to have fun together. The family council and dinner host duties will rotate among adult members, as will the
various jobs/roles needed to run the meetings efficiently and effectively.
The family council will follow an agenda, to which each family member
may contribute in advance; a final version of this agenda will be distributed to each participant at least one week prior to the meeting. Meeting
notes will be recorded and provided to all."[1]

Why Have a Family Council?

A family business is different from other businesses. Businesses controlled by stockholders not related to one another do not have the relationship advantages available to a family business. That is why public companies around the world are trying to create what family businesses already have, namely, a strong sense of commitment that comes from genuinely caring about each other, about customers, and about what the business is doing. Public companies recognize their problems:

- Most major capital decisions in a business are based on or heavily influenced by the impact they will have on shareholders' quarterly returns.
- The company's values change as the senior management team changes.
- Service quality and employee loyalty are inconsistent, depending mainly on the strength of programs and policies, rather than coming from genuine mutual respect and relationships between the owners and the employees of a business.

With this in mind, there are four reasons why family businesses should utilize a family council to take advantage of their unique opportunities.

Maximizing natural advantages. Family businesses can and already do a better job than publicly owned corporations do. Their greatest advantage is that they are family owned. Families usually already have the following values: integrity, concern about their image and their community, caring about their employees, willingness to delay gratification for the sake of long-term returns, concern about opportunities for their children, responsiveness to others' needs, and commitment to keeping their promises. These kinds of values are what the management consultants and senior managers in publicly owned companies have been trying hard to produce with reengineering, team concepts, customer-driven ideologies, continuous improvement, total quality management, leadership training, incentive programs, and the program du jour. While families that control businesses have natural advantages, they must use tools that help them capitalize on their advantages, and a family council is an excellent choice for doing that.

Overcoming challenges. While families in business easily produce results that other businesses can only reach with great effort, conducting business with family members also creates unique complexities. For example, family members in a business may be uncle and nephew and also business owner and employee. They may be father and daughter and also chairman and treasurer. They are brothers and also president and head of sales. They are mother and son and also employed shareholder and uninvolved shareholder. They are cousins and also accounting manager and general manager, and so on. As a result of living in the same family while also being business partners and coworkers, they face unique issues that are irrelevant to shareholders in public companies who do not have pictures of each other in their homes and do not share holiday dinners.

Role and emotional conflicts can quickly deteriorate the advantages available to a family business. In fact, the presence of family members in a business has the potential of being not only destructive to the business but often also to family relationships. The complexities of being a family can add conflict to the pressures that a business normally provides. A family council can proactively address these issues and can keep them from harming both the family and the business.

Utilizing evolution. Often in the second generation of a growing family and family firm, the main players in the business start to feel overwhelmed by increasing demands. The emerging input of multiple shareholders must be taken into account as the maturing next generation begins asking about career opportunities and learning about their role as shareholders; these questions can be particularly urgent during estate plan discussions. A business family might hold on tightly to centralized control of decisions (the few who run the company), or its members might see the need to involve others and make a transition to a democratic system for some issues. Often this transition is facilitated when a family employment policy is formed, and those in the business realize that their spouses have some very definite and sometimes contrary opinions about the way in which their children should be treated by the business. Furthermore, the family as a whole may realize that the business family issues are bigger (e.g., coordination of estate plans to ensure that the future ownership supports business, tax, and family relationship goals) than the scope of the business leaders' perspectives and priorities. Tensions such as these are lessened when the family comes to the conclusion that another forum (a family council) will allow for more voices to be heard, elicit greater involvement in critical issues, and ensure decisions that are not resisted by the board of directors or family members active in the business. With a family council, development and change in the business can be embraced as a means to future prosperity.

Creating solutions. Thus, family businesses must find ways to deal productively with the conflicts and demands of growth or to avoid them through planning and education. Only then will they enjoy the benefit of a family fully aligned with the business. Unfortunately, business and family experience alone offers little help in dealing with family business conflicts or maintaining an aligned group of shareholders. Something new is needed, and the family council is a structure designed for just this purpose. In order to keep the "family owned" advantage from becoming a competitive liability, structured family business meetings are essential. The most successful family businesses use them. In a study of 614 family businesses, Astrachan and Kolenko[2] found a positive relationship between the existence of regular family business meetings and survival of the business over several generations. After a few generations, most business families come to the same conclusion: we must organize ourselves as a family, organize education, communication, and ultimately manage ourselves as a unified voice of influence where the business is concerned.

Regular family council meetings, when used effectively, can help avoid many of the conflicts that frequently plague family enterprises. Families using a family business meeting to establish a policy for the sustained employment of family members will be better able to avoid dividing the family over the departure of an underperforming member. By setting expectations early for what it takes to be an employee, a family business can avoid making a hiring mistake with a family member. By establishing ownership rules early, future conflicts over control of the business during succession can be minimized. Through the skills that are built among family members who repeatedly meet to discuss family and business issues, conflicts will be resolved and emotions defused before they become destructive forces.

A family council meeting is a forum for a civil discussion about some difficult issues. For example, it is a place for a levelheaded discussion with dad, who in the opinion of his children is not retiring soon enough;

it is a forum for educating and listening to the young adults who want to make sweeping changes in part to demonstrate that they "have arrived" as business managers who want to contribute to business formalization and growth. A family council is also a forum for a spouse to understand why her mate is working so often on Saturdays even though other employees who are not family members are not required to work extra hours. It is also a forum for setting the rules regarding future ownership to avoid having two cousins independently decide they want to will their substantial holdings to their children who have no knowledge of or interest in the business.

Family business meetings deal with the gray area where business, family, and ownership meet, where it is not clear whether an issue should be resolved by the family or the business but have a great impact on both. Such issues therefore really concern both business and family and are thus appropriate agenda items for family council meetings. Crucial for success is realizing when to stop dealing with an issue at the informal family level and move decision making to the more formal family council. For example, the film *Avalon*[3] tells the story of an immigrant Polish family who work together with business success and heartbreaking failure. The tensions between the generations as well as the conflict between those in the business and the extended family are depicted with great realism and reflect the experience of many business families. At one point in the film, during a time of escalating emotion at a family gathering, an older family member slams his clenched fist down and proclaims, "Family meeting!" The message is clear to all: their informal gathering will now be transformed into a more formal one. The declaration "Family meeting" implies that family members will now comply with rules regarding who can speak and what purpose is to be achieved. They understand that the outcome of their family circle will govern their behavior and that they must comply with the decisions arrived at. At some point, the business of the family transitioned from casual conversation to a higher level of discussion requiring a formal meeting with consensus rules.

The scenes from the Krichinsky family circle meetings in the film *Avalon* are chaotic with everyone talking over one another and with several conversations going on at the same time. While not about a family business, another feature film illustrates a second point: business families who meet must adopt a meeting style that will lead to success no matter how difficult the issue. In *Dancing with Wolves*[4] a meeting of members of the Sioux tribe takes place after the discovery of a white soldier who has settled on or near their land. The issue is whether to defend their people from a threat and kill the intruder or befriend him and learn about the potential greater threat represented by those that might follow him. The meeting is a governance function of the tribe, and several members express their different views. What is noteworthy about the meeting as depicted in the film is that before expressing his own opinions and counterarguments, each member eloquently acknowledges the significance and merit of what the other has just said. This is a terrific example of respectful listening because it confirms that what has been said by a member has been heard and understood by the others, including those with contrasting opinions. This part of the film is an excellent example of the optimal process for a group to come to a decision about what should guide actions regarding a very important issue. This attitude of respectful communication is an important part of every family council, accomplished by establishing effective forms of communication then believing in them and abiding by them.

Purpose of this Book

Families in business, nonfamily board members, and managers in the business as well as advisors will benefit from this field manual. It is our purpose to provide the answer to why, when, and how to introduce and use a family council. In addition, this book will serve as a reference manual for the many questions that might come up during the course of governing the business family. In this introduction, we use the term "family council" because that is a widely used term to describe a governance forum for the family to meet outside of a business or shareholder meeting. There are several different kinds of family councils, and a family council in one family may look very much like a family association in another. One business family's family meeting is another's family council. Another term we use is "family forum," which is a general term covering family meetings, councils, assemblies, and associations. Complete definitions can be found in appendix 1.

There are many kinds of families, businesses, and business families. We begin by covering the many ways in which families come to establish family councils and the many reasons why they are resisted. Next, we define different types of business families and the different family forums that apply. In chapter 3 we then provide a description of different kinds of business families, mostly by referring to their size and the particular generations involved, and we then explain the family governance structures that commonly apply.

The chapters in the middle of the book deal with starting a family council, how to continue it, and how to utilize and preserve family assemblies and family associations. These chapters provide numerous examples, and the appendices offer additional resources. Chapters on leadership variations, transitions, family communication, and the use of facilitators provide supporting information regarding effectiveness and continuity of governance structures. Finally, even while there are many different kinds of family governance configurations, we provide a blueprint of the connections between family councils and four other entities: management, the board, the family, and the owners.

This book is designed to provide a field manual that can be accessed at any point without having to read all chapters in sequence. Thus, some repetition of concepts or definitions is intentional so that a reader might easily find the relevant information and learn how to apply it. There are many tools, examples, and case illustrations provided as this is a field manual or reference guide. The names of individuals, families, and businesses in our case examples are entirely fictional, and the situations they refer to represent the amalgamation of many different business family situations. Our intent was to combine multiple situations within each case, thereby providing an example that might be instructive to many different business families.

Finally, we hope the reader will pay special attention to both the content of the examples as well as to the processes involved. Both are vital, and generally we do not assign greater importance to one over the other; rather, in our view there should always be a balance appropriate to the situation between *what* is dealt with (content) and *how* the content is addressed (steps, attitudes and environment). Business families' success has often been due to their ability to adapt. Our hope is that our readers will adapt the information and examples provided here in a way that serves their unique and very special business family.

2

Reasons for Starting or Resisting a Family Council

What motivates a business family to establish a family council? Is it because they have heard it was a good idea from another business family? Is it because a family member read a book or went to a seminar? Or is a family council started because it was recommended by a consultant or advisor? Family councils are usually started for any or all of these reasons, among others. When we begin working with a family, we are curious to learn why a family is receptive to implementing a family council. We also like to understand why families do not respond to our recommendation to start a family council. Over the years, we have kept track of the reasons why families are ready to jump in as well as the reasons for their resistance to family councils.

Ready to Jump in: Learning from the Previous Generation

For some families a family council is a way to avoid repeating a previous generation's mistakes. Sibling business owners may encourage their children to set up a family meeting forum so the third generation does not replicate the conflict and estrangement they experienced with their siblings' families. Business families are willing to do the work of building and maintaining a family council if they see it as a way of avoiding a problem they have experienced firsthand, not a theoretical problem. They see a family forum as a way to introduce the family to the challenges of the business, to learn as much as possible, and to agree to do things in a way that will avoid problems and even find solutions to problems that are only just beginning to surface.

One common scenario involves the previous generation's males getting opportunities to work in and become owners of the business while the women did not, and this often leads to resentment that extends to the children. Cousins who grew up together as friends are no longer on speaking terms because of an unresolved injustice between their parents. Families with such a history may then ask themselves whether they can provide opportunities to all family members in a fair way, maintain business performance standards, and remain a strong, cohesive family at the same time even though the previous generation was not able to do so. Since a family council has a mandate to find a way to satisfy these competing demands, families in this situation are likely to be very interested in establishing one.

Ready to Jump in: Someone in the Family Read a Book

A family member may have been reading a book or attending a seminar or may belong to a forum (e.g., Young Presidents Organization, Vistage, etc.) and so have heard about family councils and then persuade the rest of the family to try it. When one family member is convinced of the necessity of being careful architects of the future, he or she can influence the others to pursue a specific course of action, such as establishing a family council. The process can begin with a consultant, an invitation to attend a seminar together, or family members can share an article or book or meet with another business family that has already set up a family council. In any case, sooner or later, a large enough number of family members will agree—we need to set up family governance.

Family business seminars, books, and articles that discuss family councils are consistently building awareness. Seminars, institutes, trade groups, and associations are creating interaction among business families to help them learn about the value of family governance. While listening to others talk about their family councils, an individual may realize, "In our family business, we discuss family roles only with those members working in the business while the spouses create conflicting agendas in the background. But if we get a family council going, we can address family roles more effectively." As experienced speakers, we have known for several years that the biggest value of a well-orchestrated event is not the speaker but the opportunity for participant interaction. This interaction might come at just the right time, such as when informed shareholder investment direction is needed for the business, and a CEO hears about family councils and family associations and realizes how these structures can be utilized to organize the business education of a large family.

Focus Turns from Business Success to Legacy

Many business people in their forties are running at full speed in their careers. In their fifties they are getting good at what they do, and in their sixties they are still very good at what they do but often feel that something is amiss. Whether it is a crisis of identity, a realization that the legacy needs attention, a brush with a serious health threat, a search for meaning or a second adulthood, as defined by Gail Sheehy, we see a pattern among many family business leaders in their late fifties and sixties.[1] Several find that they have accomplished many of their goals for the business, but when considering its future in the hands of the younger generation, they may think, "Our kids are no closer to take on ownership of our business than they were ten years ago!" So at a time when they are experiencing some ambiguity about their own role and purpose, some will focus on preparing the next generation. They go from "I've got to make this business the best I can" to "I've got to set the stage for the next generation's success."

While the process of handing off to the next generation involves much more than starting a family council, families in this position quickly realize that a forum is needed. Thus, assembling the family group and exploring a vision of the future is a useful activity for a family council and especially helpful for a leader who needs to adjust his or her purpose.

Tough Issues are Resolved Proactively

Family firm histories often mention a family member in the second generation quitting the business out of frustration with the founder. The result is emotional pain and often also limited access to grandchildren and avoidance of traditional holiday celebrations with the whole family. In our experience, after a period of separation cooler heads often prevail and pave the way for the angry son or daughter to return to work by promising changes. The crisis is resolved in time largely due to the deep desire for peace in the family. While there may be emotional scars, the family at least has avoided the tragedy of continued separation. Such a scenario typically makes a family realize the need for deliberate and open discussion. In many cases, the next step is to establish a family council.

Shocking resignations by key executives have also served to establish family councils. For example, not long ago a senior shareholder in control of a quarter of the shares of a distribution company lobbied the non-family CEO to make his son the next leader of the sales group. The young man's aunt, also a significant shareholder, found out about this and set up her own meeting with the CEO. In a very businesslike way, she reviewed the needs of the company and the requirements for the leader of the sales group, pointing out that her nephew was not qualified. She further pointed out that her nephew had been the subject of substance abuse rumors. The CEO saw this episode as one more instance of being caught in the middle and responded by resigning. The family was surprised and shocked, and especially family members not directly involved in the discussions were caught off guard without a qualified successor. The heads of the four branches met to consider what to do. They agreed that their best option was to convince the CEO to reverse his decision. They succeeded, but he negotiated higher compensation, and they also had to concede to his demand for an employment contract.

Once the group had averted the crisis, the CEO persuaded the heads of the family branches to meet with a consultant to conduct a postmortem on the episode. The family now has an active and productive family council. One of its first priorities was to produce rules for employment decisions affecting family members in the business and to make transparency and objectivity key elements of their process in drawing up and implementing a policy.

After a crisis, business families feel much like a person after a health wake-up call. Having dodged a bullet, so to speak, they are ready to make significant behavior changes and adjust their priorities quickly. Savvy business families are more ready to use preventative or proactive measures to avoid another crisis. A family council is a natural forum for open communication, for finding alternatives to radical or punishing actions, and for avoiding a destructive conflict altogether. Immediately after a crisis, a family is much more ready to seriously consider and commit to the effort needed to establish an effective family council.

Why Families Resist: Justifiable Resistance

Resistance to establishing a family council occurs for several reasons, among them some very good ones. It could be the wrong time or the wrong solution for a particular family to set up a family council. Not all business families need family councils at any particular time; they may need something else first. For example, issues such as a business leader's addiction or continuing resentment about an injustice of the previous generation and the accompanying emotional fallout can be handled only by the most effective, long-standing family councils. We don't recommend starting one to deal with such large-scale issues. In such cases, there is a bigger, more immediate issue that must be addressed first before a family can even think about a governance structure such as a family council.

Another justifiable reason for resistance is when a family needs a product now that would normally take a new family council six months to produce. We may think about this as, "We need a race car now, but the engineers are just starting to assemble the design." For example, a family council is a great forum to create a family employment policy, but starting a family council to create the policy in order to deal with a current family member's request for a job is too much. In such an instance it is better to deal with the request, hopefully in a manner that responds to the best advice the family can find from a source familiar with good family employment practices. The family council can then be started without the pressure of having to produce immediate results.

Other sources of resistance can be classified as objections that can be overcome. We will look at these next.

Objections to Overcome: This is a Business!

This objection to forming a family council is based on the view that the business is most important, that shareholders should act just like those holding public company equity, and that family employees are employees. Those who hold this view may prefer to see the family business as a private company rather than as a family business. A common profile is that males are involved in the business and females are not, and the women (and in-laws) are comparatively passive where business decisions are concerned and even regarding family matters that play out in the business. This view may also be promoted by non-family managers, trusted advisors, and independent board members who think of their contribution and success in terms of business performance. Those with this attitude would consider it a distraction to use financial or human resources to conduct family meetings.

Overcoming this objection requires a convincing explanation of the value of a family council to the business. Ultimately, the objecting parties may have to decide that the family influences the business and that family is thus a legitimate concern of the family business. Those who have accepted the need for organized family governance have done so by recognizing the following values and beliefs:

- Avoiding or addressing conflict productively is less expensive than dealing with a full-fledged destructive conflict.
- Investing in the education of family members for their future role as a shareholder team has similar benefits for a business as investing in employee training.
- No matter how "business first" the family is, there are still family dynamics playing out in the day-to-day business operations for the resolution of which the business is not the best or most appropriate forum.
- Costs associated with family governance are similar to the costs public companies bear for shareholder relations.

Family members may not be fully convinced of a family council's value in advance, but they may agree to give it a try. That is enough to allow the most convincing argument to emerge: evidence produced from an effective family governance function.

Objection to Overcome: It will Become Family Court

The creation of a family council in a family where members criticize each other can appear very attractive to individuals who feel they are not heard, and it can seem very generous to those who feel they have been targets of criticism. For example, the business leader's performance may be under attack from his cousin shareholders who do not work in the business, or the founder may be criticized for not letting go, or several siblings may complain that their brother's compensation package is too rich. The accused parties do not want a forum that to them may look like family court where they become the defendant. They may feel that the forum is being created for the benefit of a single agitator and allows several voices to coalesce into a real threat. Many business families begin a family council with little clarity about its boundaries. This is understandable since the council exists to deal with the complexities and ambiguities of a business influencing a family and of a family influencing the business.

To overcome this objection, it is best to focus on the boundaries and to begin by engaging family members in creating their own charter. Through the process of designing how the family council will work and defining its mission, purpose, and ground rules, individuals who feel under attack can become more secure about conquering its potential for abuse. For those in the business who may see their relatives outside the business as noncontributors, a family council can provide a forum for educating the family about their investment, business strategy, or the need for shareholder alignment and support for competitive business positions. These family members could lobby for discussions and transparency concerning management succession plans. They could discuss compensation processes and how they result in fairness for the roles of family members in the business. For individuals who feel they have been inappropriately criticized by family outside the business who are unfamiliar with business practices, a family council can be seen as a classroom with a clear set of boundaries and a good set of rules and fair processes.

Objection to Overcome: Too Much Work

When a family is comfortable with effective management of the business, its members may be too complacent to put forth the energy to build the family council infrastructure. The profitability of the company may be significant and so are shareholder returns. When family members trust each other, they may question the need for a family council. In short, there is neither enough pressure nor a perception that problems may be on the horizon, and so the need for a family council seems doubtful.

These business families may not be sufficiently motivated to commit at this time to starting and maintaining an effective family council. Consultants and seminar speakers may give them the best reasons but with little result. However, to overcome this objection, one option is to conduct one meeting per year with an invited guest speaking on a relevant topic. This is only a stopgap measure, but it is movement in the right direction and a foundation from which the family can take more aggressive steps in the future. Other families have gone forward despite their contentment by encouraging the interested parties to begin setting up formal family governance. Several individuals may not opt in at the beginning; yet, with a permanently open invitation to participate, they may join in later. Sometimes the younger generation will be encouraged to begin without the participation of the more senior generation of family members. If they are given resources, such as travel cost reimbursements and a budget for an advisor and educational materials, they can make progress governing their own generation. Again, a small step is better than none at all.

Objection to Overcome: Overwhelming Tasks with Little Leadership or Capability

Resistance to starting a family council might come from a view that the job seems overwhelming, given that the family is so large or spread out geographically. With little experience or little success with past attempts, family members may accept that they need a governance structure but lack the confidence to set it up. Perhaps there are no candidates to take the leadership role. The family may be at a stage where the candidates for effective involvement are too busy with demanding careers, young families, or challenging roles in the business.

These are legitimate reasons for concern about the wisdom of starting a family council. Everyone deserves a reasonable expectation of success prior to beginning. Business families facing these challenges have used the following tactics to overcome them:

- Begin with the individuals who are available and willing and provide them with substantial resources, usually a consultant and/

or dedicated staff from the business. Board members can also be a resource and mentor new, inexperienced family council members.

- Some families unnecessarily limit themselves by assuming that only bloodline family members can provide leadership, and some family cultures are especially prone to this. However, when spouses have relevant skills, business families are wise to consider involving them and to ask capable spouses to provide leadership. This may also be true for the younger family members. Certainly, participation is an option, and the family might also benefit from the opportunity for family leaders to emerge from the younger generation.

- Family members who are in leadership roles in the business may need to step in and consider themselves responsible for the first phase of family governance development. With their organizational experience, skills, and the support of a business, they may be the best and only option if a family council is going to be established successfully.

When families can think of a family council as an evolving form that will grow from its initial start-up phase, they might find establishing one less overwhelming; for example, they could plan on a two-year process for setting it up. Expectations should not be overly ambitious, and success could be defined as "running a lap concluding with a handoff to the next runner." A business family would be indebted to those who step forward and provide the foundation.

Objection to Overcome: Politics

Providing a forum for an open discussion or establishing democracy in the family through a family council may threaten the position of some family members. That is, they are better served by the status quo remaining unchanged. For example, if the larger family is uninterested and uninvolved in the business, an individual who wants the business to be sold may not welcome a forum that might increase pride or enthusiasm for continued family ownership. Or an individual who is in a position to promote the career of his or her daughter or son in the business without scrutiny may be uninterested in an open forum and the associated transparency. As is the nature of politics, the reasons underlying this resistance may never be fully revealed. All of the objections listed above and others may be presented as a rationale for resistance, but the real reason may remain hidden. Thus, a convincing counterargument will likely be impossible.

If there is a faction of the family that wants a family council and is convinced of its value, the only way these family members can overcome the resistance of others might be to go forward without full support of the entire family. While this is not ideal, there are many cases where business families proceed to do what they think is right without involvement of those family members who do not want to participate. In time, some will come around and want to participate while others never do.

3

Stages of Family Businesses and Types of Family Councils

What is the Appropriate Forum for Your Family?

A business that was started twelve years ago by a thirty-eight-year-old entrepreneur with children who are now seventeen, thirteen, and ten does not need the same family business governance forum as a third-generation business family with thirty-five shareholders in two generations who do not work in the business. While the entrepreneur might use a family meeting to hold discussions about the parents' expectations of the children, the third-generation business family might discuss the issue of how the second generation will be asked to participate in teaching values and business history to the fourth-generation teenagers. Since business families vary greatly in size and configuration, we need a way of categorizing them. Family businesses are often classified as (1) first generation or founder firms, (2) sibling ownership or partnership, or (3) family dynasty or cousin consortium.[1] These classifications serve us well for identifying the predictable issues arising in each stage. Also, for a complete discussion of the challenges faced by founders, siblings and cousin transitions, please see the notes at the end of the book.[2]

For the purpose of providing guidelines for developing a first family council or further enhancing an existing one, we expand these business family categories to focus on the transitions between generations, that is, the generations who are working together and the tasks they must accomplish together. We describe five stages that correspond to the issues typically faced and the associated relevant forum(s). In the first

Table 3.1 Business family forums, associated issues and challenges and corresponding governance structures

Family Stage	Family Council Forum	Common Concerns and Issues	Meeting Features
Founder Founder Parents & Some College-Age Children	Kitchen Table	Founder parents ask themselves: Who should get the business? How do we support career development for the children? Will gifting to all children result in conflict? Do the children understand what is expected? G2 may not see the importance of a family meeting.	Family meetings are informal gatherings and few in number. Irregular meetings as needed; at least annually.
Late Founder Founder Parents & Young Adult Children	Dining Room	Realization that continuity is the goal and it requires preparation. What are the children's interests: employment, ownership? Sense of wealth on paper. G1 engaged in estate planning. How to be fair to the business and fair to the children.	Full family meets 3 to 4 times per year combining family and shareholder issues. Separate Shareholder meeting if G2 owns shares.
Early Sibling Founder Parents & Middle Aged Sibling Children with Young Adult/Adolescent G3s	Negotiating Table	Siblings (G2) experience tension with founder and between themselves. Founder role ambiguity – letting go/control tension with G2. Risk tolerance tension between G1 & G2. Felt pressure to start preparing G3. Some want spouses in the forum, others do not.	Family Council is all G1 & G2 adults. Separate sibling team meetings. Separate Shareholder Meeting. May be special forums for spouses and for G3's education.

Late Sibling Sibling Parents & G3 Sibling/Cousin Children	Harvest Table	G2 Siblings have control, yet may still have unresolved conflicts. G3 involved, yet unclear vision for their turn as stewards. Spouse role ambiguity – if involved, do they have a voice that counts? May be complexities of a divorce. Branch loyalty first, whole family second. Understanding trusts. Who is family?	Family Council of all adults or Representative Family Council + Family Assembly Meetings, and separate Shareholder meeting. Possibly an Owners Council.
Cousin G3 Sibling/Cousin Parents with G4 Sibling/Cousin Children	Round Table	G3 siblings and cousins control. Questions about preparing children for wealth. Geographically dispersed family with distant relationships – communication failures. Non-family business leader? Branch vs. one family may still challenge cohesion. Who is family? Multiple paradoxes.	Representative Family Council + Annual Family Assembly/Association Meetings + Annual Shareholder meetings.

stage, the founder stage, business families use a Kitchen Table forum for family and business communications with their young children, some of whom are becoming young adults. In the second stage, business families use a Dining Room forum; the additional formality of which underscores the importance of the communication, decision making, and education needed for seriously planning continuity. In the early and late sibling stages and, finally, the cousin stage, business families use forums respectively referred to as the Negotiating Table, the Harvest Table and the Round Table. Table 3.1 illustrates different business family characteristics of each stage, the related family concerns and issues that are appropriate for a family council, and the corresponding family governance structures.

Figure 3.1 represents common business family configurations and their related issues, yet there will be many families who find they share the characteristics of two or more stages and some who will not experience all of the issues and characteristics typically associated with their stage. That is, the table presented here is not perfect but is designed as a general guideline to help business families establish enough structure without doing too much. For example, families that look like they are in the Negotiating Table stage may not have second-generation siblings in the business and may not have decided that they will keep the business beyond the founder's career. Thus, their issues are more appropriately discussed in a Kitchen Table or Dining Room forum. Moreover, many business families may be in their third generation after the founder, which might normally mean they need a Round Table. Yet, they may be served better by a Dining Room or Negotiating Table forum if the business passed from founder to one child rather than to several siblings in the second generation.

Founder Stage: Kitchen Table

To understand the difference between family characteristics and related family council forums let's consider a single business family over a span of twenty-five years. At the founder stage (Kitchen Table), there are two forty-eight-year-old parents with two children; one of them is away at university, and the younger one is midway through high school. We can imagine informal meetings around the kitchen table, without agenda or notes, introduced simply as, "your mother and father have been think-ing about a couple of matters." The growth opportunities of the busi-ness and its need for investment may be discussed in relation to college tuition costs and the resulting need for the young family members to pay some of their college expenses themselves. Other matters may include

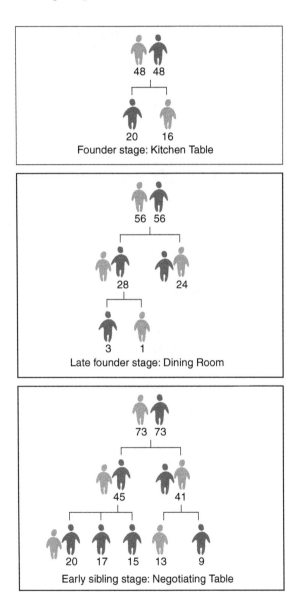

Figure 3.1 Stages of Family Councils

discussions about key trusted managers or advisors and their opinions about the business. Discussion may also turn to what the parents are learning about gifting ownership of their appreciating estates. In addition, the parents may discuss their views of their children's friends, individual plans for summer break, and how to get everyone to a cousin's upcoming wedding.

Families in this stage are owners of a successful private business and may not yet think of themselves as a family firm. The business is likely regarded more as the economic engine of the family and the founder's passion rather than as a family business. At this point, the founder may wonder whether the business will ultimately be sold or retained as a family asset, but the question may not yet be verbalized. Forward-looking founders may be interested in learning about others' experience, both positive and negative, if they choose to provide employment for their children (i.e., success factors for family employment). A founder of a successful business may initiate a kitchen-table discussion to ask his or her young adult children about their opinions regarding their own careers and to discuss the opinions of the parents.

Kitchen Table family meetings are typically infrequent and prescriptive, educational, or informational with a focus on expectations. The level of preparation and thoughtfulness varies, and they may labeled discussions in some families and family meetings in others. Some families may utilize impromptu meetings as needed and may also conduct an annual family meeting that includes an update on the business.

Late Founder Stage: Dining Room

Consider this family eight years later. The middle diagram in Figure 3.1 shows that the family is now different; two spouses have joined the family, and there are now grandchildren. The oldest son is now twenty-eight and has worked in the business for the past five years and has decided that he would like to make it his career.

Business families in this stage view the business as more than just the founder's concern and see it as a family business. Something has occurred to make them realize this: perhaps the second generation's growing passion for the business, a health worry, the arrival of grandchildren, or the awareness of the negative experiences of other business families. Thus, as the founders, the parents have determined that they will pass the business on to the second generation, resulting in new topics to be addressed in the appropriate family council forum. They are in a stage we refer to as the late founder stage and need to prepare for continuity; the family's meeting needs must accommodate that purpose and have reached the Dining Room level.

In contrast to the first stage, the Dining Room family council has more topics, challenges, and plans to address, and more formality and follow-through are needed. Like family councils at the Kitchen Table stage, those with a Dining Room family council will focus on information and communication, but they will also serve for education and decision making. The second generation, now a bit older and more mature, is expected to participate actively. More dialogue is appropriate as well as preparation for the meetings and follow-up between meetings. These meetings are characterized by greater accountability and more results than Kitchen Table meetings.

The issues of business continuity of business families at the late founder stage have some urgency because of the goal of making a successful transition. For example, families in this stage with young adult children starting families of their own will benefit from clear expectations about employment in the business and its effects on the family. A discussion about employment of family members often addresses the use of business assets as well as the determination of compensation and perks, promotions, and views on leadership of the business. By making explicit the family's values and clarifying the reasons for keeping the business, family members will create a reference for decisions and conclusions on matters where one part of the family opposes the other.

If the business is growing and has more visibility in the community, family members may discuss their views on when it is appropriate to speak of business matters in their community and with others who work in the business and whether it is wise to employ personal friends of the family. As a way of advancing every family member's business knowledge, the founder may address complicated issues emerging in the business. The discussion agenda might include the question of who is in line for a future senior leadership role as well as a conversation with the parents' tax advisor. Finally, when the parents provide the children with an opportunity to express their concerns and encourage them to ask questions, uncomfortable questions may emerge, such as the amount of time a founder spends away from the business or what amount is appropriate for shareholder distributions when the business needs capital for growth.

Education is an important purpose of meetings for business families in the late founder stage. If not initially, over time and as members of the second generation begin to think of themselves more and more as shareholders, a separate shareholders' meeting reinforces the discipline and skills needed for effective ownership. Family council meetings may still consider preparation of the second generation for the role as owner and focus on better understanding by all of the transition and estate strategy. They may also allow for a unified investment-oriented meeting of shareholders in a separate forum. Shareholder meetings would include a review of the business's financial statements and other matters, such as industry and competitor status, necessary to prepare the young family members for their roles as investors and stewards.

The dinner table serves as a metaphor indicating the additional formality and added structure needed for family councils of business families in the late founder stage. This formality is reinforced by the setting, which for many families at this stage is a conference room. The family council meetings at the late founder stage may include guests from time to time, such as professionals and key managers, and can also be a forum for participation by members of another family business to discuss what they have learned about transitioning to the second generation in their business.

The expectation is that formal family council meetings will continue on at least an annual basis, but there may also be quarterly or semiannual meetings. They are regular, use agendas prepared in advance, are conducted in a neutral meeting space, and decisions, conclusions, and plans for follow-through are documented.

Early Sibling Stage: The Negotiating Table

In business families at this stage, the second-generation siblings are beginning to form a team separate from the founder. The family council is referred to as the Negotiating Table forum because of more diverse, and potentially louder, voices at the table influenced by two family dynamics: the normal and expected tension between a founder and his/her children and that between the siblings. While the Dining Room forum was for parents who recognize they have the responsibility to teach their children to run the business and the children's task to appreciate the opportunity and to learn, the Negotiating Table is for a family struggling to determine who is in charge.

Seventeen years later, that family's second-generation siblings are in their forties and the parents are in their seventies (see Figure 3.1). The founding parents are likely very interested and active in the affairs of the business and certainly in the family. In fact the founder may still be engaged with the business and may retain legal control. If not legal control, the parents still have a great deal of influence due to their status as parents and founder(s). If their children work in the business, they are likely to have positions of considerable responsibility and are feeling more and more confident about their role as owners. All are beginning to have thoughts about the prospects for a significant transition when the second generation takes over control from the parents, and there are often differences of opinion about business priorities. In fact, control is likely to be an underlying issue in several matters, including the level of control that accompanies the sibling roles. The siblings ask "who reports to whom?" and tensions may affect family decisions ranging from where members spend the holidays to performance of the CEO. Thus, a very valuable role for the family council is to provide a forum for negotiating such differences, finding solutions, or learning how to continue to work together even while differences remain.

With normal tensions in business families as well as the normal stress of building careers and managing busy families, families at the early sibling stage may not have had time for reflective discussion among the siblings about their own children's future even though they feel pressure to get started. For example, family members may not have provided uniform guidelines for employing members of the third generation in the business even though the eldest of them will soon graduate from university. Therefore, there is pressure from the siblings to stabilize their control by negotiating with the founder, resolve the pecking order among each other, and be responsible parents by providing the answers required for their own children. Siblings often report that they desire a transition for their children that avoids the current atmosphere of uncertainty and tension. When used successfully, the family council of the siblings and parents is the forum for managing the complex transition required by a changing family and by a business experiencing a transition of owner-ship and management.

In figure 3.1 only two siblings are shown; this provides enough com-plexity and challenge, but what if the founding parents had six children instead of only two? Figure 3.2 illustrates this more complicated case.

This larger family at the early sibling stage has all of the complexities described above, but there are more moving parts. With larger fami-lies, it is even more likely that two or more second-generation family members are working in the business while others do not. These fami-lies may have begun to experience the tension between "insiders" and "outsiders." If ownership has begun to transfer to the second generation, some members may wonder what this might mean, and the question of who will control the business may have already emerged or be about to surface. With more family members employed in the business, there are going to be questions about future leadership, the mechanics of trans-ferring management control to the next leader, sharing of leadership, and the role of formal business processes. By formal business processes we mean that the rules for fair compensation, shareholder involvement in strategic planning, performance management, and human resource development are applied to family members working in the business. Business families at the early sibling stage that do not yet have a family council or any other formal family governance structure will certainly find ways to discuss these issues. Some families have a family board of directors or use informal family gatherings, and in others discussion is limited to those actively involved in the business. All of these forums usually feel inappropriate or inadequate to some or all family mem-bers, and thus a family council is often a welcome structure for properly

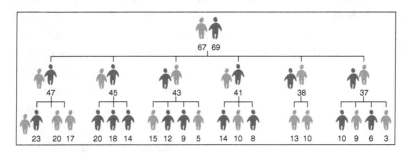

Figure 3.2   Early Sibling Stage: Negotiating Table Family Council

addressing the issues. Family members immediately see the benefit of setting aside time with the appropriate participants, thus freeing their board, their management, and their family gatherings to concentrate on their respective purposes.

In smaller families with only two siblings, deciding on participants is relatively easy except for the question of whether spouses should attend. We will cover this topic in more detail in chapters 4, 5, and 7; for now we will assume that spouses attend, which we consider preferable. Therefore, in smaller families the family council starts with six family members: the parents and their sibling children with spouses.

In larger families the original family council may consist of fourteen family members. Even though many family councils eventually include all family members over a certain age (e.g., fifteen), many business families beginning their family councils in the early sibling stage include only the founding generation and the second generation. The most common reason for doing so is that there is too much to accomplish since there has not been a forum before for the group to discuss issues and reach a consensus. Family members in the second generation want to have answers for their children to questions and explain, for example, the distinction between the roles of the family council and the board of directors, and they would feel awkward about involving their children before knowing these answers.

For business families in the early sibling stage the first family council meetings will likely be influenced by tensions between the generations and tensions among the siblings as they make progress on topics such as participation rules for the younger generation; the creation of a code of conduct for family communications, interactions, and conflict resolution; and changes or adjustments to their board of directors. Several family members will have a vision for the future and explicitly define their values for establishing a family business constitution or protocol. All of these issues present the opportunity for different views to emerge, thus win-win negotiation is a very valuable skill at this stage and the proper forum is the Negotiating Table.

As mentioned above, smaller families (see Figure 3.1) will likely include all six members of the founder and second generations, and when they are ready, they will add the oldest of members of the third generation. Age requirements vary, but if families set the threshold at the age of fifteen, then they would have a family council of ten members. Once many of the pent-up matters are resolved (some family councils meet monthly until urgent issues that have not had a place for discussion are resolved), family members may settle into a routine of two meetings per year. One meeting might be divided equally between a four-hour family council meeting, followed by to a two-hour shareholder meeting. Participants in the former may or may not be invited to the latter if they are not shareholders.

Larger families, because of their size, may begin and evolve differently. Like smaller families, they will likely begin with just the founder and the second generation at the meeting. Meetings of fourteen family members (see Figure 3.2) will be challenging to manage, and even more so when the older members of the third generation begin to be involved. However, it is better for trust and family-wide progress to initially involve all the adults and only later consider a representative family council. To manage a large group, families may form a planning/coordinating committee, or they may depend on facilitators to make their meeting productive. Many families also use subcommittees, such as an education committee, so that when the full family council meets, prepared proposals and planned education sessions can be submitted. Some special meetings may be for the benefit of a segment of the family, such as the third generation. Negotiating Table family councils often begin with some awkwardness much like when a new team forms; however, even after a period of conflict, they get organized with roles, rules, and policies, and later they achieve greater productivity.

Late Sibling Stage: Harvest Table

In business families in the late sibling stage, the founding generation may still be involved, but the siblings in the second generation are in charge, and their issues with the parents are not dominant. The siblings are more focused on dealing with each other and with their children and nieces and nephews. They may have been late in getting to this stage as much depends on how the founder transitions, or they may have been given opportunities for greater responsibility gradually and experienced an orderly transition. There is no prescribed path or pace for transitioning from a Negotiating Table forum because the founding parents' dominance will diminish at different rates in different families. The ages of members of each generation could be as illustrated in figure 3.3, or everyone could be ten years older; a larger and more complex family

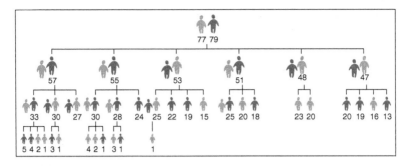

Figure 3.3   Late Sibling Stage: Harvest Table Family Council

could have more spouses in the third generation, perhaps a divorce or two, and a growing fourth generation.

In figure 3.3 most siblings are in their fifties and two in their forties. The oldest members of the third generation are in their thirties and getting settled. If the issue of their involvement has not yet been addressed, the older members of the third generation may be pressuring the siblings for answers. However, now that they are no longer focused on the parents or founder(s), the siblings may be focused on themselves. Pressure from the third generation can actually help the siblings to turn to what they can all agree on: preparing their children. Some business families find they need to allow one or more siblings to trade their shares for liquidity or exit, and some family members may be in ill-fitting roles in the business.

After negotiation provides more independence from parents and more role clarity among siblings, separating into branches may emerge as a threat to unity. As the third generation gets involved, it is natural for the siblings to think of themselves as branches, and many issues get evaluated relative to the perceived fairness toward all branches. Branch politics can emerge as a way of settling issues. Thus, a family council must be a forum that maintains trust and minimizes branch thinking.

Having made the transition from the parents and founder(s) and resolved the issues among siblings issues, business families in the late sibling stage need a Harvest Table family council, which is part celebration of a transition and part forum for preventing future disunity. It is no little thing for siblings to take control as a group and sort out their roles so they can begin thinking about the future of their children. Moving from a Negotiating Table format to a Harvest Table forum represents a type of graduation from one stage to the next, and family members need a forum that works for them and their children, the siblings and cousins of the third generation.

In larger business families in the late sibling stage not all key roles are held by the same individuals. That is, some family members are on the board, some are in management, and some are not involved. Thus, a Harvest Table family council will need to coordinate its work with these other entities as the family grows larger; a key role for the Harvest Table family council is to communicate with the entire family and build consensus for a single message to all groups. The challenge will be to bring together a large family even though not everyone will be able to participate in a family council. The Harvest Table thus represents the larger family through a smaller group; the latter must do what is logistically and organizationally impossible: produce the effect of all members coming together.

Business families in the late sibling stage that are large enough use a family assembly (the entire family) and a family association (adult members of the whole family who can elect the family council). In the time between the infrequent family assembly/family association events a representative family council does the large family's work. The representative Harvest Table family council consists of a few members, perhaps only five to seven, from the second and third generations who are well-connected across the family, can identify the right questions and decisions, and can facilitate communication and consensus across the whole family. The representative family council may meet four times per year while the family assembly and/or association may meet annually. Of course, the shareholder meeting has evolved to be separate and distinct from family governance. Insofar as branches of the family are a concern, there will likely be an emphasis on a representative of each branch participating in a newly formed family council.

A separate sibling team forum, important for consensus in the early sibling stage may no longer be needed, and its continued existence could even slow down the involvement of the third generation. Instead, the sibling group may evolve into an owners' council. The role of the owners' council is a representative shareholder group that allowing for consensus building and coordination between several owners on matters concerning them, which might otherwise be awkward to handle informally or even in the family council.

A Harvest Table family governance function suits families in the late sibling stage because it accommodates the larger size of the family, represents a change from a format that has served its purpose to one that fits a new purpose, and much like an autumn harvest celebration, it represents an accomplishment as well as a gathering of representatives from the broader family. It is a forum to build and reinforce the unity of the second generation and invite participation of the third generation.

Cousin Stage: Round Table

This stage is not defined by a generation achieving control, as the late sibling stage was. Figures 3.4 and 3.5 illustrate a smaller and a larger business family, respectively. In both cases the siblings and cousins in the third (cousin) generation are not defined by a group roughly similar

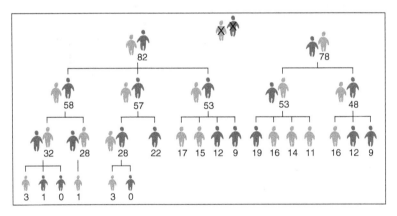

Figure 3.4   Cousin Stage: Smaller Round Table Family Council

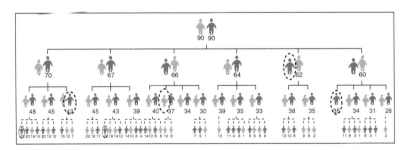

Figure 3.5   Cousin Stage: Larger Round Table Family Council. Circles Represent Family Council Members

in age. Rather, the youngest members of the second generation are not much older than the oldest members of the third generation, whose youngest members in turn are close in age to the older members of the fourth generation. As generations progress, differences along generational lines will decrease, and thus the family council forum that meets the needs of a family at the cousin stage will be suitable for generations to come. A second obvious characteristic of a family at the cousin stage is that the family is large, too large for all adults to come to many decisions as one group. We refer to the family council forum needed here and in the future as the Round Table. The Round Table is a symbol of equal participation, with members invited to participate because diversity resulting in agreement will be influential for those the group represents. Whereas a Harvest Table family council might get final agreement on many matters from the entire family, a Round Table serves a much larger family, and it is a little more like a board in that it makes decisions on behalf of the very large and growing family.

In business families at the cousin stage, branch thinking, which is a carryover from the second generation, may still be influential, but the family council's activity may weaken it. If so, the Round Table family council may for the first time not include representatives from each branch, particularly if the family is trying to include members from several generations on the council. The circles in figure 3.5 indicate members of this family's family council. Notice also that in the example spouses of lineal descendents participate as members of the family council.

Geographically, the family may be at its most scattered; some cousins may not know each other, and as new spouses join, they may not have had many opportunities to meet other members of the family. While younger family members may have been gifted shares of company stock, they may have never seen the main facilities or operations. Thus, their commitment as stewards and owners may be weak. Their level of commitment and involvement will certainly vary from one family unit to another, based on the differing approaches to education and family history. Thus, a priority of Round Table family councils is to develop strategies for connecting members of the large family to each other and to the values, shared mission/vision, and the shared source of pride in family membership. Focusing on the forces that unify the family will remain a priority for the family council.

In addition to a representative council, business families in the cousin stage will also utilize a family assembly and/or association that meets annually or every other year. In addition, the family council commonly establishes several committees, including an education committee, planning committee, and next-generation committee. The family council may work out a common vision for family philanthropy and lead the development of a family foundation. In the beginning stages, a subcommittee of the family council may lead the family's philanthropic function. Ad hoc committees or task forces might be established for specific purposes, such as studying a question and reporting the findings, e.g., recommended changes to the family employment policy or defining the qualifications of a family member representative to the board of directors. It is not uncommon for business families in the cousin stage to consider the value of a family office, and a special committee of the family council might research whether this would be suitable. When committees are formed, especially ad hoc committees, the family council may draw on resources outside their ranks to include specific skills or expertise; the family council may call on other family members outside the council for help, special knowledge, and eventual approval of and commitment to recommendations. While committees do the groundwork, just like a board of directors, the committee chairs bring their recommendations and findings to the Round Table family council for decisions and actions.

4

How to Start and Organize
a Family Council

A meeting of the entire family is an ideal way to start a family council. At this meeting it's important for the whole group to hear what the goals are, get everyone's feedback, reach a consensus, and set a course of action. However, family councils do not always begin in such an open and organized way. When starting a family council, business families must change from their current way of doing things to a new, unfamiliar, and more formal way of working together. For example, you are probably used to several traditions that are part of your family's culture, such as:

- Uneven communication—some family members have strong relationships with each other and may speak more frequently with each other, and those who are more deeply involved in the business will interact more often.
- Dominant decision making—many families follow the lead of one or two members or adopt an informal consensus approach that relies on people to speak up if they disagree with the direction being taken.
- Prevailing planning—in many cases planning works like decision making, or there may be individuals in the family who enjoy planning, and they may be the same ones who are most engaged in planning all family events.
- Informal rule making—though not typically associated with an informal family structure, unwritten rules exist for many families, often concerning traditions or holidays.

On the level of the individual, establishing a family council means that people agree to exchange their old ways of doing things for a new approach. This is a significant transition, and it takes time and trial and error because individuals are often not immediately successful in trying to adapt. For example, in an effort to provide equal access to information, a family council might adopt a process of concurrently informing everyone on its activities through a family intranet or emails. Yet, members of the new family council may also speak with their closest relatives after a meeting and provide them with much more information at a deeper level than with the formal email method. Others may not be accustomed to regularly reading their email. So the new method, intended to provide an even and equal flow of information, begins with many flaws. It is normal for families to experiment and experience failures as they transition from the old methods to new ones, and in the early stages of transition, frustration with the failures leads family members to question why they should change and can cause them to fall back into the old, familiar patterns. A new family council must remind individuals of what was agreed to and why, and then it must be patient while the shift from the old to the new gradually takes hold.

A key transition for all family members is to agree that a formal family meeting or family council is going to be empowered even though this may seem to threaten the familiar way of making decisions and plans. Resistance is natural. Accepting the transition will be different for everyone; for example, a family leader will evaluate it differently than his youngest child. The leader may need to transition from being the main decision maker for the family to complying with a democratic method for some decisions. For example, his youngest daughter may make the decision to become more involved and to take responsibility because she now has a voice in the consensus and perhaps a vote on some matters. Often, people need time to fully understand what will now be decided as a group and what will legitimately not be tampered with. "Will the younger family members now give direction to the board?" "Are we opening the door to family meddling in the business?" The transition from the familiar to more democratic ways of doing things is made possible by involving everyone, permitting objections and challenges, hearing replies, and finally reaching agreement based on mutual understanding.

The meaningful first step is involvement and understanding the extent and limitations of change. The old adage that people don't resist change, but resist being changed applies. If you involve and inform everyone, allow everyone to fully understand the benefits of accomplishing what is important to each and to the family through a family council, respond to fears and skepticism, and give everyone a choice, family members are much more likely to give participation in family governance a try.

Alternatives to the First Steps: Individual Champion

A champion is a family member who believes in the value of organized family governance and seeks support for a family council from the rest of the family. For the business leader who is also a family member and for the family leader who is not leading the business, it is relatively easy to become the champion. Both can use their bully pulpit. However, a champion of a family council can also be the youngest and least powerful family member. That is, individuals without title or role in the family business but with passion and persuasion skills have started family councils. We are often approached by young family members and spouses as well as other family members who are independently looking for ideas and examples as they seek improvements in how family members interact with each other.

How to be a champion. If a family or business leader takes the role of champion for a family council, the trick is to get it started and then back out of it. If the family council becomes dependent on the one who leads all the other affairs of the business family, then its sustainability may be problematic. We prefer the business leader champion to lead by assembling the family, giving all family members good educational resources, providing financial support to remove early barriers, and using persuasiveness to inspire others to assume responsibility and get involved.

However, leaders are in leadership roles for a reason, and sometimes they are the family's only resource for the task. They may be the only ones who can get the family council started, and they may need to be in a leadership role for the first few years until other family members can develop leadership skills or resolve other obligations (e.g., small children) so they can then concentrate on leading the family council.

A word of caution is in order if the business leader is also the champion of the family council; the level of ownership and commitment on the part of the rest of the family may be limited. Thus, if a strong leader assumes responsibility for starting the family council, other family members are likely to see it as the leader's project. There may be a limited opportunity for others to fully become involved, and at some point there will need to be a transition from a very capable leader to an inexperienced one. We advocate that the transition to a leader who is not the business leader is made as soon as possible; in fact, leadership development and succession should become one of the key priorities of the new family council.

The champion with less power has a different problem. For example, while the business or family leader can gather the family and deliver a convincing argument for getting a family council started, the enthusiastic oldest child of the youngest brother will first have to build a support base. There is an even bigger problem when the family or business leaders are not in favor of an organized family council or do not see the value of having one. The young champion must then systematically recruit all the family members who will listen and convert them one by one. This may take some time, and patience may be in short supply; thus, there may be a rush to build support before the enthusiasm wears off.

An appointed champion is very different; that is, a savvy business family may begin with a good understanding of how to develop a family council. Family members may understand the value of a family council and also realize that a lot of practical questions must be answered before the family as whole will support establishing a family council. In such cases a champion might be selected. Consultants or advisors can help a family select a champion and set expectations for that role and provide coaching and guidance for greater credibility with the rest of the family.

An appointed champion is like a task force of one; there is an expectation that a family council will be established and the needed support for a champion's success is built into the appointment. Thus, the follow-through on the part of the broader family is easier to obtain than might be the case with a young, self-motivated champion. Finally, the appointed champion does not necessarily need to be a family member; a skilled, trusted internal manager or staff member could be a candidate. We know of many family councils started by the general counsel or chief financial officers; based on their role as trusted advisors and with the mandate of business or family leadership, they can guide the family to establish a family council.

Qualifications for a champion include:

- A high level of trust from the entire family
- Good communication skills and contact to the entire family
- Ability to work with a limited goal of getting the family council to a functional level and to resist the temptation to run it after it is established
- Wisdom regarding the dynamics of the family
- Supportive of as much democracy in a family meeting as the family culture will allow
- Sufficient knowledge of family governance or a willingness to learn
- Essential organization skills needed to organize and conduct a meeting

Good connections and trust from the entire family includes all segments of the family, (e.g., all generations, branches, spouses, and those working in the business as well as those not working there). If equal and consistent connections do not yet exist, a good champion will make a special effort to reach out to everyone and being as transparent as possible so that all can see that they are being treated fairly and equally. This is very important as it lays the groundwork for the relatively equal status everyone is expected to have during the meeting.

Egalitarian Beginnings with the Entire Family

Introduction of a family council through a family meeting. Many family councils owe their beginnings to a pivotal meeting of all family members from all generations involved. Or perhaps a senior group of shareholders organized a meeting of the entire family, what we refer to as the first family assembly (see appendix 1 for a full definition), and introduced the concept based on their assessment of the family's future needs.

When the entire family is assembled, everyone learns about the concept at the same time. Material to be read in advance might be provided, and a presentation from an informed family member or an invited guest could serve to provide the educational component and answer initial questions, for example:

- Why do we need a family council and what does it do?
- Who participates?
- How do we distinguish a family council from the roles of owners, managers, and board members?

It is important for this first family assembly to be successful so that it can reinforce motivation for attending others. If there is too much pain and conflict or an agenda that is too aggressive and results in unmet expectations, the family might miss out on an opportunity to galvanize the support and commitment needed for starting a family council. Family members attending the meeting must be able to envision an important, compelling purpose that can be served by additional meetings. Some may be most interested in a forum for education and alignment to make the most of the competitive advantage of their business. Others may see a meeting as a way of quieting restless shareholders by providing them an outlet to voice their opinions, be heard, and be productive by creating a unified direction to guide the board of directors.

Through discussion, a consensus emerges that regular family meetings should be institutionalized, and the question will arise of what will be next. A method for follow-through must be provided, one that matches the egalitarian style of the family meeting everyone has participated in. The family needs a plan for the organization and leadership needed to form a family council or to conduct formal family meetings on a regular basis.

Follow-up: A family council task force. We believe that before you hire a person for a job in a business, you first must have a job description and list of qualifications. We think this is a good principle for business families when doing anything for themselves outside the business. In setting up a task force to implement the steps decided by the family, it is a good idea to clarify the task and the qualifications for the task force first.

An appropriate follow-up task after a general meeting of the entire family that includes an overview of the form and purpose of a family council is to have a task force create a charter for the future family council. There are many charters available that the task force can use as guidelines and examples, and it has to produce no more than a first draft, not a final document ready for ratification. That is, the task force has a limited objective and has useful tools available; family members should also know the outline of the intended charter before volunteering for the task force.

The task force task is to create a first draft of a charter. Since we discuss charters in detail below, we'll only provide a basic outline here:

- Purpose of the family council
- Definition of family
- Membership
- Roles—what the chair does as a minimum
- How to become a member, e.g., election procedures and terms
- Structure—number of meetings, compensation, expense reimbursement, budget, relationship to the family as a whole and to the board and to management
- Amending the charter

Predictions regarding the amount of time required vary depending on the individuals involved, the number of participants, and the task force's approach to the assignment. We have seen this process completed quite quickly; for example, when four task force members live near each other, two two-hour meetings with good preparation on the part of all members can be sufficient. On the other hand, we have also seen a six-person task force require as many as eight drafts and four conference calls, two of them lasting more than four hours. Democracy takes time, but efficient democracy takes less time, and skills and qualifications make a difference.

Qualifications of task force members. Below is a list of the qualifications we have successfully introduced over the years as general capabilities needed for a family work group:

- Ability to communicate effectively with the entire family, not just with one branch or family unit
- Recognition of one's own strengths and weaknesses and respect for others' skills—not everyone has to be equally gifted
- A healthy respect for "good enough," remembering that the purpose of the task force is to make the family as a whole more efficient in establishing its charter; its goal is not to produce perfection

- Little pride of authorship—the group produces simply a draft and there is value in inviting input from others and not meeting it with defensiveness
- Teamwork skills, including a commitment to and ability to achieve consensus on decisions
- Assertiveness, especially when there is disagreement, and a sense of obligation to find a solution to which all can agree; and
- Willingness to put in the time

It is not necessary for all individuals involved to have these qualifications, and certainly not at expert levels, but we encourage family members not to volunteer if they feel they cannot meet these expectations. It is important that everyone agrees to hold the members of the task force to standards so it can be successful and to remind members from time to time that the task force works on a charter draft rather than a finished product.

Populating the task force. A task force can then be formed through volunteers, nominations, or appointments by family groups of individuals to represent them. For the job of writing a first draft of a charter, three or four members make a good working group. Busy family members will have to schedule time together either on a conference call or in the same room together. This is also a good number for delegating sections of the charter to individuals as a quick start to an initial meeting.

Even though the task force will dissolve after it completes the draft charter, the team established to identify the process and the goals is critical to the overall success of the family council. If key family members in the family do not trust one another at the time, including one while excluding others will result in a draft that could be hotly contested when presented to the family as a whole and for the wrong reasons. If there is not enough trust between branches of the family, the only option may be to make sure that all branches are equally represented at any off-site activity for the benefit of the entire family. Generations are another consideration, especially if the transition of control is a current issue. Even though a family council is not the same forum as those utilized for business or board decisions, individuals may not know the significance of representation at this early stage. Different generations will want to make sure they are each represented at every step in order to ensure that this new feature is consistent with their overall priorities for generational transition.

A good rule of thumb, when naming specific family representatives to the task force is to consider acceptance of the task force's product, the draft charter. Family members on the task force must do their homework and produce a good product, but they must also have credibility extending beyond their product to evoke the trust and respect needed for adequate scrutiny on the part of the broader family who will be asked to consider the proposed draft charter. That is, the family's scrutiny will be informed by its respect for the individuals involved in the creation of the charter draft.

Task force leadership. We believe a task force should choose its own leader once the task force members have been identified. Thus, if four members have been chosen for the task force, their first responsibility is to pick a leader. Just as with the qualifications for membership on the task force, its leadership is facilitated greatly by an individual who has the following skills or at least endeavors to practice these qualities of a task force chair:

- Ability to facilitate the inclusion of all task force members
- Ability to assertively and diplomatically set timelines and stick to them
- Ability to balance one's own input and facilitating the integration of input from all members
- Ability to diplomatically keep the goal and its limitations in mind
- Ability to lead sensitively without being a boss

Ideally, the chair of a family task force helps the group remember its focus, divides the workload among the members in a way that fits their abilities, and summarizes as needed where the group stands with its project.

Back to the full family meeting. Business families that want to establish a family council quickly may meet again two months after their first full family meeting during which the concepts of a family council were presented and the task force established. Other families may provide the task force with more time and not convene again for six months. When the entire family assembles again—ideally, after all members have read an advance copy of the task force's draft charter—family members can then discuss the draft as a group and seek to move it toward completion. This works well with the following process:

1. The task force is identified and thanked for its role in assisting the family by preparing a concrete example the family can react to and finalize as their governing document.
2. The chair of the task force outlines the steps the family will take in reviewing and providing feedback on the draft:
   a. Review the main points
   b. Identify opinions and input and record them
   c. Minimize task force defensiveness, and instead allow everyone to hear the rationale and alternatives considered by the task force as the recommended draft was decided on
   d. Minimize wordsmithery in the large group, but record the nature of the recommended changes and produce the final wording after the meeting
   e. If opposing recommendations are presented, they may or may not be resolved in the current meeting; a way of addressing them may have to be found after the meeting.
3. During the discussion the ideas, reactions, and suggestions for changes are recorded as input, and if easy consensus is reached on a point, it is considered an agreed-upon change.
4. Once the document has been reviewed and all input recorded, the task force chair will read everything back.

Typically, in a well-facilitated meeting, with a good first draft, a business family can get to the point of adopting a charter, including the changes identified during the discussion. There is an opportunity to move on from the charter to identifying who might become a member of the family council. For some families, this might seem too sudden, but many families are able to go ahead and elect their first family council in accordance with the procedures spelled out in the charter.

Arranged Initiation of a Task Force

The egalitarian method outlined above is an example of a process that establishes self-sufficiency and builds support for a conclusion by the way in which the conclusion is reached, but it takes time and requires starting with a blank slate and a meeting of the family as a whole. Conditions do not always provide the opportunity for such a start, and we have identified some alternative beginnings:

Informal task force. Much like the task force process described above, a family task force can be formed without the full family meeting. Especially in smaller families or families with only a few leaders, a task force can be informally agreed to and given its mandate to produce a description of how a family council would function and a draft charter. For example, three members of a sibling group of owners might decide to appoint themselves to the task force or delegate the drafting to one among them to be reviewed, discussed, and finalized later by all three. Once the three agree on a draft, they might then circulate it to all family members in advance of a family meeting.

Result of a series of shareholder meetings. Business families that have adopted a regular meeting structure but meet as a group of owners may initiate a family council as an outgrowth of their meetings. For example, a group of siblings who have been meeting to establish their board of directors, create policy for family employment, and develop a shareholder agreement may conclude that for certain matters more involvement of the family would be desirable. They should follow the task force process described above, inviting specific individuals to work on a charter. Alternatively, they may bypass this process and establish their family council's membership and also draw upon their previously uninvolved spouses and children. The siblings may still meet as owners to continue their work on matters relating to ownership, and some may also participate in the new family council.

Active business employees. Alternatively, a group of the family members active in the business can start the process. Active family employees regularly working together can easily shift from a current operational issue to the matter of the full family's influence on dividends and the competitive advantage of their business. They may be complaining to one another about their cousins who do not work in the business and do not understand their responsibilities as investors. Again, on a formal or informal basis, they might establish a task force or name themselves as the task force and proceed with the steps involved to produce a charter and thus a means of educating the entire family on how to be better shareholders.

At the board level. Much like a group of family employees in the business, a board of directors could come to the conclusion that a family council would be an ideal institution for family shareholder education. The directors might also provide the needed organization and direction and establish a task force to initiate the process.

Fragmented Start

What if not all family members agree that a family council is needed? Perhaps some disagree with the potential benefits and may even feel that a family council has the potential to be damaging. Do all family councils begin with a consensus? The simple answer is: no. In many business families divisions between branches or individuals make it impossible to begin with a joint meeting involving all the owners because the wounds were too fresh. In such cases, one branch may forge ahead alone and organizes its own family council while making it clear that the other branches are invited to attend. After some time, perhaps years, the branches may be friendly enough to be part of the same family council. For example, reconciliation may begin with a cousin who specifically invites her favorite cousin from childhood in another branch to a meeting. Or the family council may plan a family trip and extend an invitation to the nonparticipating branches; a few of those members may accept and have fun. Or specific meetings to discuss employment policy may not require family council participation, but all branches are invited because all have children who might be interested in careers in the family business. The process is usually slow and may never be complete; still, keeping the door open is the policy that has led to many success stories.

For example, second-generation siblings may learn about the concept of a family council and try to convince their parents to begin meeting. The parents may only hear that there is an interest in pushing them out to speed up succession planning. On the other hand, members of the senior generation may be able to convince their oldest daughter and her spouse to begin a formal, organized process of thinking and talking about and planning for the family's future as a group even if their other three children are not interested.

To the question of whether the lack of complete acceptance presents a barrier we say no. If there is a segment of the family committed to begin meeting as a family council, this need not be a threat to the others. All of the procedures for starting a family council still apply and can be scaled to the size of the group. However, as the family segment goes forward, those involved must consider how to inform the others and keep the door open for them.

Some families prefer to meet without the faction of the family regarded as disagreeable and are not keen about an open invitation for participation in the family council. Other families may have had conflicts with members of a branch of the family but would like to maintain relationships with their children. We have seen several instances where, after long periods of estrangement, family members have reconnected with the main family group and started to attend family council meetings. What breaks down even stubborn grudges held by family members is unpredictable and as varied as the reasons for the feuds. In our experience an invitation to participate in a family council has not usually been what made the difference, but it has also never escalated an existing conflict. Most of the families we have observed in this situation have a policy of keeping the estranged group informed about meetings and even sent them agendas to keep open an opportunity for reconciliation and to demonstrate transparency.

Getting Started: Needs Assessment

There are a number of ways in which a family can address its needs and determine what should be accomplished. As consultants to business families, we often determine this through individual interviews with family members then sharing consolidated, anonymous results in a full family meeting. The discussion which follows prioritizes goals and enhances motivation for achieving them.

We use specific techniques in full family meeting settings that can also be used by families themselves as long as they are organized and willing to lead their meetings themselves. We present three methods below: the nominal group technique,[1] a SWOT analysis, and the achieve/avoid contrast analysis.

Family Council Priorities: Nominal Group Technique

The nominal group technique works best with an independent facilitator; however, it is rather self-directed, and families can use it on their own as long as one person thoroughly understands the process described below. The process was not developed specifically for family groups but adapts well for a new family council. This egalitarian process allows everyone to be heard, limits domination by one or more individuals, allows less assertive members to be heard, and helps set priorities in an organized way. This technique works for large and small families and includes the following steps, adapted for a family group:

1. **Create small groups.** If the family is small, say eight or fewer members, there is no need for grouping and the family can proceed as one group. For larger groups of nine or more members, create small groups mixing up the ages, genders, and branches as much as possible. Each group should be able to work together without being distracted by another; if the family is big, they will need a big room. Each small group should have five to seven family members. Once the small groups are formed, they will need to appoint an agenda manager, a timekeeper, and a recorder.

2. **Phrase the question.** All groups need to focus on the same question: What are the top priorities for our business family that should be addressed by our new family council?

3. **Individual ideas.** The instruction to each group is that there will be no talking for five minutes. During that time, which is tracked by the timekeeper, each individual privately lists on a tablet as many ideas as he or she can think of in answer to the question.

4. **Record ideas.** On a flip chart the recorder writes the ideas of the group members as follows: each individual gets a turn to state only one answer, which is then written on the flip chart. The agenda manager makes sure that the following rules are understood remembered, and followed:

    (a)   The idea is written as close to the speaker's original words as possible.

    (b)   No discussion of the merits of an idea is permitted, no questions about how the idea would be addressed—in short, no evaluation from anyone in the group.

    (c)   Comments from group members are allowed only to help an individual clearly state his or her idea.

    (d)   Individuals can pass.

    (e)   Individuals can say their idea is the same as one already on the flip chart, and the recorder then places a check mark next to the item. The agenda manager keeps the process moving so that everyone has a turn until there are no more ideas anyone wants to offer.

5. **Evaluation.** The agenda manager hands each person self-adhesive, colored dots[2] (10 dots per person) and each person places as many dots near an item on the flip chart as he or she wants, with greater numbers of dots indicating greater importance, e.g., members can place all their dots on one item or they can divide them among as many items as they care to. When all members have placed all their dots, the recorder totals the dots and writes the total next to each item.

6. **Reporting.** The small groups then join again as a full family group, and the recorders from each small group report on the items that gained the greatest number of votes by dot count.

7. **Priorities.** Rather than consolidating the final set of priorities at this meeting, this will be left for the new family council to do. The flip charts should be displayed for the remainder of the meeting, and recorded in some way, e.g., transcribed into notes, photographed, or saved and provided to the family council for use at its meetings.

Family Council Priorities: Family SWOT Analysis

Amy Schuman, one of the principals in the Family Business Consulting Group, has refined the SWOT method for use in establishing a family council. The process allows for a more thorough analysis of the family but still produces a consolidated list of priorities. It has the added benefit of activity, as small groups are physically moving around the room when completing the task. Her technique is useful for a large family group (twenty or more members). SWOT stands for Strengths, Weaknesses, Opportunities, and Threats.[3] A professional facilitator is valuable so that all family members can focus on participating, but the process also can be lead by a family member. The process is as follows:

1. Welcome, General Instructions, and Overview.

A leader provides the following introduction: "This activity allows us to take a strategic look at our family. Many businesses conduct SWOT analyses to move outside a tactical, short-term orientation, and identify larger, more long-term initiatives based on more than a gut feel. Families benefit from designing their family councils around such a strategic perspective. The process allows us to gather the wisdom of the group; thus, the entire family provides 'marching orders' or priorities to their representatives on the family council." Suggested time for this: 5 minutes.

2. Small Groups: Brainstorming

Divide into four groups of no more than ten members each. If the big group is larger than forty, include additional small groups of ten or fewer members. The room must be prepared in advance with four blank flip chart pages hung/taped on the wall with some distance between them. They should be in the order listed below. Watercolor markers are placed by the charts. The four charts are entitled:

1. FAMILY STRENGTHS
2. FAMILY WEAKNESSES
3. FAMILY OPPORTUNITIES
4. FAMILY THREATS

(Additional sheets of flip chart paper should be available)
Each small group is assigned a category: one has Strengths, a second has Weaknesses, and so on. Each group brainstorms ideas for one category at a time and then adds the items to its assigned list. If anyone wants to write an item that is already on the list, a check mark is placed next to the original item.

After five minutes, each group moves to the next chart on its right until all groups have had an opportunity to brainstorm and record on all four charts. The suggested time for this is 5 minutes per chart, 30 minutes total.

3. Large Group: Clarification

Once each group has had a chance to add to each chart, discussion should be allowed to make sure everyone fully understands the items on each chart. Individuals may return to their seats or remain standing by each chart, depending on the room and the energy in the group.

The leader goes from chart to chart reading the items out loud. If anything is unclear, questions are asked to clarify the item. The leader should not allow long discussions of items, permitting only questions and comments for clarification. This can go fairly quickly, and caution is advised so discussion does not bog down the process. The suggested time for this is 3–8 minutes per chart, approximately 40 minutes total.

4. Small Groups: Combining Duplicates and Categorizing

Each small group returns to its original chart. Members then combine, categorize, and generally condense the brainstormed items in preparation for voting. The goal is to have distinct items and to minimize overlap between them.

It is important that the leader emphasizes that groups should not condense the items too much. Doing so may result in losing the unique expression of an item. If members are in doubt, they should leave an item in its original form. The suggested time for this is 10–15 minutes total.

5. Large Group: Revisiting Condensed Charts

A representative of each group presents the group's condensed items to the large group; minimal discussion is allowed. Representatives should emphasize where they have combined items, so that everyone clearly understands the nature of all items on each chart, which is important for the next step. The suggested time for this is 3–8 minutes per chart, 30–40 minutes total.

6. Individuals: Voting

The leader distributes twenty self-adhesive voting dots to each individual. Individuals are asked to vote for their priorities on each chart by placing five dots by the items they consider the most important. Individuals can place their dots however they wish on each chart, i.e., participants can use all five dots on one item if desired.

For family groups of twenty or fewer members, fewer dots works better, and three dots per chart are used. For very large families, it is recommended that each individual receive six dots per chart.

Individuals who are quick at math are asked to help tally the votes and circle the items with the most votes per chart. The number varies, but typically the top priorities number between five and eight. The suggested time for this is 15 minutes in all.

7. Large Group: Announce Top Five to Eight Items per Chart

The leader assigns individuals to help write the summary flipchart that reports the top items per chart/category. The suggested time for this is 5 minutes total.

8. Small Groups: Key Family Initiatives and Family Council Committees

Each group convenes to answer the following:

- What are the implications of this process for the family council?
- If we were to have two to five committees of the family council that would best respond to the priorities of this SWOT analysis, what would they be?
- Are there items here that do not belong in the family council? Where do they belong and how would follow-up best take place?
- Other implications, next steps, etc?

The leader instructs each group to prepare a flipchart with the group's committee recommendations and a list of any other key items identified in the small group discussion. The suggested time for this is 30–45 minutes total.

9.   Large Group: Discussion

Each small group presents its answers to the list of questions while allowing for discussion and questions from the large group. The suggested time for this is 10 minutes per group and 30–40 minutes in all.

10.   Large Group: Determine the Next Steps

Steps include:

- Delegating a final listing of family council priorities and goals to a task force
- If desired, a final vote can be taken on the specific committees of the family council

The suggested time for this is 10–20 minutes in all.

11.   Evaluate Process, Self-Congratulate on Success, and Adjourn

Like many business families, the Valdez family has focused primarily on the business led by two hard-driving brothers. Their conflicts have been buried or set aside in favor of hard work. When they set aside their work, they are focused on family. Their families are close and share many traditions. They have strong values of care and respect for their business and for the many employees who work in the business. Education is one of their strongest values and all family members, including spouses, have advanced degrees; even if they do not work in the business, they are active professionals or entrepreneurs in several fields. The Valdez family's SWOT analysis resulted in the following list of priorities after voting:

Strengths:

- Highly educated family members
- Diverse skill sets and respect for all capabilities are best for teamwork within the family
- Strong conservative stewardship values shared by all family members—we have little diversity in our lifestyles

Weaknesses:

- Historically poor success with problem solving and conflict resolution within the family
- Unequal engagement in the family council concept on the part of the family leaders

Opportunities:

- The younger generation is fully engaged and enthusiastic about taking on more responsibility—the timing is right
- Spouses and less active shareholders can catch up on their education about the business at the same time we are training the younger generation

Threats:

- In four years there will be many college-aged children in the younger generation who may not make family council activities a priority for several years
- New spouses in the younger generation will likely not understand or support the time and effort needed to maintain unity and commitment on the part of the family
- Current patterns of escalating stresses on the business and reduced performance may overstress our family relationships

One initiative that emerged from these SWOT results was that the family council was asked to recruit members of the younger generation and engage them anywhere the council could use them. The family council sought to take advantage of an opportunity (enthusiastic younger generation) to reduce a weakness (unequal engagement of family leaders). The SWOT analysis gave the family direction and also provided broad support for the direction because everyone was involved in the process.

Family Council Priorities: Accomplish/Avoid Contrast Analysis

A third option for business families is to analyze their needs using a process to develop two lists: (1) what we hope to accomplish as a business family, and (2) what we hope will not happen to our business family. An interpretation of this list of contrasting futures leads to a description of the purpose of the family council and can be used to identify long-term goals. This method can be used more quickly than the two options described above, and it is better adapted to smaller families of about fifteen or fewer members.

A leader who primarily keeps the group focused on the task and the rules is also the scribe who writes on a flip chart.

1. **Chart Preparation.** A single flip chart page has a line drawn vertically down the middle from top to bottom, creating two columns. The left column is entitled "Accomplish" and the other column is entitled "Avoid."
2. **Ground Rules.** The primary ground rules are as follows:
   - There is no evaluation while items are added to the two columns, and
   - The "Avoid" column should not be the opposite of the "Accomplish" column but should provide new information.
3. **Individual Reflection.** For five minutes without discussion, individuals identify items for each column.
4. **Brainstorming.** In no particular sequence, the leader asks individuals to name items for each list and writes them down as close to the original words as possible. Individuals can contribute by

requesting that an item already listed is checked to indicate it was their item as well.

5. **Conclusions/Priorities.** When all individual contributions are on the flip chart, which could be several pages, the group as a whole discusses the lists to draw conclusions about priorities. With the goal being a general list of four to five priorities, the leader records on a flip chart entitled "Family Council Priorities" the conclusions from the discussion. The "Priorities" page and the original lists are provided to the new family council.

The First Meeting of the New Family Council

When a new family council meets for the first time, it will be a luxury to have the results of any of the three priority-setting processes described above. Those methods provide a mandate emerging from fair processes that allowed individuals to merge their ideas and opinions with those of the entire family. If the process was done correctly, the new family council can safely assume that the results from those meetings will now be its focus. This is a tremendous advantage for a new family council. The council members are empowered to act.

Yet, what about new councils that begin without the full family's mandate? Perhaps the family council was appointed by the siblings in the second generation. That is, a late stage sibling group (see table 3.1 in chapter 3) that finds itself recently free of the control of the founding generation and is working out its business partner/family relationship issues is simultaneously looking beyond its own issues as a group and wondering how to better prepare the next generation for responsible ownership. There is a lot going on with such a group and perhaps an egalitarian meeting of the entire family did not fit into a schedule crowded with more immediate priorities. Thus, it is very possible that a new family council is meeting for the first time and must do its own assessment without the benefit of the entire family's involvement and must decide on its own how to go about accomplishing its goals.

Below we provide descriptions of the first steps of two family council beginnings: (1) the one that is not empowered and has only modest goals of organizing regular family meetings to cover educational topics, and (2) the empowered group that has received a mandate to act and begins with the ambitious objective of defining the structure of family governance through the creation of a family council charter.

The Modest, Not Empowered Start: The First Meeting of the Planning Committee

For our example, we will make a few assumptions. The family is in the late founder stage as described in our classification system in chapter 3. Regarding the future, the family members have committed to the business being owned by the founder's four children, siblings in their late twenties and early thirties. The founder and spouse are both fifty-nine years old, and they have decided to include all adult family members, including the spouses of their four children, in family meetings that will focus on education about the business. Ten adults will participate.

A planning committee was formed through a combination of a request from the founder and others volunteering. The founder's spouse, her second oldest son, and the spouse of the oldest son form the planning committee and they are about to meet for the first time.

The considerations for the planning committee are very similar to what a representative family council might tackle:

1. Key decisions to address before the meeting
2. The meeting agenda
3. Ground rules for the meeting
4. Involving members in the process
5. Organizational accomplishments for the "getting started" phase:
    (1) identification of purpose
    (2) Goals—defining success
    (3) Structure (models to choose from)

Preparation for the first family meeting. The planning committee meets for the first time, and the members are organized in that they have the list of five planning items to address; this is their planning agenda. They make the following decisions:

- The first meeting will be three hours long with an agenda that covers in part education about the business and in part structure of the family meeting process; it will be followed by a dinner together without the children.

- The founder's spouse will handle scheduling, and dinner will be hosted by her son who sits on the planning committee and by his spouse. This was intentional. The family matriarch has often applied gentle pressure to get the family together, and it works; it's efficient and in this case, was needed so that the meeting would be attended by all for its entire length. The second oldest son and his spouse have not been entertainers nor have they played a leadership role in the family. By hosting the dinner, they make a point that the family meeting is different from how things have normally been done in the family. The planning committee wants to get the family to realize early on that family meetings are a significant departure from the standard way of doing things (Mom schedules) but not too different.
- A neutral setting for the meeting was selected, again to make a point. Using the founding couple's home would make this their meeting, but the meeting is intended to be a family meeting with all individuals participating more or less equally. The setting underscores this goal. Including the spouses in discussions of business-related topics is unusual for this family, and the planning committee wants to encourage broad, roughly equal engagement and commitment to the success of the meeting. A private room in a local restaurant was reserved for the meeting.

For ground rules, the family decided on the following:

- Young children and phones or other devices should not be a distraction
- Dress will be business casual
- Children will speak only when they are spoken to—the matriarch had a little fun slipping this one in
- Only one person speaks at a time
- Questions are encouraged
- Decisions by consensus
- Everyone's views are important and of value to everyone else

The agenda with a letter from the planning committee was circulated to all family members in a way they would be sure to receive it;

that is, two were mailed to work addresses, one to a home address, and the others were sent as electronic versions. The letter included a welcome, was upbeat and positive in tone, and expressed a sincere desire to introduce a responsible practice that had served many business families.

Chairing the first meeting. Options for selecting a leader, the value of rotating leadership versus selecting a permanent leader with a term of service will be explored further in chapter 5. The planning committee decided on its options. If the family matriarch chaired the meeting, everyone would be respectful of her position, and the meeting would likely be successful. If the second son were to chair the meeting, there would no doubt be success but also challenges from his three siblings as typical of their relationship of aiming good-natured jabs at each other. If the oldest son's spouse were to chair the meeting, everyone would be taken off guard by such an unexpected development. She had led a few community volunteer projects, and skill was thus not an issue, but the choice would be surprising as this family's culture had consistently excluded spouses from discussions of business matters.

The planning committee decided to select the oldest son's spouse to chair the first meeting because this would send a message that inclusion was important for the purpose of education about the business. If the committee members are to commit to serious education about issues important to continuity as a business family and family business, they would need to include all members of the family.

The first meeting: Organization. The agenda for the first meeting was as follows:
Introductions: 10 minutes

1. Welcome from the planning committee; all three members provided their views on why the meeting was important
2. Review of ground rules and two requests—are there any other ground rules and any changes to the agenda?

Business education: 90 minutes

3. Founder describes the early years when the business was growing
4. Invited guest: the director of operations describes two new products and plans for introducing them to the market

Break: 10 minutes
Structure of the family meetings: 60 minutes

5. Future family meetings, discussion of their purpose, goals, and structure
6. Brainstorming—ideas for topics for future family meetings

Wrap-up: 10 minutes

7. Set date for the next meeting
8. Evaluation of the meeting

The first meeting: Processes for success. The meeting chair is responsible for keeping everyone focused on the agenda topic, staying on time, and contributing just like all of the other family members. She served the family by using a simple introduction to each topic:

- What we want to accomplish with this topic
- How much time we have
- A reminder that I will help us stay on topic

She introduced her father-in-law in the following way:

> "Herb will now describe the early years of the business so that we can all benefit from knowing what challenges were confronted, what was learned, and what the underlying values are. Jon will record the values we all identify in the discussion. We have thirty minutes, and I will do my best, with your support, to keep us focused and on time."

At several points in the course of the three-hour meeting, individuals remembered a topic they wanted to bring up, and since there had never been a forum for such things, they felt compelled to express it. The chair was good-humored about the potential diversions, and she called upon her experience as a leader of community volunteer organizations. After the first diversion, she introduced a "parking lot." The parking lot was simply a blank piece of chart paper on the wall that allowed her to write down the off-topic items so they could later be added to a meeting agenda and dealt with properly.

At the end of the meeting, a simple evaluation form was distributed and collected by the planning committee. It asked three questions:

1. Do you think the meeting met its objectives?
2. What would you like to see us do again?
3. What would you change about the next meeting?

The first meeting: Accomplishments. At the end, at the request of the family group, the planning committee agreed to plan the next two meetings. The family defined the purpose of family meetings as meeting regularly, providing a forum for discussions of how the business impacts the family and vice versa, educating the family on the business and on family business in general, and reviewing needs from time to time and plan ways of meeting them.

One suggestion for a purpose was confusing and a little difficult to handle. The suggestion was this: to advance all shareholders' understanding of the financial aspects of the business to achieve an investor level of competence. All agreed that this was important, but everyone understood that the second-generation spouses were not and would not be shareholders. The tension arose around the invitation to spouses for the first meeting but not including them on an important issue; this felt awkward. The family members solved this issue by reminding themselves of their varied roles: they were a business family, and some of them were also owners. They agreed to hold future meetings in two sections, one for shareholders only and one for everyone, including spouses. They agreed on two meetings per year and evaluating each to make continual improvements in process and structure.

Planning Committee Recap. A week after the meeting, the planning committee met to review the evaluations and make an assessment. The committee members agreed that they got off to a good start. The background provided by the founder revealed some history no one had heard about before, and they were able to identify five values that have been consistent guidelines during the early years. The presentation on the new product had been a little dry, and they agreed in the future they needed to coach any outsiders on how to make the most of their meetings with the family.

Regarding structure, they were pleased. The committee members felt the discussion had been balanced and that everyone had been respectful of the ground rules; they'd had a rather even level of participation, which was unique for the family. People left the meeting enthused with the prospect of the next meeting and their success with handling the awkward issue of when to include spouses and when it was appropriate to include only shareholders and future shareholders. This didn't feel completely right, but the committee members agreed that they had reached a good solution for the time being. Finally, they considered the evolution of their new forum for the family. The family would still revert to traditional roles outside the family meeting; there were no illusions. However, for important learnings that must be preserved, the process of the meeting produced an agreement on what everyone saw, understood, and freely accepted, rather than merely what they were told to understand and appreciate. Thus, the planning committee determined that the process of empowerment and acceptance of the family meeting was off to a good start, but they also realized that this process would take time.

The Empowered, Ambitious Start: Creating a Family Council Charter

For this example, consider a business family in the early sibling stage (Negotiating Table family council), with the founding couple in their late sixties and their five children and spouses ranging in age from 45 to 35. The family will meet as a group of twelve adults in the first and second generation even though there are four children in the third generation over the age of 15.

This family begins with the understanding that a family council is a governance function for the family. That is, as a fully informed and involved family group the family members made the decision to use a family council for planning, education, decision making, and learning how to effectively work as a cohesive family unit. They came to the decision to try this after several family members attended seminars, circulated booklets, and then met for a day with a family business consultant. After hearing about the structure used by others, the family members decided to use a family council, but this is still new to them, and they do not fully understand how it will fit in with their business and their board of directors. They will soon have their first family council meeting where they will explore their structure; they will decide the nature of their family council. A planning committee was appointed to prepare for the first meeting.

This family has taken a significant step toward empowering itself to do things under the auspices of a sanctioned family council. Thus, making it a choice for individuals to attend or not is significant. The family meetings are about more than showing up to hear a speaker. Individuals seriously thinking this through may consider the following:

> If I attend and participate, I am choosing to abide by the decisions made in the family council. If I participate in the decisions, and a course of action is agreed to, I am committing to conforming to the authority of the council's direction. This is very different from how we have done things as a family. Will it work for us? Will it work for me?

Thus, individuals make decisions regarding compliance before they show up and then comply with rules when they participate in a meeting. Participation as a choice to comply with new rules may not be apparent to everyone and will require some time to fully sink in. Family members have a long history of dealing with one another in a particular way; for example, the parents used to be in charge of all decisions, but now the two oldest children act more like peers to the parents, and the other three siblings and their spouses usually go along with their decisions. Some may consider the power shifts resulting from meeting in a new forum, and others may expect that nothing will change. The rules may be changing, and individuals do not have all the details. They are about to go into a meeting where they will create the details in the form of established rules for self-governance; they will establish them in their family council charter.

Preparing for a discussion about their charter, individuals will consider seriously how to limit or control potential problems by deciding on the rules. For example, this family includes siblings who are of the age where they are taking on more responsibility as a team with the oldest two leading them. They see a future together, and they all know who works best with whom and in what ways they irritate each other. They are all sensitive to one or more of their siblings gaining too much power over the rest; these feelings may range from unease to angry outbursts. Will working in a family council add to their anxieties or reduce them? While not every individual may realize the ramifications at this point, they will ultimately understand them, particularly as they are in a meeting that focuses on the rules of governance (the substance of a charter). At the very least when family members prepare for their first family council meeting, they will consider the following: "I hope I get more clarity about why are we doing this as well as about what we hope to accomplish with a family council." Realizing the complexity of a shift in the dynamics of the family and the desire to be successful, this group has decided to work with a facilitator in drafting their charter.

Preparation. Creating a family council charter as a first step accomplishes two things: (1) it gives the family something concrete to focus on, and those who are more task-oriented can see the results of their work, and (2) it requires a process of development for the family so that when all work together to produce the charter, they have an opportunity to practice working together in a new, more egalitarian way. Thus, ground rules for the meeting are important. As consultants and facilitators, we have had success with business family teams by encouraging them to try the following set of ground rules. These may be provided in advance or early in the first meeting, for example:

The ROPES[4]: Family Council Meeting Ground Rules

R   Each person is **RESPONSIBLE** for getting good solutions from the meeting. This means that each family member has to work hard to find creative solutions or support those they see as effective. It also means that each family member must take responsibility for saying something if he or she feels a solution is not a good one. **R** also stands for **RESPECT**; that is, family members agree to show each other the same respect they reserve for customers and esteemed visitors. Finally, good solutions are those that are good for all family members; we all are responsible for win-win conclusions and plans.

O   Each family member is **OPEN** to the ideas and views of other family members. This means that each family member works hard to hear what someone else is saying. **OPEN** also means that each family member is open with his or her own ideas and views.

P   **PARTICIPATION** is as equal as possible so that everyone has
       an opportunity to present his or her views. This means that
       every family member always makes sure everyone has com-
       mented on important topics before a decision is made or before
       the discussion moves on to something else. **P** also stands for
       PRIVACY. Nothing goes outside the room unless everyone
       agrees.

E   Because there must be a change in how family members
       make decisions and interact, each person is encouraged to
       EXPERIMENT with doing things differently. This means that
       if one person usually dominates discussion, then this person
       should experiment by waiting until others have spoken before
       offering a viewpoint (or asking others for their viewpoints).
       Moreover, family members who usually remain quiet should
       experiment with taking the lead.

S   Each family member will **SUPPORT** other family members.
       This means that discussions will not allocate blame but will
       focus on problems to be solved. If discussion turns to blaming,
       each family member has an obligation to call attention to this
       and refocus the discussion on solving a problem. In this way,
       each person will get support from the others.

Thus, right from the beginning, individuals can see that they may be
asked to work with each other differently than they have done in the
past.

The meeting facilitator begins work well before the meeting, providing not only the example ground rules and other readings, but
meets with the planners. The scheduling of the first meeting was efficiently handled by the business president's assistant. It was planned
to last a day and a half and to consist of an evening together at a
resort that could accommodate both the meeting and social events.
Thus, all would commit to be on site for a Monday afternoon and
the whole day on Tuesday. Considering all schedules, the meeting was
planned to occur in four months time, which would place it in the
early summer.

The planning group consisted of the oldest sibling and two of her
younger brothers. Coached by the facilitator, one of the members of
the planning group worked with the parents to write an informal and
personal letter to be both informative and to generate interest. The

letter reminded everyone of the date and served as a cover letter for four advance reading items sent to each of the twelve family members in advance. The letter appears below.

Dear Loved Ones,

We are pleased that you have all worked hard to accommodate a meeting in a busy summer; we are an active family, and the meeting will be a challenge, especially for those who must arrange for child care. However, we truly believe this first meeting of our family council will be worth everyone to attend from beginning to end. All the advice we have received is consistent; the consultants have stressed the importance of full attendance for the entire length of the meeting, so please arrange your travel and child care accordingly.

As you can see, there is HOMEWORK. We have provided you with some reading material that should help you prepare for what to expect and help us all to be productive when we get together. You have four enclosures:

1. *Family Meetings: How to Build a Stronger Family and a Stronger Business*, 2d ed. by Craig E. Aronoff and John L. Ward.[5]
2. Meeting ground rules for us to consider—we will all decide at the beginning of our meeting whether we want to adopt these or not or whether we want add to them.
3. A generic family council charter to serve as an example—we will want to complete our own rather than adopt another family's charter. The enclosure will serve as an example for the decisions we will need to make together.
4. The preliminary agenda.

Our time together will be most effective if you read these materials and, if you have comments or questions, please send them to our advisor Dr. McClure by April 30.

Please plan to arrive at Eagle Oaks on Monday by noon so that you may check in and get oriented before our afternoon meeting. It is scheduled to begin at 1 p.m. and conclude by 5 p.m. Mom has been in touch with Louis, Jenny, Mia, and Tommy (oldest grandchildren), and they have agreed to explore the pool, tennis courts, maze, and game room with the younger grandchildren during our four-hour meeting on Monday. We felt they all would appreciate having some unstructured time together on the first day. Dinner will be at 6:30 p.m. in the White Oak Room—everyone is invited, including child care givers, but it will be the parents' choice whether the youngest children should attend. We will have the White Oak Room to ourselves so noise and running around will be just fine. Papa has arranged for a surprise visit from a guest who will delight the children and be fun for us older ones as well. There is nothing scheduled after dinner, but for those who want to stay around, Papa and Mama have a large suite reserved that has plenty of comfortable seating and opens onto a deck. There should be lots of room, and we will have board games and refreshments available.

For the next morning a buffet breakfast will be available in the main dining room. You may come and go as you like after 6:00 a.m., but please be prepared to begin our meeting by 8:30 sharp. On Tuesday, the children will have more structure. Our consultants have planned activities for the oldest four and for the middle group of five- to eleven-year-olds. They will be occupied the entire length of the adult meetings, from 8:30 to noon and from 1:30 p.m. to 3:30 p.m. The children's activities will be divided between experiences that teach earning, spending, and saving money, and our business (the youngest ones will create and videotape a commercial for the company). A complete agenda will be forthcoming. It should be fun for them.

We are really looking forward to this first organizational meeting of our family council. It will be different for us, but we are in a unique position to be purposeful about our future together and can listen to each other's views and create a vehicle for accomplishing our "family work" and have a little fun together while we do it. We are fortunate to have this opportunity!

With love,
Momma and Papa

We have a few comments about some of the features of the first family council meeting that were revealed in the letter. The following were intentional:

- Use of a planning committee—one sibling could organize the meeting, and that would likely be more efficient. However, three in a planning group is a good number and reinforces an egalitarian culture right from the beginning; it encourages commitment before the meeting begins. Moreover, since this is a family in the Early Sibling stage, providing an opportunity for siblings to work together as a team without parents was a deliberate choice.
- Full attendance at the entire event—commitment to a family council function is eroded by late arrivals and early departures.

It is more than the disruption caused by individuals showing up who must catch up in order to effectively participate or individuals getting out of their seats and departing at different times toward the end. A big part of the effect of a family council is that agreements, plans, and common understanding are created, and thus commitment to follow-through is greater with full participation. An individual who was not there will be less committed to abide by a decision made in his or her absence.

- Advance readings and requesting action, such as questions and comments—in other words, homework is a commitment to prepare for the meeting, and it encourages engagement. Participating in this way could be some family members' first opportunity to engage.

- An example of what will be produced—providing a sample family council charter allows family members to understand the size, scope, and content of the task. Having little prior experience with a charter, individuals benefit from seeing the final product. However, once individuals have the concept illustrated by the example, they should be encouraged to put the example away and draft an original. Greater commitment and more effective compliance are created with full participation in a struggle to define and agree on the rules and structure. It is easier to copy parts of an example, and it is also easier to forget or ignore a charter created in such a way.

- An overnight stay—there is a great benefit to an overnight stay at a meeting facility even for families that live close to one another. Doing so reinforces a focus on the family's task and helps build or maintain relationships. Also, an overnight stay allows time for contemplating the natural uneasiness and questions that form during the first day, and a second day allows time for the questions to be answered, and it also provides more comfort or the recognition that answers will come. Researchers who study groups describe this change process as moving from a frozen state to an unstable state, followed by a refreezing in a new set of conditions.

The agenda. This family has the advantage of working with a facilitator, and even though preparation is required for the meetings, all family members will be able to fully participate in the meeting. The planners will not have to run the meeting or take notes; they will participate just like everyone else. The sibling planning group together with the consultant created and circulated the following agenda two weeks prior to the meeting.

Family Council Meeting Agenda

Monday

12:00 p.m.   Hotel check-in. Lunch buffet available outside the meeting room

1:00 p.m.   Meeting begins

Overview. Review of the ground rules for the two-day meeting, establishing goals and review the agenda—any adjustments to the agenda?

Our purpose as a family and the role of a family council. What is the purpose of our family and why continue as a business family? Create the basis for a family mission statement.

Case example. A case is presented that involves a sibling business family looking back on its strengths and weaknesses, accomplishments and disappointments. From the case, we will identify our challenges and the role of a family council to assist in implementing our mission and meeting our challenges. Prioritize goals into "This Year" and "Within the Next Two Years."

Midafternoon break

Who is family? Discussion and decision regarding the membership of the family council. Who will be involved in the future, and what are the membership requirements?

Review of family council charter example. Review of the advance readings and the charter example. Discuss the meaning of each segment of the charter and action plans for the completion of each.

1. History
2. Purpose of the family council
3. Membership
4. Meetings—number and location
5. Leadership
6. Committees
7. Expenses

Overview of Tuesday's agenda

    5:00 p.m.   Conclude

    6:30 p.m.   Dinner

Tuesday's Agenda

    6:00 a.m.   Breakfast buffet available in the main dining room—come and go as you please

    8:30 a.m.   ***Review of previous day.*** Any questions or conclusions to share?

    Conflict and decisions. Before taking on any particular conflict or decision, we should decide how we want to proceed. We will identify decisions and possible future decisions and create rules. For conflict, we will review practices of other business families and decide which ones we want to adopt. There may be follow-up tasks that we will not complete until after the meeting. Develop a code of conduct?

    Midmorning break

    11:00 a.m.   ***Business update.*** Overview of the recent developments in the business, new products, competitive landscape, and market trends

    Noon Lunch

    1:30 p.m.   ***How to follow through.*** Review of action plans for finishing and making further progress on the charter and for addressing items on the "This Year" and "Next Two Years" lists. Planning for the next meeting: Who will be involved and who will lead?

    2:30 p.m.   ***The third generation joins the meeting.*** Premier showing of video commercials created by the children. Third generation updates on the work of the first and second generations.

    3:30 p.m.   Conclude

Remarks and Results of the Initial Meeting of the Family Council

Part social, part learning, part creating. In addition to the founder parents and their five children and spouses, there are eleven family members in the third generation. In addition, two caregivers were involved to help with the youngest children. Handling the logistics for 25 people is a project in itself. The planning committee got support by recruiting other members of the family to help but retained the decision-making role.

Planning for the children was accomplished by asking grandma (Momma) to organize the first day, and the second day, for all but the two youngest, was planned and conducted by consultants. For the evening between the two days of meetings, unstructured time was left with options to gather as a family or go one's own way after dinner. This has the effect of letting people decompress or recharge in different ways; no one way works for everyone. The committee also felt that there was enough scheduled time with the meetings, and they wanted a balance.

Thus, they tried to create a balance of fun or social time for the family, where the family learned from the experiences of others or from discussion, and time for accomplishment. This final part of the balanced event was supported by family work that led to the following accomplishments:

- A first draft of a statement on the purpose of the family and the role of the family council
- A first draft of a family mission statement
- Description of the definition of family (this might seem straightforward, yet it is complicated as we will see in chapter 7)
- General direction for the chapters of the family council charter
- The children created and videotaped a commercial that was presented to their grandparents, parents, aunts, and uncles

In our consulting group, based on the experience of many business families, we have found that attempting to balance these three aspects of a meeting is likely to lead to success. It is impossible to make the three segments exactly equal, and they can vary from meeting to meeting. As in this case, once the rough draft agenda was developed, the planning committee evaluated the balance and made some adjustments. The committee members found they were trying to squeeze too much into the agenda, so they ended up removing some of the items on the original agenda.

Purpose and mission. The planners understood that for the family council to survive and be useful and provide a basis for decisions about the charter, individuals had to know its purpose. They chose to focus first on the purpose of the family and then to connect the business to the family, asking the question of why they should continue as a business family. They reasoned that allowing a participative discussion on these questions would be valuable whether they created a charter or not and would in any case be vital to a charter. Based on the evaluations conducted after the meeting, this segment of the meeting was rated as the most valuable.

First drafts in the family council, wordsmithing in committees. Another decision on the part of the planners was to limit the meeting goals so that they make best use of the family being together. Rather than trying to finalize elements of their charter or family mission statement in the meeting, they wanted enough guidance and input for a committee to follow through and prepare a document for final review by the full family council. An ad hoc charter committee was created at the family council meeting.

Meeting notes. In this meeting, the consultant provided the notes. As is our preference, notes are preferred over meeting minutes. Notes include the key decisions and conclusions from the meeting, ideas and input for later consideration by a committee, and action plans with accountability identified. After the meeting, an evaluation was completed by each of the twelve family members, and these results were also included in the notes. Finally, the agenda and handouts were attached in the appendix of the notes so that there was a complete set of material for later reference.

The issues in the family. Like all families, this one has issues; the family is in the early sibling stage, and many of its challenges can be identified as normal symptoms of a business family where the founding and second generations are determining how their roles will transition. The family members provided an opportunity for the issues to be named, but they did not attempt to take them on in the first meeting. Two concerns drove their decision making.

If they ignored the fact that issues related to the family dynamics existed, they would run the risk of ignoring the proverbial elephant in the room. Someone would call attention to the issues and that would be difficult to manage. Thus, they needed a way to acknowledge their issues and be productive.

The second concern was that if they named the issues, the family would naturally want to solve them, or individuals would want to provide more background and support for their views on the topics. The planners wisely understood that a family coming together for the first time could not take on significant issues and resolve them quickly; the family had neither the conflict and communication skills nor the time.

Discussion of a case example was chosen as a way of identifying many of the family's issues in a productive way. After discussing the case, family members identified their own challenges as priorities for future family council meetings. Doing so let them know that important issues would get addressed. They produced the following list:

- What model of leadership do we prefer: a team of siblings at the top, one leader of a sibling team (i.e., first among equals), or one traditional leader?
- How do we separate the roles of owners from the roles of family employees and managers in the business?
- What do we need to do as a family to maintain good relationships and high trust?
- What is the path of the first-generation leader in the transition of management and ownership control to the sibling group of the second generation?
- What values do we agree must be maintained in the business?
- How do we want to conduct ourselves as a family in our community and in our business?
- What are the developmental needs and available resources for family members in the second and third generations?

A journey begins. The first step for this business family was a successful one. The family's meetings are not always two-day events; family members use a schedule of one day every six months followed by a two-day meeting. As a result of defining family, the family council meetings have expanded to include all family members above the age of fifteen. The family council also elected a chair and vice chair; together with the planning committee (two others) they plan each meeting over the course of their two-year term of office. The family's charter was completed in the third meeting, which was frustrating for some family members as it seemed to take too long.

Finally, this family has initiated a meeting of siblings; thus, some of the questions identified in the family council are addressed at sibling meetings. The siblings regularly report on their progress at family council meetings. The separate meetings provide siblings with the opportunity to work things out on their own, and the role of the family council is to hold them accountable for good solutions and to provide support, of course.

5

Running the Family Council

Now that you and your family have determined that creating a council is a good idea and have the basic understanding of what it takes to make it happen, you need an instruction manual on how to run this newly created council. Remember that a council meets not just one time but rather is a sustainable, ongoing process that will help keep everyone informed and involved. And it is critical that the council be a living function that can evolve over time as things change.

The family council charter is part of the operating manual; it contains a set of instructions and guidelines provided by the family for use by the family council. This chapter discusses the charter and provides practical advice for the leaders and organizers. This information will also be useful for any member of the family who wants to understand and get involved in optimizing the performance of the family council. This is not just a guide for the chair of the family council, the more family members understand effective operations of their governing body, the more a single vision of performance will be held by all and thus the greater the potential to achieve and maintain the vision. The components of a family council charter are revealed first, followed by illustrations for dealing with realistic family council challenges that are common to many business families.

We will use two kinds of family councils as illustrations; first, a family council including the entire family with more than twenty family members. It is important to remember when reviewing this case that even though all adult family members make up this family council, it is not a family association or family assembly, both of which are described fully in chapter 7. Relatively speaking, the family council example is simply big, and in the evolution of the family it will not be long before a family assembly and association are formed, with a smaller representative family council acting as their executive function. The second case example describes a representative family council of five members serving a family of over fifty adults. The family councils in the two examples are self-run family governance functions, which may have benefitted from consultants and advisors at their start and may from time to time receive help on difficult issues; for the most part, they are managed and operated by the family for the family.

Compensation of family council members and leaders is addressed next where general guidelines are provided and a method for determining compensation specific to a business family's size and complexity. Finally, we will illustrate how a self-managed family council participates in what family business is famous for: adapting. We describe feedback and assessment options available to family councils along with methods for utilizing the information they receive.

The Family Council Charter

The charter is a description of the purpose and the family council's function. It is a description of the constituency, the family that is defined in the charter, and it is a description of the rights, authority, and responsibilities the family assigns to the family council. As we have indicated in the previous chapter, a good way to start a new family council is to work on the charter together because this builds necessary group work skills. It is also a good practice for developing family councils that have operated without a charter, especially right after they have made significant changes, such as when transitioning from a council of the full family to a representative family council.

Below we describe the major sections of a charter and offer the choices, rationales behind some of the options, and recommendations where we have preferences and where we believe there is a right way and wrong way. (A short version of a sample charter appears in appendix 2.)

Purpose of the Family Council

Purposes can vary from succession-oriented function to a very broad scope of serving the family's well-being. We advocate for a family council's purpose being specific to its constituent family. While there are several examples of charters available, simply adopting the language of an example will provide little commitment, meaning, and value. Instead, we recommend using one of the techniques described in chapter 4 to prioritize a purpose and create a custom charter.

For a comprehensive description of the family council's purpose, we believe the best way to begin is to use what was developed in one of our consulting group meetings by John L. Ward,[1] who identifies six purposes of a family council as follows:

1. **To promote family mission and meaning**
   - Support shared values
   - Understand and respect history
   - Steward the family's enterprises
   - Pursue philanthropic interests

If the family does not yet have a mission statement, then it would be a purpose of the family council to help articulate it. If the family already has a mission statement, we recommend making it a part of the charter. The same is true for the family's values. Even though stewardship is almost a universal value for business families, it is not always fully understood, and a family council will assume responsibility for advancing an understanding of stewardship and the other values of the family. It will also enhance appreciation for the family and business history, especially among new members of the family and younger family members. Whether there is a separate family foundation or all philanthropic activities are handled entirely by the business, families may depend upon the family council to guide philanthropic education and development, and they may even go so far as to use the family council for consensus formation on philanthropic goals.

2. **To promote understanding of the family's enterprises**
   - Review status, strategy, and performance
   - Discuss opportunities and challenges
   - Explore new visions

An update on the business or news about the enterprise is often a memorable segment of a family meeting, and a valuable role for the family council is to find and maintain ways for the family to remain informed. However, an even more important role is to set the stage for a productive discussion among informed family members that respects the lines between owners and operators, and between family and owners, yet provides valued direction for a board and management.

3. **To promote communications and mutual understanding**
   - Exchange information
   - Strengthen friendships
   - Share good times
   - Learn from each other
   - Recognize and appreciate each other

One very common responsibility a family will delegate to its family council is to promote dialogue within the family. Thus, a critical part of helping a family continue healthy discussion is to provide the forum and tools, work the back channels, build the skills, balance appreciation with a respect for differences, and monitor the overall strength of relationships throughout the family.

4. **To promote problem solving**
   - Address family grievances
   - Deal with one another
   - Make decisions on family matters
   - Address common problems

Similar to the purpose of ensuring communication and mutual understanding is the need to address problems, preferably before they cause damage to relationships. A business family will be served well by a family council that counts among its responsibilities the institution of proactive measures, such as conflict resolution and negotiation education, and a policy for addressing conflict and a code of conduct. Families may even go so far as to make the family council a decision-making body for the resolution of conflict.

5. **To promote family education**
   - Learn business and family business
   - Explore ownership and wealth
   - Enhance interpersonal skills
   - Study family dynamics

Among a family council's responsibilities is general education beyond learning about the business, the shared history, and communication and conflict skills. The family council may also be charged with anticipating the educational needs of the changing family, the growing diversity within the family, and especially the needs of new members and younger family members; the family council provides access to or coordinates delivery of appropriate education.

6. **To promote family and ownership continuity and succession**
   - Develop and review the family's constitution
   - Initiation of the next generation

It may seem counterintuitive that this last purpose is listed last. It is certainly an important role for the family council in the eyes of many families; however, successfully accomplishing most of the previously listed purposes paves the way for a transition. Still, the family council is a forum for monitoring the goals and progress of generational transition. For example, a family council may be the coordinating body for education, specifying the nature of resources and providing the gentle nudge that gets family estate planning accomplished; it may also arrange for signed shareholder agreements as well as establish the vision for ownership, governance, and the critical role of the family in the next generation.

Membership in the Family Council

Constituency. This next section defines who can serve on the family council and defines the constituency; that is, we define the sometimes difficult concept of the "family" that is served by the family council. The factors to consider and the options available for defining a family are covered in chapter 7 and will not be repeated here. Generally, we are in favor of the broadest definition, if only for the reason that inclusion rather than exclusion makes for fewer problems and more opportunities to deal with the problems and potentially resolve them. Aside from this practical reason, the other practical and philosophical considerations are fully explained in the section that discusses family assemblies and family associations.

Thus, as an example, we might define the family to be served by a family council as:

All descendents of the founders who are shareholders or will become shareholders or the beneficiaries of shares held in trust, including their spouses and children, together with bloodline children, adopted children, and children from blended families.

The charter may further clarify that participation of a spouse or blended family children begins after a marriage. The charter may also specify that children who are adopted or those who join the family before the age of ten[2] are welcome to participate in the family assembly and be represented by the family council. Many families believe this degree of clarity prevents awkwardness or hard feelings arising from multiple interpretations about when it is appropriate to invite a new member of the family.

Voting eligibility. Typically, age is the key consideration in distinguishing voting from nonvoting members of the family represented by the family council. Thus, a charter may specify that "for all matters requiring a vote, an individual must have reached the age of fifteen." However, this item is more appropriate for a family association charter.

Configuration. Once the constituency is defined, the family council configuration may be defined. Typically, the following are considerations for establishing the configuration of a family council:

- Generations—how many members from each; this also covers age distribution
- Family branches—should all branches be represented or not
- Family or business roles—members of business management or the board, spouses, and lineal descendants

For example, a large family with several potential candidates may establish a six-person family council specifying that one person should participate from each of the six branches and that at least two of the members should be from the third generation. This configuration emphasizes broad representation and ensures participation from the youngest generation. This same family might have one more member than the number of branches, i.e., a seven-member council, with the seventh seat an at-large position elected without respect to branch but based on qualifications. Over time, more and more at-large members of the family council and fewer branch seats can move a family away from branch politics.

Another family might emphasize maximum diversity and de-emphasize branch representation. Thus, family members might specify that of the six family council members at least two should be from each generation, at least two should be non-lineal descendants, and at least one should be or have been employed in the business or on the board of directors.

Qualifications. In addition to the configuration, the next source of guidance for membership would be qualifications. What skills, experience, or abilities are desired? Examining the purpose the family council is to serve, we suggest the following qualifications:

- Willingness to provide time and commitment throughout the term
- Communication skills—listening, persuading, and informing
- Win-win negotiation and group diplomacy skills
- Maturity
- Understanding and support of the family mission and vision
- Accessibility to the entire family
- Respect and trust from the entire family

Most families considering the requirements for an effective family council establish an age and/or experience requirement candidates must meet to qualify for service on a family council. For example, the cutoff for voting eligibility in the family assembly may be fifteen, but the minimum age for participation on the family council may be eighteen or twenty-one. The minimum age for the chair may be even higher. Many families opt to require service on an ad hoc or standing committee of the family council as an experience and commitment qualification for family council membership.

Elections

Who participates in the council can be determined by either a formal election process or appointments. For example, a family in the early sibling stage focusing on developing more trust across the branches might opt for appointments; that is, each branch selects its own representative. A large family needing to choose among many good candidates will need a fair process for nominations and elections similar to a process used by a board of directors. Procedures for establishing initial membership were covered in the previous chapter; here we present an example of procedures for a Cousin Round Table family council, that is, a family with adults in the third generation who are taking on significant responsibilities. They are working less with their second-generation parents, aunts, and uncles, and focusing more and more on the young adults in the fourth generation.

Nominations. To replace members whose terms are ending the chair of the family council will appoint a three-person nominating committee from among the family and/or the family council and set a time frame for its work. The nominating committee will choose its chair whose role will be to coordinate the function of the committee and to serve as its spokesperson. The committee is expected to:

- Conduct an assessment of the family council's configuration and the upcoming needs and priorities of the family council; this includes asking for input from current and outgoing members of the family council;
- Inform the full family of the vacancy, provide the list of desired family council membership qualifications and a summary of views on the needs of the family and corresponding requirements for family council candidates and ask for volunteers and nominations; and
- Determine as a committee a recommended slate of candidates, contact each one privately to establish willingness to serve, and submit the list to the family council chair.

Election Procedures. To replace outgoing members at the end of their terms, the chair will appoint a two-person election committee from among the remaining family council members. The election committee will inform all members of the family who are eligible to vote, explain the procedures for a secret ballot, provide the nominating committee's assessment of needs, the list of qualifications, and a list of the candidates. Voting eligibility is defined above in the membership section of this charter.

The charter may not go far enough to answer all of the questions about specific procedures. It is thus a good practice to use written policy to augment the direction provided by a charter. For example, the specific voting procedures may be set forth in a policy that could indicate that if there are several candidates for the same seat, the one with the most votes will be determined the winner, and a run-off procedure will be used for breaking a tie. The election committee will collect the ballots, count the individual votes, and inform the family council of the winner(s). The chair will make the announcement to the individual candidates and to the broader family.

Replacements in the event of resignations. For members who resign from the family council prior to the end of their term, a special procedure will be followed. The chair will convene the family council to identify their needs and the desired qualifications of a new member then identify candidates and make a decision as a family council. The replacement member will serve to the end of the term, and at that time standard election procedures will be followed.

Election of the chair. Many families prefer to select the chair from among the representatives who have been elected to membership on the family council. After establishing the criteria for the chair role, candidates are selected from the group and elected through a vote. Terms may or may not coincide with an individual's term on the family council. We prefer that the chair leaves the family council at the end of his or her term as chair of a representative family council. Doing so provides for an effective handoff of leadership. That is, it is easier on both the incumbent and the new chair when the former is not confronted with changes to his or her way of doing things.

An alternative approach is for the entire constituency to elect the new chair; that is, all eligible voters who are members of the family association elect the new chair. A nominating committee is useful and follows the steps described above: (1) needs assessment, (2) qualifications communicated with openness to all volunteers and nominees from the family, (3) recommendation for a slate presented by the committee, and (4) election, usually by secret ballot.

Council Structure

In this section of the charter, a description of the family council configuration is provided, along with officer positions, the terms of members, and the standing committee structure.

Officers. We have seen charters provide detailed job descriptions for the chair and vice chair roles, but we prefer that these be maintained as separate documents. We prefer a general statement about the role of the chair, such as the following outline:

The role of the family council chair is to be a servant leader of the family governance function. That is, he or she must build support and commitment for family council initiatives by encouraging input and participation from all family council members and also from the broader family whenever feasible. Specifically, the chair's role is to:

- Lead the family council by developing goals, maintaining focus, coordinating its work, and providing follow-through to optimize performance
- Moderate discussions in family council meetings to develop conclusions, decisions, and actions
- Remain aware of and manage the balance between the family council's work and topics that must be addressed by the full family
- Act as liaison and spokesperson for the family council with the board of directors and serve as the primary conduit for communication to the family council from all others, e.g., business management and constituent family members

If a family council wants to have a vice chair, that role's purpose is often to assist a chair through division of labor, e.g., one leads some committees and the other coordinates the work of the remaining committees. Another purpose of the role of vice chair is to provide an opportunity for an individual to gain experience. For example, the vice chair position could be reserved for family council member from the younger generation.

For some families, term limits are important because they want to encourage rotation and broad participation and also share the responsibility of family council service. After one or two terms individuals may then have to sit out for a term before standing for election again. For other families, their rationale for not imposing term limits is to make it possible for those who are highly qualified and willing to serve to have the opportunity to do so.

Configuration. If branches are to be represented, the number from each branch is specified in this section as well as the number from each generation and any other description of a representative that is important to the family, e.g., the ratio of lineal descendants to spouses. The total number of family council members is determined and also whether the number can vary. For example, some families prefer to have a set number, often an odd number so that tie votes do not occur. Others indicate a range, usually five to seven, which is a good range from the standpoint of group performance.

Terms. Members' terms of service often range from two to three years and are staggered; that is, they do not all end in the same year. Like terms in the US Congress, terms of family council members may expire but only a third of the members come up for reelection or replacement at any one time. Also, this section of the charter will specify if there are term limits. We are advocates of merit and qualification considerations for membership on the family council. For small families, we are not in favor of term limits. For large families with lots of qualified members, we are in favor of individuals having to sit out one term before renewed candidacy for membership on the family council.

Committees. Committees are an important part of the family council, and the charter should provide guidance for their use. For example, a family council for a family in the late sibling stage might be a Harvest Table family council and have the following committees:

- Next generation—For and of the junior generation to specifically address its integration into family governance and development as a group
- Education—To identify and coordinate the education of the entire family and provide for the unique needs of segments of the family
- Philanthropy—To provide family input regarding corporate philanthropy and to coordinate among family members who desire a combined strategic approach
- Planning—For planning and organizing family association and assembly meetings

For the purposes of drawing up a family council charter, we prefer leaving it to the family council to decide about establishing, continuing, or retiring standing committees so they may adapt to the shifting needs of the family. The same is true for ad hoc committees and task forces. It is typically the responsibility of the chair to coordinate the activities of committees, which involves appointing a chair for each committee or ensuring that one is chosen, clarifying the goals and time frames for committee activity and outcomes, following up to ensure progress, helping to resolve challenges, and scheduling committee reports. We also prefer charters to specify that standing and temporary committees can be staffed by at least one member of the family council with no restrictions on other members. Thus, broader participation and contributions is encouraged.

Meetings. How many times will the family council meet, what will be the procedures for informing the family of the agenda in advance? Will the meetings be open, and how will the family council communicate its conclusions? The minimum number of meetings can be specified in a charter and is often two, three, or four per year, with more meetings scheduled as needed at the discretion of the chair. Transparent procedures work best for many family councils; common practices include advance notification of the agenda made available to all family members, invitation to submit topics to the family council, and access to the notes following a meeting.

Furthermore, in support of transparency, family council meetings may be open for observation by any member of the family association who would like to attend. It is usually a good idea to give the chair discretion for determining if any matter on the agenda would be best addressed in a session without observers. The chair is also responsible for maintaining the order of a meeting with two sets of participants if observers are provided an opportunity during the meeting to address the family council.

Budget. Regardless of how the family council is funded, the expectations regarding planning, gaining budget approval, and managing costs should be explained in the charter. Many family councils are funded by the business, and a statement such as the following is common:

> In November, the family council will develop and submit to the chair of the board of directors a budget for the following year's expenses. The chair of the family council will be invited to the December board meeting to present the budget and to respond to questions.

A separate written policy describing the cost reimbursement procedures for individuals' travel and meeting costs, while not a charter matter, is a good practice.

The Accomplishment Horizon:
Long-term Goals and Plan

Like a business, a long-term planning horizon for a family council will increase the odds of achieving the most important and rewarding accomplishments. Attempting to accomplish too much too quickly may overwhelm family members and too few accomplishments will erode support and interest. Whether the accomplishments concern development of knowledge and skills, creation of greater cohesion, or determination of common goals and plans, family councils must always consider the pace of the activity and work. The family council must know the family well enough and be aware of its own tolerance and desire for the work that needs to be accomplished in order to evaluate the appropriate pace. What to accomplish first, second, and third is just as important to decide as what projects can be done concurrently and what the timing of the introduction should be.

Strong family councils utilize family association meetings, surveys of family members, and direct inquiries to identify long-term priorities. In addition to asking for direct input, family council representatives are the elected leaders of the family and thus may come to their own conclusions about the family's long-term needs and priorities. These can then be broken down into manageable parts. Over several meetings, the family council can maintain continuity as members address priorities and achieve goals at an appropriate pace. With long-term plans, attention to a logical sequence and the number of projects that can be accomplished concurrently is important. Continuity can even be extended beyond the terms of current members when long-term goals and priorities are established.

Examples of long-term goals for different family situations, any one of which could occupy the agendas of several family assembly meetings and require multiple methods for successful completion, are as follows:

- Developing an understanding of shareholder responsibilities and skill development to allow a unified voice regarding investment goals for the business
- Reintegrate an estranged family member or branch of the family
- Connect the family that has grown and drifted apart and reestablish connections between members and with the enterprise

- Understand the meaning and implications of a transition from family-managed to family-governed and enhance the family's capability to adapt

Example of three-year priorities. For one family in the late sibling stage with young adult children in the third generation, the ultimate goal was to prepare the younger generation for its future role of steward shareholders. After prioritization, the family council created a list of expected accomplishments to be pursued and monitored over the next three years:

1. Make resources available to support the next generation's career development—mentoring, coaching, and family education;
2. Plan succession for the CEO and board chair—identify a vision for the future management and governance of the business;
3. Create a family constitution—identify the principles and values for the future of the family and family's involvement in the business;
4. Develop the responsible owner skills of the third generation— provide readings, make available financial seminars, and develop an internal university staffed by family and management; and
5. Develop a balanced business and family philanthropy function directed by the family—create a committee that provides input for the charitable needs of the business and accomplishes the family's philanthropic goals.

Based on this list of priorities, family council members determine how often they need to meet, how they would use themselves as resources, and what outside resources they would need in the form of information and education; they determined the goals and the sequence in which to accomplish portions of the list. Based on their list, they decided to meet three times per year and evaluate at the end of each year whether they should continue with that schedule or change it to two meetings per year or meet more frequently to manage the appropriate pace for the family.

Priorities in terms of goals for one year. Based on the above list of accomplishments family council members determined three goals for the coming year. These could be achieved because they were manageable even for busy people on a family council and reflected the most important and time-sensitive priorities.

1. Provide the appropriate support for mentoring, coaching, educational, and networking resources as well as creative experiences needed to support current endeavors for seeking one's "life's work." Make available assistance to match appropriate progress for each individual so as not to overwhelm or pressure anyone but encouraging continued development and progress at an appropriate pace. By the end of the year, report to the family council on the program status for each individual in the family who chooses to participate.
2. Develop a family mission/vision statement and the table of contents for a family constitution. In addition, complete the family employment policy and shareholder agreement segments of the constitution.
3. Identify educational resources and conduct or make available at least two financial skills sessions with each third-generation family member.

Goals segmented into a sequence across meetings. These same goals can then be converted to the planned main points of family council meeting agendas spread out over the three meetings planned for the year.

January Agenda: Rough Draft of Potential Agenda

- Advance readings and examples to fit the agenda topics
- Definition of a family constitution and goals for elements—perhaps make progress on some elements
- Create an initial draft of a family mission/vision statement for the constitution
- Educational component—focus on what complements the other items on the agenda
- Define the scope of a career assistance program for young family members—research what other family firms have accomplished
- Fun component—perhaps connect this with the business

May Agenda: Rough Draft of Potential Agenda

- Advance reading materials and drafts as outlined in the previous meeting
- Finalize the family mission/vision statement
- Significant progress on the family constitution draft
- Educational component—financial skills
- Draft charter for the family career assistance program
- Fun component

October Agenda: Rough Draft of Potential Agenda

- Advance readings and drafts to date of constitution and career assistance program charter
- Finalize constitution
- Educational component—financial skills
- Finalize charter and program features of the career assistance program
- Fun component

Planning a Successful Family Council Meeting: Preparing the Agenda

In business, the leader usually calls a meeting and sets the agenda. Typically, the boss has something to say and assumes all responsibility for the meeting; the meeting is either a success or a flop depending on this one person's skills in conducting it. However, the objective of family business meetings is for all participants to be fully involved in the meeting. In fact, one of the key ground rules for family business meetings is that every participant is responsible for the success of the meeting. Showing up is not enough of an effort; every person needs to feel that the topics covered in the meeting are important and should commit effort to preparation or at least formulate their thinking on topics prior to the meeting.

For family members to feel ownership of the meeting and develop their interest in the meeting's success, they must be involved right from the beginning in setting the agenda and in determining what the meeting will be about. Involving everyone takes the pressure off the leader to entertain or perform and produce a successful meeting. As a result, all family members are encouraged to really think about what the family needs to focus on in the upcoming family business meeting and to think about how to treat each issue. To summarize, sending out an advance request accomplishes three purposes:

1. To allow broad participation in creating an agenda for the upcoming meeting
2. To inform all attendees of the topics to be addressed in the meeting and to allow and encourage preparation for the meeting
3. To help distribute the responsibility for ownership of the meeting among all family members and to motivate everyone to make the meeting successful

A Responsive Agenda: Amanda's Case

Amanda, the third child of four, was elected to be the family council chair a year ago, and one thing she vowed to accomplish was to improve the agenda-setting process for family council meetings. Her family council consists of her parents, her three siblings and their spouses, her own spouse, and her niece who recently became old enough to participate; they form a Negotiating Table family council of eleven members from three generations (see chapter 3 for definition of Negotiating Table family council).

The significant current family dynamics that impact this next meeting must be taken into account by Amanda. Mike has his own agenda with the family; he feels that the family is much too involved in management matters at the board level and that the independent directors are not doing enough to manage the separation of governance from management and vice versa. There has been a conflict that everyone is talking about except the two in the conflict. Specifically, James and Ellen are both employees of the business, and rumor has it that they have had a blowup during a management meeting over a compensation issue. No two stories circulating in the back channels of the family match. The family has invested time and effort on their family council with good results to date. Amanda is the fourth chair preparing the third meeting of her two-year term. She is building upon the work of others. The education committee has been working hard; however, its members are dismayed by the lack of response (and appreciation) they are getting. Recently, they sent out a request for volunteers to help with an upcoming event and got no replies.

Before becoming the family council chair, Amanda had been openly critical of the way in which meetings were planned in the past; specifically, she saw too little input from the family and too much dependence on the previous chairs to make or break the success of the meetings. After taking office, she adopted a standard form that has received good feedback from a few family members. Family members have now come to expect to get the form as an advance memo a few weeks before each meeting.

Advance memo. Three weeks before each meeting, Amanda distributes a memo to the ten other participants. It includes the date, time, and place of the meeting and in bold letters the requested date for getting ideas back to her with reactions and suggestions for the agenda. She also lists the purpose of the family council, which is taken directly from the family's charter. She reasons that listing the purpose each time she requests input can serve to remind everyone of the kind of items that are appropriate for family council meetings.

She also lists on her form the agenda items previously established (e.g., topics individuals were asked to prepare for, a presentation by a guest professional such as the business's lawyer, or previous action plans calling for updates at this particular meeting). As the family council chair she is free to add items to the agenda as she sees fit, and she usually does so when there are emerging issues or developments about which she feels the family should be informed. However, in her advance agenda memo she does not include the regular items that appear on every agenda, namely, "Review of the Ground Rules" and "Meeting Evaluation and Summary of Items for the Next Meeting." One of Amanda's advance memos appears in figure 5.1.

The use of this agenda-setting format has resulted in significant discussions that might not have emerged otherwise. She now looks for two kinds of feedback in the responses she receives to her memos and uses these questions to help her decide how to be successful with agenda

Memorandum

Date: August 20
To: Family Council Members
From: Amanda
Subject: Ideas and input for our September meeting agenda: **PLEASE REPLY BY AUGUST 25**

Time Date and Place of Next Family Council Meeting:

9:00 A.M.—3:00 P.M. September 15 (Thursday) at Morris Woods Golf Club— Lunch in the dining room

Our FC Purpose Statement

The purpose of the Family Council is to educate and facilitate communication between family members and to provide a forum for constructive discussion, problem solving and decisions about the family as it relates to Smith Company as well as the business as it relates to the family. Further:

1. We want a forum for constructive discussion to deal with the known and unknown challenges that confront us as a family in business together. Our intention is to deal with challenges directly and the family council will be the forum.
2. We expect the council, as an informal body, to afford regular contact among family members and to be used to nurture relationships among members of the extended family and members of the next generation of owners.
3. The council will provide a place for general communication between family members involved in the business. It is a place for questions to get answered and for us all to learn what we each think about issues that affect us all. Our intention is to encourage and to make it okay for family members to bring up issues and have them addressed properly.
4. As we go forward, we will need to learn. The council will provide an opportunity for individuals with special expertise affecting our family relations, investments, or the business to address us and help us learn.
5. The council will be a place for decision making. We will benefit by a forum where all members have a voice in decisions that affect them. Our council will provide that opportunity.
6. And finally, for decisions that directly impact the business, the council will serve as the family's voice and provide this input directly to the board of directors. Therefore, for issues in which the board needs guidance from its shareholders, the council will serve as a forum for family decision making and consensus on the direction that is provided to the board.

Previously Established Agenda Topics

The following are items that were planned at our March meeting:

1. **Balance between family shareholder influence and independent director influence on the board**. Mike will make a presentation and lead the

Figure 5.1   Continued

---

discussion based upon his research and conversations with other families he met at a recent governance seminar and from a YPO/WPO webinar.

2. **Shareholder investment skills.** Sam Jones, the company CFO, will be invited to join us to provide a workshop on what we need to understand and master as responsible shareholders.

Your Reactions and Input—Please get back to me by August 25

1. What are your comments and ideas about these agenda items? For example, you might wish to comment and provide the chair with input on the appropriateness of this item for the family council or an outcome you hope we achieve.

2. What else would you like to see on our agenda? I'll try to accommodate as many ideas as possible, but please understand that I will need to make the final decision based upon our goals and priorities and the time available.

Thanks very much for your thoughts, ideas, and your contribution to the success of our family council meeting.

Figure 5.1   Example Advance Memo Requesting Agenda Input for a Family Council Meeting

topics and how to prioritize them:

1. Is the topic, and its explicit or implicit goal, appropriate for the family council, or do we need to address it in another forum instead/also?
2. With respect to our goals, purpose, and mission, what is the most important issue we should be addressing right now?

Amanda was recently surprised by feedback written in response to her latest memo by her niece:

"It is my understanding that James and Ellen are no longer speaking to one another because of a compensation argument at work. I don't know what it was about, and no one else I've asked has much information or details. However, two family members not speaking is a serious breach of our goal of family unity. Thus, we should have it on our agenda for our next meeting."

This issue raised by her niece concerns the second criterion; it is central to the mission and purpose of the family. However, for this specific issue, Amanda also considered the first question of whether the issue fits well in a family council meeting or could be better addressed elsewhere. As a result, she noted that the family council was not the first place to go and, based on the conflict resolution policy for family disagreements and her own sense of how to tactfully handle this situation, she wrote to Ellen and James.

"My request for topics resulted in a sensitive issue being raised. The point was a good one: Family unity is paramount, and it has been pointed out that you two have an unresolved conflict and progress toward a solution is dormant. I have no choice but to add this issue to the family council agenda if it remains unresolved, but the sequence of events and protocol must be followed. According to the policy on family conflict resolution, the first step is for both of you to work this out. The policy clearly states that it is not acceptable for a conflict to go unresolved. How can I or anyone else help? We are available for you individually, but our overall objective must also be remembered: 'a unified family with no unmanaged or unaddressed threats.' My thinking is to place this issue on the agenda as an update with your names attached, again consistent with our family conflict policy, but I hope that you will have made good progress prior to our meeting. Does this sound right to you? Our meeting is three weeks away."

After hearing from James and Ellen that they had agreed to work with a neutral third party to try to patch up their differences before the family council meeting, Amanda wrote to her niece:

"Thank you for your recommendation for our family council agenda in September (see your original comment copied below). According to our conflict resolution policy adopted by the family council two years ago, this is an issue that should first be addressed and resolved by Ellen and James. They have been advised and reminded of our policy and been encouraged to make progress toward a resolution. The family council has the responsibility to follow up and will become involved if there is no action or if efforts on their part are unsuccessful. Therefore, I am contacting Ellen and James to invite them to reply and to provide the family council with an update on their progress at our September meeting."

For the meeting in September, Amanda also received a few other replies to her advance memo:

- "We need to add the results of Don's investigation into how other family businesses deal with spouses working together."

- "Regarding planned agenda item #1, I know Mike will have an opinion about what he sees as the proper balance between family and independent shareholders on the board. We need to make sure this topic is handled so everyone's opinions emerge. I hope you will do that."
- "Thank you once again for handling this challenging job. I thought that in the last meeting you participated only as a moderator. It would be nice to hear your opinions on the topics."
- "We haven't gotten any ideas for the education committee's request for volunteers to help with this year's third-generation meeting. Can we make time for this and also get everyone's ideas on the meeting itself?"
- "I'm really looking forward to Mike's topic. I know there are some of us who have been reading up on the role of family members on the board. I think we have been very unclear about what we expect."
- "I know the education committee is feeling like they are not getting enough support. Perhaps we should give them some time on the agenda."

Consolidation and finalizing of the agenda. The two extremes Amanda must deal with are that either no one offers any comments or recommendations or that others offer so many ideas that she will be overwhelmed with all the input. Some family members may take the opportunity for input very seriously and offer lots of suggestions, and some may offer none. Whatever the response, a critical step has been taken: all individuals were given the opportunity to participate in setting the agenda. Even if some offer no input, the benefit of involvement is felt ownership on the part of all members of the family council just because they were asked for suggestions and because their input is genuinely considered in the preparation of the agenda for each meeting.

Whether too little or too much input, a decision must be made about what gets included on the agenda to fill the time available for the meeting. With respect to time estimates for each item, our experience in working with family groups is that there are some that will run over the time limit by about 50 percent and some even more than that. That is, a good practice is to assume a strict time schedule will not be kept and that items at the end may need to be postponed so that high-priority items can be addressed fully.

Smith Family Council Agenda

Thursday, September 15, 20xx

The Board Room, Morris Woods Golf Club

Wednesday, September 14 : (5–7 p.m. Dinner at the Rapid River Grill for all those who can make it)

Thursday, September 15

8:00 A.M.	Coffee, light breakfast, and catching up with one another
9:00	Underage children will depart with caregivers and coaches. Family council meeting begins.

Educational Component: *A Primer on Shareholder Investment Skills*—Sam Jones

Review of the acquisition of San Antonio Supply and Distribution. Using the acquisition as a learning opportunity, Sam will lead a review of the planning, decision making, and projections from the perspective of an investor. Topics include:

1. Legal structure—choices and the decision
2. Capitalization of the acquisition—choices and the decision
3. Cultural and other considerations
4. Role of the board
5. Negotiations and the deal with the owners of San Antonio S & D
6. Management oversight and operational changes
7. Projections for payback, future growth, and profitability

10:30	**Break—Sam will remain to answer questions throughout the break, but will depart at 11:30**
11:00	*Overview of the Remaining Agenda Items*

- Welcome, overview, and opening remarks—Amanda Smith
- Approval of notes from previous meeting and selection of today's note taker
- Review of meeting ground rules
- Key goals for today's family council meeting

Application of the Family Conflict Resolution Policy—Ralph Thompson

We will review the policy and explore its application and value to our family relationships. Ralph has worked with the family for several years as an advisor and counselor and will lead us for this part of the meeting.

Noon	*Lunch* together in the dining room
1:00 P.M	*Education Committee Update*—Rosanne and Tom

Third generation meeting planning and other news

Figure 5.2 Continued

1:30	*Scheduling Future Dates*—Please bring your calendars
1:40	***The Role of Family Directors and Independent Board Members*— Mike Smith**
	Mike will make a presentation and lead the discussion based upon his research and conversations with other families he met at a recent governance seminar and from his participation in a YPO/WPO webinar. Discussion may result in action items.
2:30	*Next Steps and Evaluation*
	• Review of today's action plans needing follow-through, decisions, and conclusions • Evaluation of the meeting
3:00	*Conclusion of the Family Council Meeting and Beginning of the Fun*
4:30	*Golf Cart Scavenger Hunt*—Meet at Smith Farm main barn for team assignment and instructions (babies will stay with caregivers; Tim and Sara will join the older children and adults in the scavenger hunt)
7:00	*Dinner at the Farm*—The nature of the entertainment will not be disclosed in advance. All offers or attempts to bribe the chair for information will be considered.

Figure 5.2 Amanda's Final Family Council Meeting Agenda

In some cases, items may be assigned into two categories: primary agenda items that will definitely be discussed in the meeting and alternate items that may be added to or may replace primary items based on the group's decision at the beginning of the meeting. The list of alternate items shows individuals that their recommendations have been considered even if these topics are not addressed until the subsequent meeting.

Commonly the chair's role is to decide on the final agenda, taking into consideration the family's input and his or her evaluation of the current needs of the business family. In some cases, the decision on a final agenda can be made in consultation with others. For example, if Amanda wants feedback on the final draft after receiving input from everyone, she could send a preliminary version of the consolidated agenda to one or two influential members of the family, a business leader invited to attend a portion of the meeting, or a selected member of the board of directors. In the end, Amanda developed the agenda that appears in figure 5.2.

Common Agenda-Setting and Planning Mistakes to Avoid

Reading and approval of the minutes. We know this is standard operating procedure for meetings, but we advise against it for family council meetings because we see it as sapping energy, inviting needless discussion on fine points, and possibly opening the door for political positioning as specific wording is debated. Using meeting time to engage in wordsmithery with the minutes of the previous meeting diverts from the core purpose of the family council; it works against unifying discussion and engagement on genuinely important issues. We recommend as an alternative that the chair send out the notes from the previous meeting not only right after a meeting but also together with the agenda and invite comment each time. If there is an issue that cannot be resolved by the chair interacting with family council members between meetings, then this can and should be raised as an agenda item in the next meeting. We also advocate notes rather than minutes of family council meetings. We cover that distinction more thoroughly later in this chapter.

Old business and new business. We also have an opinion about the standard practice of breaking up an agenda into old business that needs follow-up and new business, which comes before the family council for the first time. We have witnessed too many dysfunctional discussions about old business, everything that has not received closure, at the expense of what is most relevant and what is going on with the family right now. Too often, the old business was just that, what had been going on three months to a year ago. The compulsion to include this category so as to not forget about follow-up can sap energy from what is current and important now. Thus, we recommend to our clients that they not include this as a standard agenda item and thus avoid exploration of a historical element that can play out in today's dynamics. A savvy chair will evaluate what needs follow-up in a current meeting and what does not. This is not to suggest that a list of unfinished business should not be maintained. On the contrary, without such a reminder a family council may lose a key benefit of the structure, namely, accountability for accomplishing what is most important to the family. We are here only concerned with the agenda, and there we prefer an organization that considers priority topics and a balance of education, accomplishment, and fun.

Too much intensity on the agenda. We rarely see the error of not enough planning, which makes family members wonder why they had to have a meeting about matters of little importance; yet, it does happen. The more common challenge is to trim down an agenda that includes too much. We've already indicated that a good rule of thumb is to organize a meeting of the family into roughly three categories: (1) learning and development, (2) accomplishing, planning, or deciding, and (3) fun and social activities.

We also advise balancing weighty items with lighter ones in order to manage the intensity of a meeting. Generally, a meeting's agenda can be analyzed for intensity; the toughest topics should occupy about 33 percent of the concentration and energy, another 33 percent should be reserved for topics of medium intensity, and a final 33 percent should be set aside for easy, yet productive topics. Therefore, a savvy chair will apply his or her knowledge of the family and how they are likely to respond to each topic and structure an agenda accordingly to balance the intensity. Amanda's agenda, shown in figure 5.2, applies the principle as follows:

High Intensity

- Application of the conflict resolution policy
- The role of family directors and independent board members

Medium Intensity

- A primer on shareholder investment skills

Low Intensity

- Education committee update
- Agenda overview, ground rules, goals, meeting evaluation, and scheduling of future meetings
- Meals together
- Golf cart scavenger hunt

For general purposes, we like to evaluate topics and plan a meeting's agenda to balance the categories and the anticipated intensity of topics as illustrated in figure 5.3.

Remember that Amanda's agenda is for a family council consisting of all family members. Alternatively, for a representative family council that acts more like a committee between meetings of the full family, the same rule of thumb for balancing intensity would be applied as follows:

- Tough issues currently causing tension in the family that are expected to be a challenge to productive discussion among family council members: 33 percent
- Moderate issues, which for a representative family council may include work of committees and listening to reports from committees, developing policy, and preparing for a joint meeting with the board: 33 percent
- Easy issues, such as scheduling and planning a family assembly meeting, especially the fun parts: 33 percent

Finally, we emphasize that these are rules of thumb, and strict adherence to three even divisions will usually not be possible.

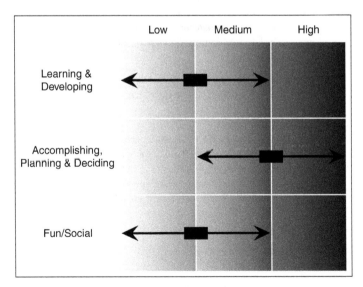

Figure 5.3 Matching the Content of a Meeting and the Overall Meeting Intensity

Beyond the Agenda: Preparing for Meetings

Planning the sequence and balancing out the agenda goes a long way toward a successful family council meeting, but there are additional steps to take in preparing. To hold an effective meeting, the chair should prepare both content and processes for addressing each item on the agenda. Setting an agenda involves topics, the content of the meeting. Thus, for a family council chair, a very useful tool is a meeting design document. This is not circulated among family members; it is prepared in advance by the chair and referred to during the meeting. To illustrate this, Amanda's agenda (figure 5.2) would be the outline of her meeting design document. Figure 5.4 shows her meeting design with process notes in italics. She would refer to this throughout the meeting, using it as a private guide, unless she was working with a cochair with whom she would likely share it.

Smith Family Council—Thursday, September 15

Meeting Design

Board Room—Morris Woods Golf Course

Early September

Meet or hold phone conference with the two guests Sam Jones (CFO) and Ralph Thompson (family counselor). Also check with family members, Mike, Rosanne, and Tom. Work with them to determine their desired processes, and associated audio-visual needs, handout copies, flip charts, and special room requirements, if any.

Send out agenda, copy of the family conflict resolution policy and notes from previous family council meeting out by September 6.

Meeting Day

7:00A.M.　*Arrive early to meet with the banquet manager on the day's facility and meal plan. Check meeting room setup and to make sure audiovisual equipment is working. Provide copies of the agenda. Write out the ground rules and meeting goals on flip charts and hang on a wall—leave ground rules exposed but cover goals so they can be revealed to everyone after Sam Jones departs. Check with golf pro to ensure number and time for transportation of golf carts to Smith Farm for scavenger hunt.*

9:00　**Educational Component: A Primer on Shareholder Investment skills—Sam Jones**

Arrange for Sam Jones to arrive at 8:30 to check audiovisual equipment and to allow for mixing with family before meeting begins. Sam's plan—he will use a PowerPoint presentation, provide his own handouts, and use

---

Figure 5.4　Continued

	exercises. His expects 50 percent presentation and 50 percent discussion and interaction. He has been asked to prepare in advance several questions to use to promote discussion.
10:30	**Break**—**Sam will remain to answer questions throughout the break, but will depart at 11:30**
11:00	*Overview of the Remaining Agenda Items*

- Welcome, overview, and opening remarks—Amanda Smith
  —*Thank Mike, Rosanne, and Tom for preparing and presenting*
- Approval of notes from previous meeting and selection of today's note taker
  —*Thank Mike for notes from last meeting, reinforce the nature of notes to differentiate from minutes*
- Review of meeting ground rules
- Key goals for today's family council meeting. *List the following on flip chart and ask for input (are there other goals for today or modifications to these?). Assure consensus on the following:*
  1. *Advance everyone's appreciation, knowledge, and skills as investors, stewards, and shareholders.*
  2. *Tastefully discuss Ellen and James's conflict with one another and their steps to resolve it, revealing what can appropriately be discussed while maintaining privacy. Reinforce the use of our policy and, using this recent case, determine if any changes or elaborations are needed.*
  3. *Bring everyone up-to-date on the progress of the education committee's work and plans for the upcoming meeting on the third generation, making sure we have enough resources and support for a successful event.*
  4. *Provide more clarity about the roles and expectations of family directors versus independents.*
- Ask if any changes to the agenda are desired.

Application of the Family Conflict Resolution Policy—**Ralph Thompson**

Ralph asked to arrive during 10:30 break to mingle. He is invited to stay for lunch and depart by 1:00 p.m. Ralph will contact James and Ellen in advance of the meeting to prepare each. During the meeting, he will interview James and Ellen and facilitate their discussion to reveal the history of their recent conflict. Ralph will manage the boundaries, e.g., individual compensation levels will remain private.

Expected learnings:

1. *Facts to replace the rumors and hearsay that have circulated throughout the family.*
2. *Any of us can potentially be in James's or Ellen's shoes, and we need to adhere to our policy, learn to better use it, and understand how to encourage each other to be successful with its utilization.*

Noon	*Lunch* together in the dining room
1:00	*Education Committee Update*—**Rosanne and Tom**

Figure 5.4 Continued

Update time target: five minutes. Presentation will focus on upcoming third-generation education session. Rosanne will lead. Remind at lunch about request that she presents in a tactful way, without blame, guilt, or resentment regarding lack of volunteers. She will positively promote the role and value of volunteers to help with the education session, indicating their role in the past with time estimates for activities. Tom and Rosanne have decided they will not ask for volunteers during the meeting. Rather, after the meeting, they will approach individuals they wish to have participate, those who have the skills but have not volunteered in the past.

1:30 **Scheduling Future Dates**

Schedule two more dates for the following year. Announce the rule first—there are two kinds of existing calendar conflicts, when a date is called, use a raised hand with one finger up to indicate a low-priority conflict or one that can potentially be rescheduled, and use a raised open hand for a rigid conflict. We will first attempt to find dates with no conflicts, then go to dates where there are the least number of low-level conflicts.

1:40 **The Role of Family Directors and Independent Board Members—Mike Smith**

Mike has been informed that he must work hard to minimize his bias. He will provide the results of his inquiries using a PowerPoint and will supply his own handouts—time estimate is 20 minutes. He will then lead a brainstorming process to identify two lists:

1. High-value contributions of family directors that only can be provided by family directors
2. High-value contributions only available from independent directors

Expected follow-up: Mike will ask for two volunteers to work with him to write up a summary of the brainstorming results plus prepare a set of guidelines to define the boundary between board and management with examples. If they agree, ask that their results be sent out within two months with a request for feedback. Schedule time for this topic on agenda for the next family council meeting.

2:30 **Next Steps and Evaluation**

- Review of today's action plans needing follow-through, decisions, and conclusions—Get consensus on items for next family council agenda
- Evaluation of the meeting

3:00 **Conclusion of the Family Council Meeting and Beginning of the Fun**

Figure 5.4 Example Meeting Design Indicating Process for Each Topic on the Agenda in Figure 5.2

Running the Family Council: The Robinson Family Council Case

To illustrate the activity of a chair running a family council, we will track George Robinson as he prepares for and conducts a family council meeting. George is chair of the Robinsons' family council that represents members of the second, third, and fourth generations. It has five members, four of whom represent four family branches defined by the second-generation siblings' family units, and the fifth member is an at-large member who is elected by the entire family. Members of the third generation are in their late forties and fifties and now dominate family governance and also hold most of the family seats on the board of directors. For the Robinsons, the primary issues that have recently dominated the agendas of their family council meetings include:

- Leadership of the business after the current family member CEO retires—should the business be family managed or family governed?
- Succession to chair of the board who is an octogenarian—the family feels the need to get the chair of the board to retire, and the family council wants the family shareholders to consider the possibility of the replacement being one of the non-family, independent directors.
- There is pressure from one branch of the family to add a member to the board who they feel would better represent them—the family council has been active in trying to get the shareholders aligned so that family groups do not feel they must have their own representatives on the board.
- There are many college-age children in the third generation who have not been connected to the family or the business for several years because they are geographically dispersed and focused on their university work and other interests.
- The family shareholders are not aligned on a single capital strategy—some are interested in buying homes and want more liquidity options, and some are legacy capitalists preferring reinvestment at a time when the business is competing in a stressful market dominated by consolidations.

Preparing for the Meeting

George Robinson can prepare the agenda for his five-member family council much as Amanda does for her family council with over twenty members. An advance memo or request can go to the family and others asking for input well in advance of a meeting. Once input is received, George will circulate a draft agenda to the other four family council members. Even though the group is smaller, managing the intensity of the meeting's topics is just as important as it is for Amanda's larger group. Finally, using the rule of thumb of about 1/3 of the time for each of the categories of (1) learning and developing; (2) accomplishing, planning, and deciding; and (3) fun and social activities will be different for the Robinson Family Council. A representative family council is more like a working committee that moves forward with the important work of the family in between family assembly meetings. Thus, while the three categories are still important to manage, a different proportional rule is typical; over a year about 70 to 80 percent of the time the Robinson Family Council is engaged in accomplishing, planning, and deciding. The remaining 20 to 30 percent are devoted to learning and developing and fun or social activities for building family relationships. Usually, this family council combines the fun and social and learning and developing segments into an annual tradition, namely, attendance at one of the family business conferences in North America at a place selected for its relevance to the Robinsons' primary issues.

For its next meeting, to which everyone will travel to meet in the family business board room, the family council has two items that are carried over from the previous meeting:

- How to increase the fourth generation's involvement and connection to the business; and
- Addressing the Carmen Robinson family's desire for its own board member to represent their branch.

Of these two items the first is considered low intensity, and the second is a high-intensity matter for the family and is also expected to be so in the next family council meeting because Carmen's son is a member of the family council. Ned Robinson has indicated to George that the issue has remained unresolved for too long and that members of his family are talking about hiring an attorney to "explore their options." George has decided that Ned representing Carmen would be too indirect and has invited Carmen to attend the first part of the meeting. It is expected that this portion of the meeting could take the entire morning. George is prepared to allow this if there are signs of progress. He plans to contact Carmen a week before the meeting to hear Carmen's views and, most importantly, find out why she feels the current family representation on the board is inadequate. George is also prepared to invite other members of Carmen's family if it appears that transparency and openness will enhance their willingness to find a mutually agreeable solution.

Based upon the input received from George's advance request for ideas and his own ideas about the best use of the family council, there are two other items that will be added to the agenda:

- A suggestion that the family council conduct a survey to determine the highest priorities of the family to include in the family council's long-term goals; and
- A suggestion that a new Task Force be assembled to study and make recommendations regarding leadership succession at the board and at the helm of the business.

Both of these items are relevant, but the second one is potentially a tough issue for the family. The family council will not discuss succession at its next meeting; rather, it will establish a process for dealing with the issue that engages selected family members in a process using a task force structure. With committee reports, George analyzes the time required and notes to himself that with the Carmen Robinson matter the meeting will be tense, but all the other items are relatively low in intensity. Satisfied that he has achieved as much balance as possible, George proceeds with the agenda, which appears in figure 5.5.

The meeting design notes will not need to be as extensive as Amanda's were because there are fewer people to manage in the smaller Robinson Family Council meeting. However, George needs a process for the morning session with the Carmen Robinson family. He decides to call two others in advance of the meeting, his Uncle Sheldon who is chair of the board and Sydney, a loyal independent director whom he trusts to take a balanced view on most subjects; Sydney is an attorney by training and a people person everyone turns to when things get tense.

Robinson Family Council Meeting Agenda

Robinson Industries Board Room
Denver, Colorado
September 21, 20xx

9:00 A.M.—4:00 P.M. MDT

I. Overview
  1. Confirmation on note taking
  2. Review of the agenda—are there modifications?
  3. Goals for the meeting
  4. Review of housekeeping matters, i.e., lunch, breaks, etc.
  5. Ground rules review

II. The Carmen Robinson Family Business Governance Request
  We have invited Carmen to join us for this part of the discussion

III. The Fourth Generation's Connection to the Business Issue
  1. Please come prepared by reading the summary of interviews conducted by Megan
  2. We will brainstorm methods to advance the connectedness between family members in the fourth generation and between them and the business (and advance ideas for consideration are welcome—please circulate)

IV. Reports from Subcommittees and Task Forces
  1. Family council development committee—Sandy
  2. Education committee—Roderick
  3. Other reports
     i. Family office study task force—Jamie
     ii. New task force on succession—recommendation from Dan Robinson
     iii. Budget projection for next year

V. Family Council Priority Goals for the Next Three Years
  1. Consideration of methods and plan to update three-year-old family council goals

VI. Review and Planning for Future Meetings
  1. Summary of actions and follow-up
  2. Evaluation of the meeting
  3. Confirm agenda and dates for future meetings

Figure 5.5   Robinson Family Council Agenda

Meeting Forum

Unlike Amanda's larger group, the Robinson Family Council has successfully used a pattern of two face-to-face meetings and at least two conference calls or videoconferences each year as well as a family business conference trip together. The council members reasoned that because they were so geographically dispersed and to be cost-efficient, they would hold three-hour conference calls for half of their meetings alternating with daylong face-to-face meetings in locations that rotate among the members' home cities. They are fortunate in that two live in one city.

Early on they discovered they needed ground rules to make their conference calls and videoconferences effective. George developed a policy they call conference call and videoconferencing etiquette that includes everything from eliminating background noise and using proper phone equipment to announcing one's name before making a comment. If the family invites a guest or if members of a committee who are not on the family council participate, George will provide them with copies of the policy together with the agenda. There are a lot of examples of etiquette for such calls so we will not provide one here, but we recommend that a family council that relies on conference calls adopts its own policy.

George has also learned from previous family council chairs about meeting room selection. The family council never uses a member's home, preferring instead to use a neutral location for each meeting. They have, however, taken members up on their offers to provide conference room facilities located at their place of work. While not completely neutral, the facilities are typically low in cost, and this appeals to the Robinsons' conservative culture. They have also used the board room at the business, Robinson Industries. Family council members reason that it is useful for employees and managers to see the family working on matters that they have come to understand as directly influencing the continuity and long-term success of the business. They view this as modeling responsible behavior, and the family council members have often insisted on using a conference room when the board room is booked for a business meeting. George and the other family council members feel this too sends an important message, namely, that they are there as guests to take advantage of the facilities and that business management has priority over the family council in the use of the business offices.

Generally, the Robinsons' requirements for an effective meeting include privacy, a meeting room with partial natural light (no basements or windowless conference rooms), and the possibility to obtain meals nearby so that the relatively short time they have together can be best used for meeting time. Finally, the Robinsons have adopted a rule that if a member must decide between leaving the meeting early to catch a flight or remaining overnight, the individual is encouraged to stay. Their reasoning is that the meeting and the individual both suffer if anyone leaves before the meeting concludes. In making such decisions, the family council members typically come to quick consensus by asking themselves how they would explain their decision to the broader family and especially to the younger generation for whom they are setting an example consistent with family values.

Facilitating the Family Council Meeting

Books, courses, coaches, and seminars are available for teaching facilitation methods and skills. We will not attempt to recreate them here, but we will highlight some specific useful tools and skills that particularly apply to family council meetings. We encourage family council chairs to obtain as much knowledge and practice as they can from all sources available.

Part of facilitating a meeting is to have a good plan. The meeting design document created by Amanda for her large family council meeting was a process planning tool. For his difficult meeting, George Robinson needs a good plan. His Aunt Carmen, whom he respects and dearly loves, is angry to the point of considering legal action. She will join the family council, and George is in charge of a meeting he would rather not even attend as a participant.

George's advance conversation with his Aunt Carmen went well; he was able to get good background information, and he also got the impression that the implied threat of legal action was not as imminent as he had been led to believe by her son, Ned. Basically, Carmen related issue after issue that never made it to the board agenda. She blamed her brother Sheldon, the chair of the board, and remarked that she assumed he had too much control of the board and was only interested in serving his own agenda.

George's conversations with his Uncle Sheldon and the key independent director, Sydney, were inconclusive and inconsistent in their interpretations of Carmen's concerns. George did not hesitate; he invited both Uncle Sheldon and Sydney to attend the morning session of the family council meeting with Aunt Carmen as the other guest.

Ground rules. Ground rules help keep the peace at a meeting and focus the family council on its role and purpose. Thus, the rules provided in the example in chapter 4 (the ROPES) will be covered at the beginning of each meeting. However, an additional consideration is the use of ground rules for a particular topic. What is available to George for dealing with his problem of holding a productive meeting on a matter that could next go to lawyers and courts if the discussion was not successful?

Ground rules for an issue of board configuration were basically that the family council had no authority to reconfigure the board of directors. Accordingly, whether or not family members agreed with Carmen's solution to place a director on the board who would be loyal to her family, they were powerless to do anything about it. The board and the shareholders make such decisions. Thus, a specific ground rule for this issue was:

> We will not make a binding decision because we do not have the authority on this matter. Therefore, through an open discussion we may identify a workable solution we like, and if we reach a consensus, the family council may make a recommendation to the board that we can share with the family.

While the Robinson Family Council does not have direct authority, it does have power, the power of finding agreement among family members. In this case, George is attempting to provide the forum and the format that will produce a consensus among those who hold the power.

Decision making. Early on a family council must decide on how it will make decisions, and sometimes this is part of a family council charter. We advocate an efficient consensus process; described in appendix 4. Essentially, this is a voting method that, if used well, helps a group make a decision everyone can support.

Before introducing an agenda topic, family council chairs may find it helpful to refer to the specific ground rules that apply for the topic (see above) and to remind everyone of the way in which a decision will be made. For example, George may make the point, "I assume that after open discussion we find a solution that we can all support, then essentially we will have a consensus. This is how we typically make decisions in the family council."

There are many facilitation tools available to help solve problems and to move a group toward a consensus decision. However, one facilitation tool that regularly helps advance discussions in a family council is the go-around. While this is not a decision-making procedure, it often yields a conclusion because the go-around provides an opportunity for individuals to hear what others have to say, especially the ones who have previously been relatively quiet. One common result is that the issue that has not been directly addressed and its resolution (obvious to some) emerges with a go-around. The go-around is used by a chair to gather the uninterrupted comments and conclusions from all participants in the meeting. A go-around works well after a topic has been discussed to the point that issues have been raised, and they are getting raised again, without any apparent conclusion. The chair simply asks: "I'd like to hear from each person one at a time what you are thinking. Let's begin with Samantha; what are your conclusions on this matter?" The chair may further clarify that each individual should not feel compelled to react to what someone else has said, but it is okay to do so. The rule is that there are no interruptions or challenges; each individual gets a chance to speak his or her mind. The go-around is also a good way to close a topic that may not lend itself to a conclusion today; crystallizing the key issues is a way of documenting the progress that has been made in today's discussion. Individuals can conclude, "While we did not solve this one today, we did refine it to a point where we can take it up again without going back to the beginning."

Accountability. We are regularly asked what authority a family council has to enforce its resolutions. A family council is the governing body of the family, but it does not make laws that can be enforced. The authority of a family council rests in the way it operates to achieve a consensus. Briefly, if there is broad participation and genuine consideration of input, if there is a fair and transparent process for making decisions and coming to conclusions, then there is a legitimate expectation that peer pressure and integrity of the individuals involved will lead to all members supporting a single direction. Adhering to these principles regularly and consistently will get results. However, results are not guaranteed, and patience is needed on many small but important matters.

We have already referred to ground rules; using them is a way to hold family members accountable to meeting rules. By covering the ground rules at the beginning of the meeting, the family council chair is essentially saying, "Do we all agree to follow these rules, and do you give me permission to help us remember them from time to time?" If a ground rule is repeatedly broken despite the chair's reminders, we advocate that even in the middle of a meeting the chair reminds everyone again after a break, "Before we begin again, I'd like to ask if we should change our ground rules. Since we are not following them, which ones do we want to follow?" Through patience and group consensus, the original ground rules will usually get a renewed commitment. The chair will also get additional support from other family council members to help keep the meeting consistent with the ground rules.

In addition to ground rules for meetings, other agreements that families use for accountability are written values, a conflict resolution policy, and a family code of conduct. It is within the scope of most family councils to bring the big issues to the table. As with Amanda's family, if family members are not following the agreement they freely made with each other regarding the handling of conflict between family members, then the family council is the forum where this is put on the table to find a resolution. When family members know that this is expected practice and trust that it will be followed because their family council has been consistent, they will be encouraged to hold themselves accountable. Ellen and James knew their conflict was going to be on the family council's agenda in three weeks, so they got busy resolving the conflict consistent with their policy, just as Amanda knew they would. George does not have a policy to which he can hold his Uncle Sheldon and Aunt Carmen accountable, but he does have a forum where he can promote the family's commitment to open discussion and resolution of differences.

Open meetings. Some family councils hold meetings that are open to any qualified family member who wishes to attend. By qualified we mean any family member who participates in the family assembly represented by the family council or all those defined as family by the family council charter. The meetings are held by and with the members of the family council, but all qualified family members are invited to attend and observe.

An open meeting requires a family council chair to be clear about the rules. At the discretion of the family council chair, individual observers may be allowed to make a statement, but they are primarily observers. Some chairs may not permit interaction by the observers, which is justifiable when facilitating the productivity of the family council meeting is a challenge. The benefit of open meetings is great; there is an open invitation to directly observe the work of the family council. Individual family members, even if they do not attend, have more trust in the work of their governance function because they know they can attend.

Time management. One of the toughest challenges for a family council chair is to manage the discussion on each topic and keep it on time. A rule of thumb when planning the agenda is to estimate the time discussion should take, and then add 50 percent. Some groups have had success with a time clock. A timer that can be reset at the beginning of a discussion may help, especially if everyone can see it.

Family council members can easily get offtrack in their discussions and lose sight of the original goal for the agenda topic. Family council chairs who use meeting design notes, such as those Amanda used, will at least list the goal for each topic and the process for achieving it. In George Robinson's family council, there is an item on the agenda under the heading "Reports from Subcommittees and Task Forces" referring to a succession task force (see figure 5.5). For better time management, George will remind the group of the goal and process as the discussion begins. "Our goal for today is to do two things: (1) listen to Dan Robinson's recommendation on the use of a succession task force, and (2) decide if we would like to establish one or not. We do not have enough time to create one if we decide to proceed, so we need to think in terms of another time slot in a future meeting to create one. One potential outcome is that we could agree if we like Dan's idea that he and perhaps another member of the council come back with a specific recommendation on how we could implement such a task force."

Meeting notes. We have made the point before that rather than meeting minutes, we prefer that the meeting record be meeting notes; that is, it should be a summary of conclusions, decisions, and action plans with all the meeting materials (e.g., agenda and advance documents) in an appendix. The appendix can also include ideas that did not lead to conclusions but should be preserved because they might be useful later. A good example is the lists that come from brainstorming and analyses of benefits and disadvantages in problem solving.

A very helpful facilitation tool is a flip chart or white board where the group can see the ideas and options under discussion. The conclusion reached should also be recorded on a flip chart, but the conclusion would also be included in the notes; everything else entered on the chart or board would go in the appendix. Using such a tool helps facilitate productive meetings, and it also helps determine how much to record.

Following process. The Robinson Family Council did what a family council is supposed to do. It did not step in and assume a role reserved for the board and shareholders. It was not a "family court" to make a judgment after hearing all sides. The family council did not even research the facts and come to a logical conclusion and rational recommendation. George and the family council provided a forum for Carmen and Sheldon to work out their differences, yet George provided assistance by involving an independent director they trusted and respected, Sydney. George introduced the first topic of the meeting by indicating that the purpose was communication and problem solving. He indicated he had spoken with both Aunt Carmen and Uncle Sheldon and he believed that differences existed, but he also thought that there had been lapses in communication between them and perhaps even some unfounded assumptions. He further stated that he had full confidence in their ability to talk things out during the meeting. Finally, he thanked them for their willingness to do so and thanked Sydney for his time and commitment to the family. Then he suggested that first Carmen and then Sheldon state their view of the problem. The discussion was respectful, and in the end each person's perspective was better understood, and both agreed to redouble their efforts to communicate effectively.

George was hoping for an additional benefit from the discussion between Carmen and Sheldon. The family council would soon need to address the succession of the chair of the board. In the past, this had been a position for the leader of the company who left management and assumes leadership of the board. Carmen was accusing her brother Sheldon of ignoring her wishes and desires for the board agenda. Sheldon felt he was doing his job in making decisions about what was appropriate and what was not appropriate for the board's agendas. The incident provided useful background material that would later be integrated into the discussion of the value of the next chair being an independent, non-family director.

Compensating Family Council Members

The first question to ask is whether to compensate or not; it is a philosophical question, and whether the answer is yes or no, it will be correct as long as all family members are in general agreement. Their agreement is largely determined by a preference for one philosophy over another. We typically see two competing philosophies; one view is that the work of the family council is critical to the business' long-term success and members should be compensated. The other view is that family council members should not be compensated because they are either shareholders, will become shareholders through inheritance, or are spouses of shareholders and are already paid in dividends or distributions. Those who determine that it is inappropriate to pay for family council service reason that individuals should not be paid to add value to an investment that already provides them with a return on their invested capital. Further, some business families have been trying to withdraw from a period of too many family perks from the business in the form of autos, fuel, health insurance, and false jobs; to them paying for roles outside the business may look like a reversal of efforts to discourage entitlement expectations. Others see it as aggravating an existing conflict between family members who work in the business and nonoperating shareholders; the insiders may see it as an unfair dividend.

Business families deciding to compensate family council members reason that it will inspire greater commitment and associated performance from family council members. Payment makes a significant statement that good family governance is believed to add value to the business. These families believe that conflicts can be minimized or managed and that when passive shareholders become active stewards and when the family council ensures that younger family members effectively prepare for future ownership roles, the business will be stronger, and more likely to continue as a family enterprise. To them, these results are worth compensation. With respect to jealousies or insider/outsider conflicts, families that compensate family council members feel the potential risk is worth the expected benefits.

Unfortunately, there are few guidelines for those wishing to establish fair compensation for family council members. At this writing, compensation surveys to provide benchmark data are unavailable for family council members or for leadership roles. While we expect data to be developed as more and more business families gain sophistication with family governance, we currently rely on our own observations in client firms and those from our consulting group of over 20 family business consultants.

Generally, most of the business families we've observed do not compensate family council members and instead rely on volunteerism and the perception among those who serve on a family council that they are doing it for their own benefit. If travel and other costs are required for preparation and attendance at family council meetings, most will reimburse for expenses, and several businesses have written policies governing the type of expenses covered, limitations, and reimbursement procedures. While many business families do not compensate their members, a more common practice is to compensate the family council chair. Amounts increase as the families move from the younger to the older family stages (stages are described fully in chapter 3) and as family size grows. Larger families are more likely to pay their chairs, and the larger the family the greater the amount.

In founder and late founder stages we typically do not see compensation for anyone serving on the family council. Founders may pay their children for family council service, yet their purpose is more to provide income for their children than to compensate them fairly for their service. For early sibling and late sibling stages with larger families, compensation of the chair becomes more common. Pay ranges from small stipends to honor and respect the role of family council chair to amounts matching those received by family directors who serve on the board. Pay on a per-meeting basis is a common practice, yet many families also pay quarterly or annually. Some follow board practices of an annual retainer amount plus a stipend per meeting attended.

Large families in the cousin stage more regularly provide compensation to the chair. The amounts vary widely with some providing a small honorarium amount on one end of the spectrum to those who match what they pay independent directors who serve on their boards. Also, family council members are more likely to receive compensation in larger, older families, and as with chairs, the amounts vary significantly. Activity levels may be very high with chairs contributing 20 hours or more per month, and members, particularly committee chairs, contributing half that amount. In such cases, the family council members may be paid half of what the chair receives.

With the lack of external benchmarks, it is challenging for business families to determine fair compensation for their chair or their family council members. Some rely on a senior family member or a group of elders to make a recommendation that is then adopted out of respect or for lack of a good alternative. Others rely on internal equity principles, comparing the job of family council chair to roles on the board and in the business, considering time requirements and qualifications of comparable positions. For example, the coordination and diplomatic and leadership skills of a family council chair might be similar to those required by a senior regional sales manager in the business with direct reports roughly equal to the number of adults in the family. Comparing part-time hour requirements of the family council chair to the regional sales manager's full-time salary would provide one data point. A second reference could be taken from a similar hours-based comparison to the board chair, and a third comparison might be to independent directors chairing a board committee. The use of three sources of data would provide the basis for a discussion from which a consensus could develop on fair compensation for the family council chair's role. If family council members are to be compensated, their pay could then be linked to the chair's compensation, e.g., half of that amount. This method of using internal benchmarks is a common practice among compensation professionals, who begin with a job description specifying projected work load, qualifications, and responsibilities; for our purposes begin with a family council chair job description.

Assessing the Performance of the Family Council

We strongly support the practice of evaluating the effectiveness of family councils to obtain feedback for making improvements and adjustments. In doing so, we are basically asking whether the family council provides what was intended. If it does not do so, what are the reasons? Perhaps the family has outgrown an original structure that worked well in the past. The primary purpose of an assessment should always be positive with the focus quickly moving from what is imperfect or missing to what adjustments the family will make. Most important, family members need to recognize and appreciate the contributions and effectiveness of the family council functions that are working well.

Even in a business setting, where assessments and feedback are good business practices and individuals have training and experience, family members evaluating the performance of other family members is rarely conducted well or received well. Thus, we do not advocate evaluation of individual family council members by the family. We see much more positive potential value to the family in assessing the family council as a function. However, in making this distinction, we recognize that it might be difficult for those on the family council to avoid defensiveness and inferences that it is their performance that is being assessed. Therefore, an overemphasis on the purpose and intent is appropriate to minimize the potential for misinterpretation. Finally, even when it is understood that concerns about poor functioning of the family council are related to an individual or specific individuals, the use of an individual assessment procedure is much too open for the culture of most families who prefer to handle such matters in a more discreet and respectful manner. In such cases, it is more appropriate for a chair to privately confront a disruptive individual and encourage compliance or resignation.

In contrast, we work with business families who effectively utilize a feedback procedure for the family council chair. In many cases, they will utilize a consultant to maintain anonymity and to ensure that the focus remains on feedback and development. An example assessment questionnaire appears in chapter 9 under the section titled Leadership Feedback. Figure 9.5 is an example questionnaire, which can be completed by family council members and/or adult members of the whole family to provide the chair with useful information about his or her performance.

The steps for assessing the family council function and providing feedback include:

1. How will we define effectiveness of the family council?
2. What are the options available to measure effectiveness?
3. After measurement, what will we do with the results?

Step one: Defining effectiveness. Effectiveness must be defined for each family council. While two business families' governance functions may be similar, it is better to assume that each is uniquely formed for the purposes and goals of each family and business. Thus, we do not advocate a standard form that can be applied to all family councils. In considering the definition of effectiveness for a particular family council, we suggest family members use the following questions:

1. Based on our charter and other written materials, what is the purpose of our family council?
2. What are the practices we have adopted based on the needs of our business family?
3. What are our stated, written family council goals and priorities?

Sources for these answers include the family council charter, written policies that are often part of past notes of family council meetings as well as the family's mission, vision, and values statements, which may or may not appear in the charter. In addition, information on the structure, operations, scope, and activity of the family council may be found in documents that are available from the family assembly, the board of directors or the management of the business. However, taking advantage of all possible sources may still not provide the complete answer. Thus, embarking on a process of regularly assessing the family council's effectiveness, even if the assessment is never complete, provides something very valuable: a definition of the effectiveness of our family council and thus a goal to aim for.

Business families may want a consultant to assist initially in providing a definition of effectiveness from multiple sources. The consultant could also conduct the assessment and provide written feedback, ensuring anonymity to the sources. After the first time, future assessments could be conducted with limited or no support from a consultant. The advantages of utilizing an unbiased consultant the first time is that he or she can get input from many sources to provide a definition of family council effectiveness combined with efficiency and confidence in the product. Moreover, there is greater perceived confidentiality if the assessment is also conducted by a consultant. An additional advantage is that the consultant, in addition to interpreting existing written material to define family council effectiveness, may provide recommendations based on his or her experience with other business families, and these may expose the business family to previously unrecognized options regarding the function of its family council.

Alternatively, the definition of effectiveness could be established by a committee of the family council that includes existing family council representatives and members of the broader family. This committee would also be asked to prepare an assessment form and recommend procedures for collecting information.

Step two: Assessment. Once family council effectiveness has been defined, alternatives for assessment are the format utilized and the sources of effectiveness input. Regarding formats, a written or computerized questionnaire or survey document are common options. If a consultant assists, interviews may replace or be added to a survey. We like the format of a rating scale used to register the level of agreement or disagreement with a statement. For example, if one of the purposes of

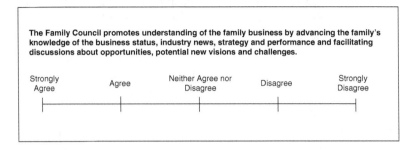

The Family Council promotes understanding of the family business by advancing the family's knowledge of the business status, industry news, strategy and performance and facilitating discussions about opportunities, potential new visions and challenges.

| Strongly Agree | Agree | Neither Agree nor Disagree | Disagree | Strongly Disagree |

Figure 5.6   Questionnaire Item Assessing Family Council Performance

the family council is to promote understanding of the family business, the questionnaire item might appear as in figure 5.6.

An example assessment survey using this format appears in appendix 3, but we recommend not using it as a ready-made tool because it does not apply across the board to family councils. Again, a key question to be answered is, "Does our family council accomplish the purposes for which it was created?"

Several online options are available for a survey of this type to be created so that respondents can quickly provide feedback anonymously. The results are easily tabulated and analyzed without identification of the source. Other family councils will prefer a paper survey collected and analyzed by a trusted, neutral resource such as a consultant who can also write up the findings.

Regarding who is asked to complete a questionnaire, there are several options. The least intrusive way and perhaps the way most should start with is for the family council to do a self-assessment. That is, the council members would define effectiveness just as it is described above under step one, then they would complete a survey or respond to a consultant's interview questions. The summarized findings are then used in a family council meeting for an open discussion. This process serves the purpose of identifying and recognizing what is working well and also pointing out what the family council sees as areas for improvement.

Beyond a self-assessment, the potential sources of input include:

- Family members who would participate in a family assembly
- Family members who are shareholders
- Family and independent members of the board of directors
- Selected members from business management

If there are enough individuals in each of these segments, an additional benefit of the assessment process may be to identify differences between these groups. That is, a result may be that the family may see room for improvement in one function of the family council, say "keeping the family appropriately connected to the board of directors," but the board may not be as positive about the same function.

Asking the family council to conduct a self-assessment or to add other sources to the assessment must be weighed considering the cost and benefit of each option. The method of assessment may vary or alternate. Initially, the family council might do a self-assessment followed two years later by an assessment that involves the entire family. Two years later, the family council may ask members of the board and selected managers in the business to participate. Thus, with experience and greater confidence, less ambitious assessments may evolve to produce results of multiple feedback sources.

Step three: Using the results. The assessment results are commonly used by the family council in a session designed to appreciate its success and to learn and consider the potential value of changes or adjustments. A representative family council can then summarize its conclusions and make the report available to the broader family, perhaps including it in a report at the next family assembly meeting. The report can also be provided to the board and to management; if these latter did not participate in the assessment, receiving the results would have the added benefit of finding out their reactions to the self-assessment and thereby expand the assessment. For example, an added benefit might be management responding with: "We understand the urgency on the part of the family council to connect the college-aged family members with the business. Your own critical assessment of your success on this front does not fit our experience. On the contrary, since the family council has initiated the summer cousin meetings, which include the social mixer and education session put on by management, we have experienced growing personal relationships and increased interest and passion about the business from the cousins."

If individuals are asked to participate in a survey, questionnaire, or interview, there is the implied expectation of follow-up. That is, before asking a family member or a member of the management team to participate in an interview or to complete a survey, the family council must think through how it intends to include them once results are consolidated and a response is prepared. The process and results of a family council assessment will have greater value if there is a commitment to letting participants know how their information has made a difference. There is greater accountability in doing so, and there is also a moral obligation involved. Even with assurances of confidentiality, participants who provide information may consider it risky to offer honest assessments, and many will have given considerable thought to their answers to questions and recommendations in the comment sections. By including them as a part of the response to the assessment, a family council signals appreciation for what they have provided and gives evidence that the process is important and that participants have made a valued contribution. Practically, this step lays the groundwork for effective participation in the next family council assessment process. A final practical consideration is that a summary report provided to the family assembly might be different from one provided to members of management. That is, it may be appropriate to provide more of a summary in a report intended for the management.

6

Committees of the Family Council

This chapter is intended to support family councils and their chairs in the development and use of supporting committees and task forces. It provides definitions and descriptions of how to use committees efficiently and effectively and be respectful of family dynamics in doing so. The chapter concludes with examples and descriptions of common committees and task forces as well as some that are not so common.

Committees are the key to preparing for topics that face the family council. They are also a tool for bringing together different groups and promoting consensus and teamwork; committees are also a good vehicle for training the younger generation.

Just like a board of directors, a club, or a legislative body, a family council needs committees to focus on a topic and develop it, then bring it back in a way that allows the family council to productively advance on the issue. Most new family councils will get to a point where they delegate some work between meetings to a segment of the group. They find that involving everyone in everything is inefficient, and then they begin to rely more on committees and task forces. Typically, what is delegated is research. A committee or task force works to gain a deeper understanding of an issue, such as finding the best seminar on family boards of directors. The committee or task force then reports back to the family council.

For active business families, there are always questions and issues emerging in the same areas, and family education is one of the most common. For example, if a member of the family council has been talking with her family about a particular seminar that she would like to attend with her cousins and wants the business to fund the cost, having an education committee the family council can turn to is efficient and makes a better response more likely. If the committee has been active for a while, members are likely to have established a philosophy, precedent, or even a policy on the matter they can refer to for their reply.

Family councils use committees to do the homework necessary to help the full family council make an informed decision, adopt responsible plans, or develop consensus on a policy. A common task for family council education committees is to consider the distribution of ages and experience across the family, interpret the direction for education from the family mission statement, and design and recommend to the family council age-appropriate educational content and resources for all levels of experience.

Committees are of tremendous value to family councils as they can produce sophisticated strategic direction to their goals. For examples of approaches to the goal of developing a large family, consider the Ramirez and Thompson families:

The Ramirez family. The Ramirez Group's family council is a representative family council which can be described as a Round Table (see chapter 3). The Ramirez family is a large family with several adults from the third and fourth generations qualifying to sit on the family council. The council has had an education committee since it was formed in a family assembly meeting five years ago. Sophie Calderon is the chair of the education committee. There are five areas of educational focus for the Ramirez family:
1. Learning about the company and industry
2. The history of the business and family and the related values
3. Entrepreneurship, investment and financial competence
4. Relationship, team, communication and conflict skills
5. Awareness of the relevant aspects of the family business field

These five core areas of competence are used to help guide investment and decision making and track the development of family members and spouses who join the family. The family uses outside sources, such as seminars and conferences, for some needs and creates and delivers content for other parts of the curriculum itself. The education committee develops an annual budget that is submitted first to the family council, which attaches it to its own budget request submitted to the board of directors.

The Thompsons. A much smaller Dining Room family council (defined in chapter 3) includes a founder couple in their sixties, their four adult children, and spouses (ten total). They do exactly the same thing as the Ramirez family, but with fewer steps and less formality. Nancy, Zack, and Blake Thompson are the volunteers who at the last family council meeting agreed to think through the family's educational needs and opportunities and make a presentation at the next meeting in two months. The family council includes all ten members from the first and second generations. Nancy, Zack, and Blake are not really a committee; they are more of a task force operating without a charter or anything more than an action plan documented in the notes from the last family council meeting. The Thompson group of Nancy, Zack, and Blake does not have a family mission statement to interpret, yet the three involved know that continuity of the business as a unified second generation sibling partnership is assumed by all. That is why they formed the family council. Furthermore, these second generation parents feel the pressure of their children getting older, and they want to anticipate the third generation's educational needs. Thus, their recommendation to the family council is to pursue two educational priorities:

1. All four sibling and spouse pairs advance their business financial acumen.
2. All family members learn about family business success and successful succession in particular.

Standing Committees, Ad Hoc Committees, and Task Forces

Standing committees are permanent and may include committees for education, communications, philanthropy, and social events and, for some, also a planning committee. The difference between an ad hoc committee and a task force is a fine distinction, and the risk of misnaming either one is small in our opinion. However, we'll attempt to define the difference.

We typically think of an ad hoc committee as composed of current members of the family council, assembled to accomplish a specific purpose for the full family council after which the committee dissolves again. When creating an ad hoc committee, it is important to be purposeful about membership and consider the configuration of the committee in terms of family representation, the skills needed for the purposeful functioning of the group, and the membership configuration that might increase the potential for greater acceptance of the committee's recommendations. For example, three members of a newly formed seven-member family council might be designated as the ad hoc charter committee. They might meet a few times between two family council meetings. They would conduct the research, review examples, come up with a philosophy, and prepare a draft charter as a recommendation. Once the full family council takes on the project of finalizing the charter, the ad hoc committee would no longer meet.

Generally, we talk about a task force when we need a multidisciplinary work group composed of members with specific talents or backgrounds. With task forces we will often step out of the confines of the family council's membership, selecting from the broader family, across generations, and perhaps even draw in members from the ranks of the business. For example, to create a family employment policy recommendation for the family council, the task force might consist of two members of the senior generation who work in the business, one of whom is on the family council, two junior generation family members who are college-age, and the company's human resource manager.

In practice, a standing committee, ad hoc committee, or task force may all include members who are not active on the family council, but we generally name a group a task force when we go *well beyond* the ranks of the family council. In addition to getting the specific skills and backgrounds needed for the purpose of the task force, selecting the right members creates huge advantages in eventual acceptance of their solutions and could even strengthen frayed relationships. If the topic is a contentious one for the family, drawing task force membership from both sides of the issue would be a strategy to achieve an accepted consensus. That is, if one family unit had a bad experience with employment in the company and there are several in the family who do not understand what happened, involving a carefully selected member of the unhappy family group might be useful in overcoming emotional resistance to a fair policy developed within the task force.

Starting and Managing a Committee: The Chair's Role

Depending upon the job description or the family council's charter, it is typically a responsibility of the family council chair to recommend establishing or dissolving committees and task forces. It is part of managing the effective functioning of the family council, the chair's main focus. In practice, a chair does not unilaterally have the authority to establish and dissolve committees; rather, it is the chair's job to always be thinking about these options and to be well-versed in selecting and implementing them. Any member can recommend the use of a committee, but savvy chairs will ask questions.

Do we need one? If a chair is considering the use of a committee or task force, some questions to ask in testing the value of a committee for a particular task are:

- Is this task clearly within the scope of the family council? It is better to be sure before dedicating the resources of a committee. Other potential domains are business management, the owner group, or the board.
- Could this task be better handled by the family council as a whole or might it fit into an existing committee's charter? A new committee requires resources (time and effort of individuals who might be doing other things) and should be established only if the task cannot be accomplished in another way. For example, for small family councils that have been newly established and where understandably there is lots of confusion about the family council's role, it might be best to have the entire family council focus on a charter, rather than forming a committee.
- Might an individual be better suited than a committee? A committee can divide the work and provide for participation that supports acceptance. It is also slower and less efficient and requires coordination that an individual does not need. Weighing the cost/benefit of a committee versus an individual is a good final assessment step before proceeding with a committee or task force.

How to Get Performance from a Committee?

Once it has been decided that a committee is needed, the question is how best to support it and assist it to be productive. For example, would there be a benefit by providing resources, such as consultants, or access to company management or administration? Certainly, there are funding and permission channels to be considered for both options, and it is a family council chair's role to follow protocol and provide clear direction. For example, if an ad hoc committee is established to create a historical archive of the family's history, and it is expected that a videographer or writer will be needed, procedures should be clear in advance for a proposal, a budget and funding approval, and a contract. Similarly, if a task force is created to study the potential value of a family office and assistance from the company CFO or comptroller is expected, then it is appropriate for the family council chair to check in with the company CEO, and possibly the chair of the board before initiating contact with the CFO.

Perhaps even more important for committee performance is clarity about what is expected of the committee. For standing committees, a good practice is to produce a written charter as a first step. Just as a family council charter specifies its purpose, goals, and operations, the same is true for a committee. The Goldman family's first step in establishing its education committee after selecting the members was to ask the committee to write its preferred charter. They were short of time when the matter surfaced, but a savvy family council chair reasoned that clarity of role and enthusiasm for the job might be increased by the family council listening to a recommendation from the new committee rather than providing a mandate. The committee had a very concrete first task, which helped the members to develop a sense of working together as a team.

Moreover, in the interest of specific instructions and clarity about role, purpose, and outcomes, a committee, especially an ad hoc committee or task force, needs to know if it is expected (1) to produce research only and report findings to the family council (e.g., how many family councils compensate their members and how much?), (2) research and make a recommendation (e.g., based upon research into the prevalence of family council compensation and amounts, the reasons for why or why not compensate, what would be the committee's recommendation for our family council?), or (3) implement or do something, (e.g., your responsibility as members of this year's ad hoc planning committee is to plan and organize the next family assembly meeting, including managing all aspects of the event). Furthermore, specific action plans with dates for output will not only clarify and align expectations between the committee and the family council; they will allow the committee to schedule steps with an end goal in mind. Committees may be made up of individuals who may not have experience with action planning on a regular basis, so the additional structure will not just increase account-ability (i.e., your report is due on this date), it will be a helpful and con-structive aid to their productivity.

Finally, the chair should not just accept that the clarity of expecta-tions is sufficient; a request for an update or interim progress report is perfectly appropriate if only to ask the chair of the committee how much time will be needed for the report at the next family council meeting. Some committee chairs are asked to share the notes of committee meet-ings with the family council chair or the full family council. The message will be clear from a request for notes or from a call to check on progress. These are some of the most common ways a family council chair holds a committee accountable for progress and results as agreed upon.

How Might We be Purposeful with Committee Membership?

We are often asked if the family council chair should automatically be a member of each committee or a nonvoting participant. We are not in favor of making this a standard requirement or even an expecta-tion. On a case-by-case basis there may be good reasons for the family council chair to sit on a subcommittee—special expertise, coordination with other projects, and enhanced productivity. There are also good reasons to avoid the practice: greater autonomy and opportunity for others to provide leadership, and the family council chair may already have enough to do. In addition, limiting the chair's involvement in com-mittee work will allow for the chair to be more objective and focus on the ability of the full family council to effectively address a committee's recommendation.

A good rule of thumb for the size of a family council committee or task force is to include three to five members. Depending upon the fam-ily involved, the biggest difference between three and five seems to be degree of added difficulty with more members to schedule a meeting, videoconference, or conference call. This is not a hard-and-fast rule, it is just that we see a lot of family council committees operating and per-forming quite effectively with three or four members.

The configuration of membership is more important than the num-ber of members on the committee. When the family council is discuss-ing membership of a committee, resist calling for volunteers as a first step. Instead, try to have the discussion of what will make the committee a success. For example, if you only need an ad hoc committee to summarize ideas and document the family council's ideas on a family mission statement, it would be helpful to discuss the following qualifications: (1) time available, (2) writing skills, and (3) low pride of authorship. For standing committees, think about the qualities that will serve them in their task and also as a team. Consider and agree on qualities such as ability to work in a team setting, collaborative style, communication and problem-solving skills, and special familiarity with, interest in, or expertise regarding the topic. Of course, representation from all the family and all generations should always be considered. The question whether aside from all other criteria, it might also be useful to balance the generations or family branches should at least be considered. For example, one family council considered overall family dynamics, specifically the existence of low trust between two branches, when assembling an ad hoc committee to plan the first meeting involving the third generation of young family members. The committee included dominant members from the two branches in the hope that they would complete the task successfully and make some progress toward reconciliation and rebuilding their relationship. At other times, it is a better idea to make sure two feuding members are not on the same committee.

Another consideration when establishing committees and task forces is the option of drawing members from the broader family. Creating a committee or replacing members who are rotating off is an opportunity to accomplish more than the committee's primary purpose. That is, adding members who are not part of the family council to a family council committee can strengthen communication and involvement and possibly offset a weak connection between the family council and a part of the family. It is also an opportunity to tap talented members in the family who might otherwise not have done so to participate on a committee even if they would not be willing to serve on the family council.

Committees, Task Forces, and their Purposes

As previously indicated, the number and kind of committees is completely a function of the needs of a particular family type, their current priorities, and other idiosyncrasies that must be taken into consideration. However, most families are resilient and can accommodate the lack of perfect customization when deciding upon what and when to use committees of the family council. Thus, below we provide an overview of the most common types of committees and a few that are less frequently used.

Common Family Council Standing Committees:
Education Committee

For many family councils, the education committee is one of the most important. Most family councils see the development of family members as owners, future owners, and responsible, successful members of their business family as a priority. Thus, an education committee is often one of the first standing committees to be established. Purposes may vary from family to family, in general the education committee's responsibilities include:

- Interpreting the role and philosophy of family education supporting family and family business goals, vision, or mission
- Assessing the education and developmental needs of different segments of the family
- Setting goals and expectations for education and development
- Developing budgets and specifying methodologies
- Identifying educational and developmental sources and providing access to outside or internal
- Making recommendations to the family council based on the above

The committee can be formed to include family council members as well as family members who may not be members of the family council. The committee is a good place to invite participation of multiple generations, particularly since the younger generation will be a primary target for education. One family established its education committee and even before the family council had agreed to its charter, the education committee had developed its own. Its second task was to read a copy of Joline Godfrey's book, *Raising Financially Fit Kids.*[1] The committee then charted family members' ages and worked on interpreting the mandate for family education and development. As a result, the committee developed the matrix that appears in figure 6.1, an age-appropriate developmental program for five critical educational areas.

Age	Basic Financial Skills	Interpersonal/Family Communication Skills	Our Family	Governance	The Business
9–12	Understanding of earning		Family values applied in family units		Visits to properties, projects to expose
13–15	Understanding of time/money; begins to earn; savings goals; philanthropy; reading bank statement; understands interest and dividends	Basic conflict resolution, accomplishments as part of family team	Family history	First exposure to family employment policy	Familiarization with the corporate structure
16–18	Saves & invests, goals & savings connection, taking responsibility for self & others, can talk about money & future, understands money is power, reading a paycheck and completes a simple tax form, shows developing capacity for economic self-sufficiency	Intermediate conflict resolution, more accomplishments as part of family team, self-awareness feedback, stewardship opportunity provided, participation in FC committees and ad hoc groups encouraged	Family history presentation from family members, books provided and group video showings with discussion	Overview of family investments governance structure—how, who, and what decisions are made, basic roles/ responsibilities of effective owners; understanding of family employment policy and other governance policies	Summer employment option. Exposure to senior management—introduction to company strategic initiatives and our industry

19–22	Basic financial report understanding	Win-win negotiation, initial leadership role in family team, more self-awareness feedback, more responsibility for Family Council tasks	Project to make a contribution to the archives	Advanced roles/responsibilities of effective owners—mastery of items on reading list	Summer internship option. Presentations from senior management—further exposure to strategic initiatives and our industry
23–30	Advanced financial report understanding-course completion			Board volunteer to understand governance & management distinction	
30 +					

Figure 6.1　Family Education Matrix

The Family Business Consulting Group did an informal survey of all consultants to catalogue their experience with clients who were working on educational programs and opportunities. Many of the initiatives on this list were implemented and facilitated by members of the group. Figure 6.2 shows a list of the variety and multiple avenues for family development. Many education committees have used this list to get ideas and to customize programs to fit their needs.

Common Family Council Standing Committees:
Communications Committee

The purpose of a communications committee is to facilitate communication across the family and between the family and the business. These committees are tasked with analyzing what is usually a challenge for most families, namely, how to strengthen the quality and appropriate quantity of information flow. For example, one common complaint heard in family assembly and family council meetings regarding information about business events is the following: "I am hearing about a development at the company now and appreciate being informed. However, it would have been much better to know about it before it was developing."

This comment is negative but often applies to a positive development, such as an exciting new product release or new service, exceeding expectations on the opening of a new facility, or an exceptional achievement on the part of an employee of the business. A communications committee's purpose is to ensure that opportunities for family members to take pride in and be involved in exciting events and developments are not missed, thus turning into a source of dissatisfaction.

Communication of family news is facilitated by this committee as well, and at this writing, many are developing or enhancing family websites or intranets and dealing with security, confidentiality, and access issues—that is, owner versus nonowner privileges regarding access to company information. Sharing anything, from pictures to news, across the entire family is facilitated by this committee's focus on maintaining and strengthening the relationships in a growing family. The committee keeps a current list of contact information for family members and provides members with guidance on how best to

---

A sampling of ideas and experiences from *The Family Business Consulting Group*

Developing Effective Owners
- Study the buy-sell provisions and the rationale for each one
- Learn about the corporate structure and by-laws
- Participate in identifying the major policies of the company and explain the rationale of each one at a family meeting
- Become competent with financial statements and major investor-related definitions commonly used in comparisons between businesses (e.g., debt/equity ratio, ROA, ROI, EBITDA, etc.)
- Learn to read and interpret the family's company financial statements
- As a committee or family group, define the role, responsibilities, and authority of shareholders/effective owners, the board, and management as well as their interrelationships
- Exchanges—attend other family companies' board meetings and family council meetings or interview others who have been active in the development of such
- Make observation board seats available to shareholders in the next generation (i.e., Junior Board)
- Learn how to conduct a private company shareholder meeting
- Compare performance of our assets with other assets, i.e., S&P 500, shares of similar public company stock, land appreciation
- Study tax and estate planning responsibilities related to responsible ownership
- Learn about the evolution of the board of directors and where the current owners see it evolving to
- Understand the values that drive the family and its responsibilities as owners
- Understand the nature/purpose of trusts as well as the role of trustees and beneficiaries
- Develop a job description and qualifications for family board members
- Create opportunities for family members to interact with independent directors
- Hold a mock board meeting at a family meeting using the agenda from a recent board meeting

Family Relationship and Individual Skill Development
- Arrange for training on win/win negotiation skills
- Develop a family code of conduct
- Arrange for mentors or coaches for young family members working in the business
- Provide feedback to individuals on their family meeting behavior
- Perform a community service project as a group
- Engage in defining and separating business and family issues—then make an action plan on how they can be appropriately separated or appropriately meshed

---

Figure 6.2 Continued

- Obtain communication training
- Obtain training in conflict resolution and problem solving
- Arrange for everyone to be evaluated on relationship, communication, conflict, and other personality factors as a basis for self-awareness and development and family group development
- Build opportunities for "getting to know you" exercises, such as mixers, three truths and one lie, speed dating; do this especially with spouses and larger dispersed cousin groups
- Analyze the family's genogram together, then discuss patterns and conclusions together
- Have members of the younger generation meet with grandparents without parents involved around a meal or around a big bowl of popcorn or M&Ms, with or without questions prepared in advance
- Develop effective meeting management skills and learn to use meeting management methods and tools
- Foster a culture of attendance and participation at family meetings, retreats, and other events
- Create opportunities for the family to interact and learn from other business-owning families

Understanding/Appreciating the Business
- Learn the strategic components of the business (external and internal factors, goals and competitive advantage) and develop a tracking instrument, then regularly report on the effectiveness of each component, e.g., balanced scorecard
- Observe board meetings, board retreats, and strategic planning presentations by management
- Obtain outside work experience before applying to the business for a job
- Document or report on important points in time or major events that affected the company's history and relate it to family values
- Learn how to assess your industry—the short-term and long-term trends and where your business and family fit in
- Attend conferences in the company's industry
- Provide subscriptions to key trade publications
- Arrange for tours of the facilities, presentations from employees, interactions with non-family employees, and hands-on experience with products, services, or tools of the business
- Develop a marketing plan for a product or service now provided by the company
- Participate in part-time seasonal jobs or internships arranged specifically for family members
- Conduct a key competitor analysis and make a presentation
- Attend or arrange for an innovation and creativity workshop with a focus on your business—define processes that will encourage entrepreneurship in the later years of the controlling as well as the succeeding generation
- Have a panel of experts from the business field questions, some of which can be prepared in advance

Figure 6.2 Continued

- Develop board training and orientation programs for family members
- Create session opportunities for family members who are interested in updates from the CEO or other senior managers, e.g., a quarterly luncheon

Learning about the Family's Heritage and Family Values
- Define all the policies, key decisions, and historical choices in the business that are/have been consistent with our family values
- Write the history of the family or create a video documentary with interviews of family members and others—use all significant memory sources, such as letters, photographs, and memorabilia or artifacts
- Storytelling—senior family members relate historical events with discussion of the implicit values and principles behind the actions of the family and/or company
- Coach other family members in the application of the family values to work and family activity
- Develop new family values—identify among the existing values those to keep, those to discard, and then new ones to adopt
- Create a history wall together with post-it notes or other graphic representations of key moments in the family's history then discuss as one history even with divergent perspectives
- Do a collage together or individually that expresses the family's history and key values
- In small groups, act out key events in the family's history. Can give each group a small bag of items to use in the miniplays (i.e., paper bag dramatics)
- Oversee the development and management of a family newsletter or website

Developing the Next Generation
- Give the next generation as a group an interdependent problem to solve, one that is respected as a potential valuable contribution by those engaged in solving it and by those in management, on the board, and in the family arenas
- Create individual career path and/or individual developmental plans
- Provide mentors or coaches for family members who work in the business
- Attend or arrange for personal development workshops
- Provide family scholarship/education funding vehicles
- Provide entrepreneurship/venture seed money to qualified family applicants
- Create a community service plan
- Family-sponsored leadership/management development (nondegree)
- Establish a compensation and family employee development committee of the board of directors, dominated by independent board members
- Make available a range of activities for members of the next generation with varied difficulty levels, time requirements, areas of focus, etc., with each person required to choose one or two activities each year

Figure 6.2 Continued

- Start a simple family website to share experiences, photos, etc.
- Establish a family education committee
- Provide funds to invest and learn about asset management
- As a next generation group attend a family business seminar and provide a report to the family/family council on ideas for improving family functioning

Learning about the Family Office and Family Philanthropy
- Review estate plans and get updates from experts on estate and tax laws
- Understand types of investments and risk/return associated with each
- Develop family vision for philanthropic giving
- Participate in philanthropy education provided by community foundation or other resource
- Two or more attend a private family foundation conference together
- Assign a rotating individual role to research and circulate readings or articles on family philanthropy

Figure 6.2   Topics and Activities for Family Education and Development

access information about the company. Finally, this committee may get administrative and technical support from individuals in the company, especially with maintaining lists and website/intranet matters.

Common Family Council Standing Committees: Next Generation Committee

The name of this committee seemingly implies education, and thus the difference may not be clear between this committee and the education committee. While education certainly occurs, the purpose of this committee is to give the next generation a forum of its own. The education committee is designed to assess the development and education needs and to plan ways to fulfill them. In contrast, the next generation committee focuses on developing independence and interdependence through practice. This committee includes only members of the next generation who meet to help their generation train for their role as a future team of family owners. The existence of the committee offers the new generation an opportunity to practice self-governance.

When this committee first assembles, writing a charter is the first step, as it is for any new committee of the family council. The purpose of next generation committees can vary depending on the generation, the family, and the matters members consider most urgent. However, typical purposes include:

- Planning combined developmental and social events. As a separate segment of an annual shareholders meeting or when it is likely that many family members are in one place, such as during traditional vacation months or on holidays, the committee will organize and conduct a meeting of the next generation.
- Organizing communication, seeking opinion, building consensus, and making decisions. When it is appropriate for the younger generation to provide input on matters, this committee will manage the process, for example, compile responses to a new draft of a family employment policy.
- Conducting team projects.
- Setting its own rules. The committee will act as a representative group for the entire younger generation and will make the rules that apply within its scope of responsibilities, such as deciding whether spouses or friends can attend the meetings, setting standards for pages on social network sites, determining what technology to use at a meeting, and deciding how to deal with phones during a meeting.

Committees of this kind are often set up when many members of the next generation are in college, some have graduated already, and some are still in high school. That is, the younger generation consists of three very different groups, and this diversity presents a realistic and worthwhile challenge. The experience gained in taking on the challenge is one of the most important benefits gained by the participants.

Common Family Council Standing Committees: Philanthropy Committee

If a family foundation exists, this committee's purpose may be served by the foundation board. However, once a family council has been formed, some families recognize that the organization and formality of family governance can enhance their philanthropic efforts. A philanthropy committee also gives family members an additional avenue for involvement; some may be more interested in philanthropy than anything else related to the business, and this committee thus broadens their opportunities for participation, which enhances unity and commitment among all family members.

One way of beginning is for the family to weigh in on the charitable contributions the business makes. Initially, this can be a challenge because there are two objectives that may conflict: the business's philanthropy objectives based on tradition and business development and the philanthropy priorities of family members. However, these conflicts can be managed, and one purpose of this committee is to consider both objectives and to work effectively with management. As an example, one committee identified its purpose and structure as follows:

> We believe it is the duty, obligation, and privilege of our family to give back to the community. Contributions should reflect the Smith family's values while keeping in mind the strategic needs of our company, including employee relations. The purpose of the philanthropy committee is to ensure that our long-standing tradition of philanthropy continues, that it integrates priorities of the business and family, and that we achieve good results.
>
> The family-owned company's management and board of directors shall determine the amount of money available for philanthropic donations on an annual basis. The philanthropy committee shall include at least one member from the family council as well as two other at-large family members, a director of the board, and a manager appointed by the company. The committee shall communicate with the family and company to determine the values and priorities to direct corporate donations within the community and then make recommendations to the family council for approval of a set of priorities for grants and gifts. For charitable contributions from business proceeds, management will make the final decision. The committee may also be involved in the distribution of gifts and grants and in tracking their ultimate utilization and effectiveness in the community.

Some committees may coordinate strategic philanthropy from family assets, much like a foundation. That is, in addition to the duties of coordinating with management to direct business donations, the committee would create a philanthropic strategy for all family members who choose to be involved in creating a common fund. At the simplest level, they might contribute to a community foundation. Yet, they may completely self-direct their donations and perform many of the functions of a family foundation, such as establishing procedures for grant applications, decision making, and follow-through. At this level, family members could also establish ways for younger members to become involved. For large funds a family may seek to establish an administrative function to assist with the operational aspects.

Common Family Council Standing Committees:
Planning Committee

This committee's purpose includes meeting logistics and could also include agenda responsibilities, depending on a family council's leadership structure. Particularly valuable for larger full-family family councils, a planning committee, which works between meetings, provides a family council with efficiency and continuity from meeting to meeting. While many business families are careful to define this committee as something less than a representative family council, even as a hybrid, it can be a stepping stone toward adoption of a representative structure. Typically, however, particularly when trust is low in the family, the transparency needs are high, and a planning committee offers increased efficiency and logistics planning. Planning committees will facilitate decisions by making possible effective and frequent access to communication channels involving the broader family.

Unless specifically directed otherwise, these committees assume limited decision-making responsibilities; they are like other standing committees in that they make recommendations but leave the major decisions to the full family council. Planning committees are particularly useful when there are rotating chairs of family council meetings because they can ensure continuity from meeting to meeting.

Common Family Council Standing
Committees: Social Committee

Sometimes referred to as the fun committee, this group primarily provides opportunities for enjoyable recreation and social interaction so as to develop pleasant memories and to build and maintain relationships between the generations and across the extended family. The committee may plan vacations and trips for small as well as larger families and fun events and activities to be combined with meetings of a family assembly, association, or council. Social committees are typically concerned with the sequence, variety, and appropriateness of social and recreational events for the changing needs of the family and the various needs of its members. That is, they will adopt guidelines for regular functions that have worked for all ages of the family and are adopted as meeting traditions, such as a full family dinner the evening before a family assembly meeting. Social committees also come up with new and unique events, such as the surprise appearance of a magician during a dinner or a golf cart scavenger hunt.

Social committees will also plan and manage or oversee the management of logistics. They may be responsible for everything from site selection to menu decisions, and they may or may not receive administrative support from the company or family office for these tasks. These committees will also be concerned with developing an appropriate annual budget and getting it approved by the family council. In addition, they may also be responsible for developing applicable policies, such as travel reimbursement and payment for babysitters during meetings.

Regarding logistical planning, social committees may gather input and then make a recommendation; yet, some family councils will give authority to the committee to make decisions as long as certain conditions are met, such as keeping within budget limits. Coordination is required with a chair or with the planning committee if there is one, depending on who or what committee creates the agenda.

Social committees provide a good opportunity for reaching out and involving several family members for short periods of time. For example, a core committee of two can remain for a term of two to three years and be complemented by three or four recruits or volunteers who join to plan an event and then are replaced by others for another event.

An example of a purpose statement for the charter of a social committee is as follows:

> The social committee of the Goldman family council is responsible for providing opportunities for the family to engage with one another in social, recreational, and other enjoyable activities and events. Typically, the events and activities will be in conjunction with other business family meetings, yet will not be restricted to such. The committee's objective is to make available at least two events per year with the hope that

all family members will participate in at least one for the purpose of integrating new family members, building and strengthening relationships, and increasing the general enjoyment of being a family.

Common Family Council Ad Hoc Committees and Task Forces

Charter Ad Hoc Committee

Charter committees are established when there is a change in the family governance structure, for example, when a family council is first formed, or when there is a significant change, such as a transition from a full-family family council to a representative family council. Charter committees are also formed to prepare charters for family assemblies and family associations. Charter ad hoc committees are formed to study and recommend and facilitate necessary amendments, and then they disband. Depending on the frequency of family council meetings and the degree of diversity involved in the project, charter committees may exist from two months to a year.

While we have not seen charter committees used for this purpose, they can develop into governance committees, still performing charter duties and also adding family council evaluations and making recommendations for fundamental changes to the family governance structure and functioning. As a family changes, the governance functions must adapt also. Being familiar and comfortable with an ad hoc committee that makes regular assessments would facilitate changes in family governance and allow fine-tuning as well as fundamental changes when needed.

Historical Archive Ad Hoc Committee

Historical archive committees conduct projects to assemble historical material and decide how to best preserve it and make it available to the current and future family. They typically oversee or directly engage in the collection of both family and company historical information and artifacts. Many families will seek options and select from alternative services and multiple media choices to assist in the organization and preservation of their history. Archive committees are tasked with making decisions about how best to represent the history when there are multiple perspectives; their work is especially difficult when the family completely separates into branches or when there were perceived inequities and unfair treatment in the past. In such cases, the composition of the committee may be more important than when there has been little controversy. Moreover, great care should go into the initial directives regarding critical decision points when family council approval will be needed and also regarding the ultimate purpose of the final product.

Project Task Forces

Task forces can be set up for multiple purposes and vary widely from one business family council to another. Among the many possible issues, two topics in particular lend themselves very well to being handled by task forces reporting to the family council: developing a family constitution and investigating the viability of a family office.

Constitution Task Force

A family business constitution[2] is a family agreement stating critical beliefs, principles, values, and aspirations of the family, owners, and business; it also spells out key policies that support fairness. For a family that is ready and decides to undertake this task, drafting a constitution is a commitment to make an important contribution to the family and will require significant effort. Thus, an alternative to a constitution task force is for the family council to take on the project supported by one task force each for the following areas: (1) beliefs, principles, and values; (2) visions for family, owners, and the business; and (3) key policies.

Special Family Meeting Task Force

At the other end of the spectrum, a task force is an equally valuable method for tasks much less weighty than writing a constitution, such as planning a special meeting. In some business families, when the adults who have been working together in a family council reach a significant agreement affecting their children, they want to announce it to them. They may be reaching out to their children as a group for the first time;

of course, they want to do it well and in a manner that appeals to all ages involved. For example, when the family council has completed its draft of a family employment policy, a task force might be used to plan a meeting during holidays when all of the children will be together. The task force would be responsible for finding a date, choosing a venue, sending out invitations, and planning all other aspects of the meeting including how to follow up.

Three Task Forces Where the Family Council is Working for the Owners

Sometimes the organization of the family council can work to the benefit of just part of the family. This is the case when the family council, accustomed to establishing task forces for research and gaining input from the family, conducts a project for the owners that is, of course, sanctioned by the owners. Three examples follow.

Family Office Task Force

As a business and the number of family members grows, many business families ask themselves if services now provided by the business might be more equitably provided through a family office. It is a good question for a task force that might conduct the viability or oversee and collaborate with a consultant who accomplishes the task. The task would be to provide the family council with a report containing the results of analyses and their recommendations.

Family Director Task Force

Some family councils are asked to nominate or select directors from the family to serve on the board of directors. If it is a challenge, the council may establish a committee, much like a nominating committee of the board (and certainly the board may choose to nominate all directors, family and independents, without the help of the family council). However, a project that fits nicely into the task force structure is the development and documentation of the special requirements and qualifications for the unique role played by a board member who is a member of the family. Establishing the job description for the family director greatly assists with the nomination process. Thus, the family council's task force could provide direct support to either the family council or the board of directors.

Owner Dividend Task Force

Finally, a task force can conduct an owner project under the banner of the family council, such as making a recommendation on a dividend or distribution policy. Perhaps a guideline or a policy exists at the board level and is in need of revision, or it may be that one is needed because there are no guidelines. A task force would make its recommendation to the family council, whose job then becomes finalization of a recommendation and submitting it to the board of directors. By use of a task force made up of family owners and future owners, who conducted research and communicate well with the shareholders, the family council's recommended policy is likely to have broad support when it goes to the board.

7

The Family Assembly and the Family Association

As families grow through birth, adoption, and marriage, eventually it will no longer be feasible to have all family members make all decisions together. For larger families, family assembly and family association meetings help to organize the family and to make decisions and are flexible enough to allow smaller decision-making groups to serve in an executive capacity. This streamlines the decision-making process provides a forum for education, development, and some shared decision making in larger groups.

Definitions

We find that many families use many different terms to describe the same organized bodies. Here are some terms and definitions that are a useful for thinking about family organization.

The **family assembly** consists of the founders and all of their descendants (including young children and infants), and this body rarely makes decisions. For example, Dave and Judy Christoff's family had grown to 45 members spanning three generations. They needed to get organized, so they began by defining who will be part of the family. They defined the Christoff family assembly as follows:

> The Christoff family assembly consists of Dave and Judy Christoff as well as of their lineal descendants, whether born into the family or adopted, and of all spouses of lineal descendants.

> The purpose of the Christoff family assembly is to nurture the bonds that connect the family and to provide an opportunity for members of all generations to share in the supportive environment of the family.

When calling all 45 of their family members together for a portion of a meeting planned for the following year, Dave and Judy announced that the Christoff family assembly would be meeting, and everyone knew which family members were invited, and all knew to bring their spouses and children. A family assembly typically meets only once or twice per year, due to the logistical challenges and expense involved in gathering such a large group.

The **family association** consists of a subset of the family assembly and is usually the largest decision-making body of a business family. To be part of the family association, family members must meet certain milestones or qualifications, and family association members usually have a vote. A typical family association will meet two to four times per year, depending on the needs of the family. In the Christoffs' case, the family decided that once children reached age 18, they should be entitled to vote on matters concerning the family. They defined the Christoff family association as follows:

> The Christoff family association consists of Dave and Judy Christoff as well as of all their lineal descendants, whether born into the family or adopted, and of the spouses of lineal descendants, who have reached the age of 18 and who have observed at least one Christoff family association meeting as a nonvoting member. Once formally admitted into the Christoff family association, each member will be allowed to vote on matters of the family.
>
> The purpose of the Christoff family association is to ensure that all generations of the Christoff family are educated about the assets shared in common and are prepared for the roles they will each play as well as to make decisions that will help the family achieve its shared goals.

The family association is still a large body of people. In the Christoffs' case, it included Dave and Judy, each of their 5 children and their spouses, and 14 members of the third generation, 26 people in total. Moreover, several of the third-generation family members were going to be married soon, and there were an additional six third-generation family members who would shortly become old enough to be members of the association. While the Christoff family association is an excellent forum for education, development, and cultivation of relationships, making consensus decisions on all decisions with this ever growing body of people would make it difficult for the family to function effectively. The Christoff family council was formed to address this need.

The **representative family council** in the context of a large family group is the executive leadership group of the family, usually chosen by election for specified terms. It is understood that council members would rotate from time to time, as defined in the family council charter (see chapter 5). The Christoff family council was defined as follows:

> The Christoff Family Council serves the needs of the Christoff family by ensuring that the family's purposes are pursued with energy and that the goals of the family are achieved in a timely manner. The Christoff family council consists of seven family members (at least two drawn from the second generation) who are elected by and are standing members of the Christoff family association.

The representative family council is responsible for more day-to-day decision making and for advancing the overall family agenda. From an organizational framework viewpoint, a larger family will be organized using the three bodies we have described in figure 7.1.

As shown, the family council may accomplish its work through either standing committees or task forces that are formed from time to time to accomplish a specific task or project. The family council has the authority to make decisions in between family association meetings but will generally bring substantive topics or decisions to the family association

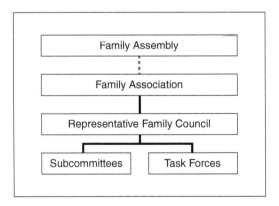

Figure 7.1 Family Organization Picture

group for discussion and approval. Decision making will be discussed in more detail later in this chapter.[1]

Who Gets to Define Who is Part of the Family?

One of the stickiest situations that many families encounter is trying to define exactly what the term "family" means. For some family members it refers to the founder and the founder's direct descendants and may or may not include spouses. Other family members may believe that a live-in partner who has been introduced to the family over a period of years should be included as a family member, and still others may exclude anyone who is not connected to the family by marriage. The matter is further complicated by many large families having advisors who are so close to the family as to be also included in the family meeting processes. Ultimately, the family itself must make the decision of how it will define the term "family." But how can the family define who family is when members cannot agree on who should be included in that discussion. This can create a conundrum for some of the healthiest families.

We advise that the founders and their lineal descendants who are involved in the enterprise be considered as the initial group who will define family. On this basis, this lineally related group can begin to clarify which family members will compose the family association. In the long run, we encourage a broad definition of family for inclusion in the family association. While there may be times in the formative years of the enterprise in which a family meeting or a family group may be composed of the lineal descendants only, enterprising families that are serious about moving to a third and fourth generation of ownership and beyond will find it critical to bring spouses into the fold on matters pertaining to the family enterprise. After all, they are 50 percent contributors to the genetic makeup of the future generations. Excluding them will create problems in the long run from which many families cannot recover.

Special Friends

We find that many larger families with offspring in the early to mid-twenties develop close and loving relationships in which they feel that

1. What purposes are we trying to achieve as a family?
2. What values do we wish to perpetuate in our family?
3. What are our deepest hopes for future generations?
4. Who needs to be part of our family association to accomplish our purposes and pass on the most enduring traits and values within our family?
5. Are we at a stage where we are ready to include all those necessary for us to achieve our purposes, or would a smaller group be more effective in building momentum?
6. If we are not ready for total inclusion, what do we need to accomplish before we include all?
7. In seeking to achieve family goals, are we at greater risk by including or excluding those who are not committed to lifelong relationships?
8. In seeking to achieve family goals, will we include those adopted or stepfamily members?

Figure 7.2   Eight Questions to Determine "Who is Family?"

their companion is on track to become a formal member of the family. Our experience has been that these families will discuss important business matters in family association meetings only with those who are in committed lifelong relationships. Family members may feel quite vulnerable when a person who is not committed to lifelong family membership eventually leaves the group knowing the family's deepest hopes, goals, and inner workings. However, much effort may be taken to include girlfriends, boyfriends, and fiancées in family gatherings that do not deal with the business of the family, such as gatherings of the family assembly. For both family assembly meetings and family association meetings it is important to clarify who is eligible to participate. Ideally, decisions about who will attend will be made by being very clear about what the family is trying to accomplish; this can lead to a better understanding of whether special friends should be part of the process or not.

Advisors

As families become more sophisticated and grow, many have advisors who participate in family association events. While these advisors are not members of the family, clear boundaries should be drawn to define what type of events advisors are welcome to attend and what events are limited to family members only. We find the following rule of thumb helpful:

> If an advisor works with the entire family and is seen as a resource for all, that advisor is valuable to the whole group and therefore attendance at family functions may allow him or her to get to know family members, family hopes, and family goals and ultimately to see how he or she can best serve the family. Still, most families operate on the assumption that an advisor to the whole family should only be at events when there is a reason for him or her to be present.

What about situations in which one family member has an advisor and wants to bring him or her to all or part of a meeting? If an advisor is specifically advising an individual member or branch of the family, that advisor's presence may be dividing, distracting, discouraging, and sometimes detrimental. Typically, a member or branch of a family will want to have his or her own advisor present when technical subjects are being discussed. Be aware, however, that having an individual advisor present can feel to many family members as if that person is trying to protect himself or herself from the rest of the family, and this can lead to a cycle of distrust that results in each family member bringing his or her own advisor to family functions. For example, when a family member requests that his or her attorney be present at a family meeting, other family members naturally begin to feel unsafe because a person is present who represents only one member of the family—potentially to the detriment of the group. For example, the person who invited his or her attorney was perhaps primarily interested in making sure the latter understood some complex estate planning that was in process but did not limit the attorney's presence to that portion of the meeting. Other family members might become wary and less candid in group discussions, and this reduces the quality of the time spent together.

We feel that it is critical that families understand clearly in advance who will be invited to what events, and individual advisors should participate only infrequently and only regarding technical topics.

Family Association Decision Making

Once a family has decided who will be included in the family association, the next task is to clearly articulate how decisions will be made. The family association will need to explore decision-making models that will work best for the family association. We offer the following previous work on family decision making as an exploratory method.[2]

Establishing rules for family decision-making can be complex and cumbersome. We have seen families choose to use a simple majority for the sake of ease; however, when families have a means of dealing with potential cutoff situations by using some of the tools presented in appendix 4, referenced above, they have an opportunity to grow together rather than apart. In adopting a decision-making model, we strongly encourage the use of the broadest method of inclusion to reach agreement on how the family will make decisions. Ideally, a broad consensus on what decision-making model will be used should be reached before group decisions are made. If the family is broadly in agreement that decisions will be made based on the principle that a simple majority rules, family members can usually live with group decisions and will abide by them. However, if a family is not in agreement and uses a simple majority decision-making model to establish the family decision-making method, there can be tremendous problems down the road when the family faces difficult decisions, as it is sure to do.

> Henry Cho had been unhappy when the Cho family first met and voted 11 to 7 that all family decisions would be made by a simple majority vote. He felt that his family branch, which was the smaller branch, would be at a disadvantage if his cousins tried to take advantage of their larger numbers. He had raised the issue, but the family had insisted that simple majority would suffice, and he was voted down. Now his worries were coming true.
>
> The regional grocery chain owned by the Cho family was being threatened by a new competitor, a national chain that had previously ignored the ethnic niche the Cho's served. Henry and his branch of the family felt that reinvesting in the stores was particularly needed at this time to secure customers' satisfaction through excellent product offerings, product layout, and modern technology. His cousins believed that the new competitor was not a serious threat and proposed an increased dividend distribution, but Henry believed this would weaken the company at a vulnerable time. The majority ruled.
>
> Henry began to dwell on how the initial decision to use a simple majority for decision making had been "rigged" by his cousins so they could get their way even when it was not in the best interest of the company. Soon rumination turned into distrust, fuelled by Henry's anxieties. Henry began to see his cousins as enemies and found that his own siblings agreed with him when he shared how the cousins had rigged family

decision making in their favor. The family began to split as Henry's branch perceived little value in dealing with the tyranny of the majority, and disenfranchisement followed.

The fuel that propelled Henry, and later his branch of the family, to pull away from the family was not the economic decision of raising the distribution. The real fuel was Henry's belief that he and his branch had been duped by a voting system that gave them no voice. In practice, most family associations will attempt to reach consensus prior to voting on a matter. This gives each member a chance to be heard and feel respected in the process. Consensus need not be 100% agreement, and it is important that the family agree on what process or mechanisms will be used if 100% agreement is not possible on matters before the association.

The Family Association Charter

When a family group goes through these steps to determine who is part of the family, articulates its deepest goals, beliefs, values, purposes, and clearly defines who is included in the decision-making process once a model of decision making has been chosen, we refer to this as the family being in the process of creating its association charter. The family association charter serves to unify the family group around a common understanding that will guide its behavior. While answering the questions necessary to complete the charter can be seen as cumbersome and time consuming, families who do not make this initial investment of time will spend exponentially more time in the long run trying to resolve difficult challenges and threats as tough issues emerge.

We strongly advise the family group to create its own charter and not simply duplicate the charters of other families. We have seen many families that have taken ideas from another family and then faced a difficult issue but lacked confidence in the very charter that was supposed to guide them through this challenge. In these cases, the families found it difficult to make decisions together because of their frustration and lack of cohesion.

Nevertheless, it may be helpful to review how one family created the charter for its family association. The Sheay Family Association charter was created to guide the descendants of Daniel and Amy Sheay in productive decision making. Below are excerpts from their charter.

The Sheay Family Association Charter

Our Family Purpose

The Sheay Family Association is created to make several dreams a reality:

- A faithful family that honors our Creator and the commitments we make to each other
- A unified family that values time together
- A supportive family that strives to honor our common values but supports individual differences in family members
- A challenging family that helps each family member be the best version of himself or herself
- A loving family that asks, "How can I help?" when a need is seen
- A family committed to stewardship that leaves our shared assets in better condition than when we received them
- A decisive family that follows clear guidelines on how decisions of importance will be made

Sheay Family Association Membership

All descendants of Daniel and Amy Sheay, including biological children and those adopted into the family by their sixteenth birthday, and spouses of descendants will be active members of the family association when they have reached their twenty-first birthday.

If family members are in a committed, lifelong relationship they have declared to the Sheays' family council, their partners will become members of the family association.

All Sheay Family Association members are expected to share in the pursuit of our purposes, respect our governance, and strive to do what is best for the family even if it is not always in our individual best interest.

Sheay Family Association Governance

Our family has a strong history of reaching consensus on decisions and will follow this method as a first course. In the event we are not able to reach consensus, a motion may be passed according to *Robert's Rules of Order*, and a vote by the majority of the group, with each association member having one vote, will carry the day. However, in the event that there is an objection voiced by a member of our family association, the family council will delay the vote, if possible, and create a task force to propose alternative solutions to the issue for the sake of creating a more unifying resolution to the issue at hand. The task force will report back at the next family association meeting, and the issue will be deliberated and a vote retaken, which shall be the final vote.

A quorum of at least 60 percent of family association members present at a meeting announced at least 14 days in advance and whether held face-to-face or electronically is empowered to make decisions on behalf of the family association. Proxies may not be used for family decisions.

Sheay Family Association Leadership:
The Sheay Family Council

The Sheay family's family association shall elect up to seven of its members to serve as members of the family council, which will serve as the leadership arm of the family association. Terms will be staggered so no more than three family council members rotate off at any one time, thus ensuring greater continuity among the family.

The members of the family council will elect one of their own members to be chair of the family council as well as a vice chair, a secretary, and a treasurer. Other officers may be installed as needed. Each family council member shall have one vote, except in the case where the family council has an even number of family members serving on the council, in which case the chair shall serve as the tiebreaker.

A quorum of the family council shall exist whenever there are four members of the family council present for a vote.

Gathering Family Association
Perspectives and Opinions

Communication and mutual understanding are critical purposes of the family association. While much of this understanding happens during face-to-face meetings, families will occasionally need to use other resources to gather perspectives.

In small families, gathering a collective opinion is a very simple task. However, as families begin to grow and scatter geographically, gathering opinions on important matters becomes more complicated, requiring more time and resources. Below are a few of the techniques that we consider the most effective ones:

The Survey

Let's say you desire to gain input from every member of the family association regarding a topic of interest. For example, the company is considering modifying its risk profile to accomplish an expansion, and the board seeks the family's input on the matter. A reasonably quick method of gathering input is a survey. Surveys are made up of four different types of questions.

1. Simple Yes/No Questions

Example:
Would you be open to increasing the company's targeted debt/equity ratio to accommodate an investment that is projected to provide a greater investment return than the company currently returns? Yes or No

This question is to the point and usually results in a clear response. It is considered a closed question in that there are only two responses to choose from.

2. Multiple-Choice Questions

When we want to go beyond yes and no and would like to know the family's opinion on a number of options, we can use a multiple-choice question.

Example:
The following represents the highest debt/equity ratio I am willing to consider for our company as it pursues higher returns on investment (we currently are targeting .30 as upper threshold):
   (a)   *.30*
   (b)   *.50*
   (c)   *.70*
   (d)   *.90*
   (e)   *I need to learn more about debt/equity ratios to answer this question.*

By giving multiple choices we gain a little bit more information, but because there are multiple responses, it is unlikely that we will determine a clear majority position for any question asked. In asking questions of this nature, we should first determine whether or not we need to have a specific response or whether simply gaining the input of the association members will be enough to allow the leadership group, usually the family council, to make the decision with the information gained.

3. The Rank Order

Let's assume that we wish to determine what priorities family members have regarding their risk profiles. One way to determine each individual's strength among several options is to have them rank their preferences. We can provide several options and ask family members to rank their preferences.

Example:
In thinking about what factors are most important to you in determining the company's targeted debt/equity ratio, rank the following factors in order of your preference from most preferred to least preferred, where 1 is most preferred and 5 is least preferred.
1. Ensuring stable dividends
2. Increasing opportunities for our key executives and employees
3. Reaching our growth goals
4. Preserving our investment
5. Passing the business on to the next generation

The family council or family member interpreting the survey can then assign a point value to the strength of responses. For example, a respondent's first choice will get five points, a second choice will get three points, a third choice will get two points, and a fourth choice will get one point. Point totals can then be used to guide decision making.

The ranking method helps us understand the will of the larger group, but there may be impassioned individuals in the group who get special consideration. For example, let's say that 5 points were awarded to each person's first choice, but what we don't know is whether or not a person's top choice was extremely important to him or her or was just a preferred response among the choices given. It's quite possible that the second option or even a lower option would have elicited great passion by a rater if that person had been given a chance to speak before the entire group. It is possible that a person's passion and speaking skills may garner the group's support for a decision that is to be made by the group.

If the family council conducts the survey to find out the ideas of family association members as a guide for discussion at the next meeting, then closed questions are more useful because they are designed to limit the options the family association may choose from; thus, it can quickly get a sense of the group's opinions. Sometimes more information is desired in order to make a final decision. For this type of information we typically use one of two different open-ended techniques.

4. Open-Ended Questions

Questions asking respondents to fill in the blanks and open-ended questions give them much greater flexibility when providing input into family business matters.

a)   Fill in the blanks

When we are not sure what is truly important to family members, giving them the opportunity to express their own ideas is an effective tool. For example, let's say the family council did not want to overly influence family ideas related to risk and instead wanted family association members to have total freedom to express their hopes and goals relating to company risk. The following format for filling in the blanks could be used.

Example:
When considering modifying our company's risk profile to take on more risk, what are the top three factors that should be considered by the family association?

Through this technique family association member's immediate hopes or concerns are identified, and their answers are not restricted by the question's designer. There is also some risk because some family members may consider options that are not realistic in terms of the management's ability to grow the company, or some may wish to take on dangerous levels of debt. Thus, the above question could be modified to still ask about the hopes of all family association members without creating false expectations about the future.

Example:
The board recently explored the health of our company and indicated that, based on the strengths of the firm, debt/equity ratios ranging from our current conservative .30 to as much as .90 could be considered, depending

on owner's goals. What are the top three factors the family association should consider in determining how much risk to assume in the form of a debt/equity ratio?

By presenting the realistic criteria the board has put forth, family members are encouraged to curtail their imagination as they answer the question because they know that not all risk levels are open for consideration. At other times, however, the goal of the survey team is to get as much input as possible without limiting options. This is when the survey designers should consider open-ended questions.

b)   Open-ended questions

The broadest possible leeway that we can grant family association members is the open-ended question. Here a question is designed to allow for any response at all.

Examples:
- *What is your philosophy of taking risks in investments?*
- *When thinking about the family business, how would you describe your risk tolerance?*

These questions allow respondents to answer without restrictions and thus provide the maximum amount of information—if people respond. In our experience, open-ended questions are frequently answered by those with strong verbal skills and usually with strong opinions on a particular subject. It is not uncommon that in a large group of 30 or 40 only about 20 percent of respondents take the time to write more than a few words in answering an open-ended question. Therefore, we feel that these questions are an excellent tool but should be used realistically by the family council because they tend to favor responses from those most emotionally charged regarding an issue and from those with the highest verbal skills.

Putting It All Together: Utilizing Surveys Effectively

Now that we have discussed the different ways of gaining information from a survey, let's look at how these different styles of questions can elicit information that can be used by a family council in guiding a family association. Let's say a family council is interested in obtaining several important pieces of information from all family association members about their interests in continuing ownership of the enterprise into the next generation. The following survey is created to gather information using several styles of questions.

Sample Ownership Continuity Questionnaire Using Multiple Question Formats

1. Is it your desire that our family business ownership pass on to the next generation?
    a. Yes
    b. No

2. Which of the following principles is most important to you regarding transitioning ownership to the next generation?
    a. *Senior generation owners will begin transferring their stock by a set age.*
    b. *Senior generation owners will complete their ownership transitions by a set age.*
    c. *Stock transitions will be made known to all family owners.*
    d. *All transitions will occur at the price set in the last annual valuation.*

3. Rank the following reasons why you think transitioning ownership to the next generation is important
    a. ___*It continues the family legacy.*
    b. ___*It provides opportunities for next generation family members to work in the business.*
    c. ___*Our return on investment is superior to that which can be achieved in other investments.*
    d. ___*Our parents would be disappointed if we did not*

4. When it comes to the next generation as possible owners or managers of our family business, I most hope:_____

Who Will Administer the Survey?

The question of who should compile the data is a critical question. This question must be answered prior to determining how the data will be collected because the answer will impact the administration of data collection. There are some surveys that can be administered easily by a member of the family council but others will require guaranteed confidentiality if they are to result in honest input. Sometimes a neutral party is needed to administer the survey. A neutral party is someone who will be trusted by the family to summarize individual answers without revealing who said what, thus protecting confidentiality.

If the person reading the completed surveys knew how a respondent had answered the survey, a "yes" response to any of the following questions would require a neutral party administrator.

1. Would this in any way cause embarrassment to the respondent?
2. Would it change the way the reader sees the respondent?
3. Would it potentially cause bitterness toward the respondent?
4. Would it hinder honest responses by the respondent?

The neutral party could be a law firm, an accounting firm, consultants, university faculty, or graduate students.

Questions on Paper or Electronically

When your family council is sending out a survey to the entire family association, you will need to make a decision as to whether to send this survey out through traditional mail or by e-mail. E-mail is easiest if the family members receiving the survey use e-mail regularly. If not, either traditional mail or a combination of electronic and traditional mail can be used.

If using e-mail, you can either send out a form that is to be returned by e-mail, or if you have the technical capability, you can create a link to an electronic form that can be sent via e-mail, and the recipient can simply open the link and complete the survey. When the survey takers are finished, they verify that the survey is complete, and the data is sent directly to a database, which can automatically gather and compile the data.

In a traditional mail format, the survey is typically sent out with a self-addressed return envelope so that the surveys can be quickly filled out and sent back. It is important when using traditional mail to include a cover page that is brief and succinct in terms of what is being asked of the respondent. Below is an example of a cover letter that will succinctly tell respondents what they need to do and by when.

Dear Shareholders,

In an effort to confidentially assess owners' desire to continue ownership into the next generation, the family council appointed a task force to determine shareholder commitment toward continuing family business ownership into the next generation. The task force, lead by Hal, Loren, and Stephano, is asking you to complete the attached survey by

February 7 and mail it in the enclosed envelope to Smith & Smith law firm, which has been hired to gather survey results and compile the responses for the family.

All individual responses to survey questions will remain confidential! The law firm has been instructed not to share individual responses with anyone in the family or company but only to aggregate the responses and present them to the task force. The task force will use the information to plan a presentation at our next shareholders meeting, and all shareholders will receive a copy of the aggregated responses at that time.

Each survey has been coded to allow the law firm to track who has returned a survey. The law firm will share the list of which owners have completed the survey with the task force, which will allow the task force to make necessary reminder calls to those whose surveys are outstanding. Your prompt completion of the survey will help minimize reminder calls and reduce the work of our task force; this will be greatly appreciated. The family has set a goal to achieve a 100 percent response rate.

If you have any questions, please call Hal at 234–567–8901.

Thank you,
The Continued Ownership Task Force

After you have taken the time to create a survey to gather information critical to understanding the wishes of the family, get ready to have your expectations jarred a bit. In a large family it is quite normal to get only 50 percent of the surveys back by the due date. Remember, while it may have taken you hours of deep thought and focused work to create this data gathering instrument, the person you are sending it to sees it as just another piece of mail. You can boost the response rate by sending by either paper mail or e-mail (or both) reminders that the due date is approaching. The person in charge of assuring a high response rate can be guided by the following schedule:

Sample Survey Schedule

- **January 1–15**: Family council deliberates on the purpose and goals of the survey, creates the survey, and appoints an individual to generate a high response rate for the survey. (Yes, somebody always has to be in charge if you want to get something done in a family.)
- **January 15**: Cover letter is sent out to the family indicating that a survey will soon be coming to each family association member to

gain valuable input. An e-mail message is an excellent way to get this information out quickly.

- **January 20**: Survey is mailed out through traditional mail to family association members.
- **January 27**: A reminder letter indicating that each person has the survey is sent out to all family association members. Due date is clearly highlighted.
- **February 4**: An e-mail reminder is sent to all family association members indicating that there are 72 hours left to complete the survey and get it in on time.
- **February 7**: The survey is now due. A list is compiled of all those who have completed the survey and those who still need to complete the survey.
- **February 8**: An additional day is allowed as a grace period for those who got the survey completed on the due date and are mailing it.
- **February 9**: The survey leader makes phone calls and sends e-mails to all those whose surveys are still not in.
- **February 13**: Depending on the response, survey leaders should either begin summarizing the data or make a second round of phone calls to stimulate response.

Depending on the issue that is being considered by the family council, a response rate of 50 percent or 60 percent may be adequate to fulfill the family council's purposes in sending out the survey, but other items many require a response rate closer to 100 percent. Depending on the response rate that the family council determines is needed, the survey leader will need to devise a reminder and follow-up system that maximizes the number of respondents.

Remember that a survey asking for 10 pieces of data from 20 family members will return 200 pieces of data that must be summarized. If we are asking 20 questions of 50 family members, we now have 1,000 items of data that will need to be presented in some usable form. Our experience is that many families find it cumbersome and overwhelming to aggregate the results. Using electronic surveys can help manage the results, but to reach those of varying degrees of sophistication, the survey leader may wish to use a combination of e-mailed surveys and paper surveys. A good strategy is to mail the paper survey and follow it up one day later with an e-mail survey explaining in the cover letter that family association members can choose which format they would like to complete.

If you send the survey using multiple forms, you'll quickly note that those surveys that come back to you by e-mail can be quickly cut and pasted into an aggregated form.

Online Surveys

There are several Internet survey tools that family council members may wish to take advantage of when surveying family association members. For example, Survey Monkey (www.surveymonkey.com), and Zoomerang (www.zoomerang.com) are tools family association members can log onto to complete the survey. Then the survey information can be aggregated immediately by the site. For some senior generation family members, this online experience is a bit intimidating, and it will be useful to have other family members volunteer to help guide them.

When using an online survey program, the survey leader will have access to the information and can summarize data quickly. The online service can also quickly tell who has completed the survey and who has not yet completed the survey. It is possible to allow each person to complete the survey anonymously even though the survey leader will have access to the list of those who have completed it. If you are able to get your family to complete an online survey, the task of assembling all the information is easier. The challenge will be to get family association members to put sensitive information online; for this they must trust that the information will be used only in the manner stated (that is, it will remain anonymous). Family members may prefer some other method.

Confidentiality

Nevertheless, somebody or something, such as a computer server, must tally the information and will see individual responses. For this reason, some families will hire an outside firm to tally the information so that no family association member will have access to responses of other family association members. This can be useful for the most sensitive pieces of information and opinions family association members may express, but for most family council information, a trusted family member can serve as the survey leader, and that member's promise of not sharing who said what is enough to secure a high response rate. Including a statement of confidentiality and being extremely transparent as to who will or will not see the data as well as who will and will not see the responses is an important part of the cover letter to accompany the survey.

Less Formal Surveys

Let's say you need to get a sense of the family's views on a specific topic but it is not critical to have everybody in the family respond, and you're looking for a highly efficient means of asking questions. We have found that a quick question sent out by e-mail to all family members that clearly articulates who will see the responses and what will be done with them is a good way to get answers to a question that is on the family councils' mind.

Internal Web Survey

Another informal means of gathering information is to post on a family's website a survey or series of questions and ask those who go to the website to answer the questions. But remember that if you do this, only those people who frequent the website will be giving responses, which may not reflect the views of the whole family.

Real-Time Survey

If a quick response is needed and a family association meeting allows time, it is also possible to use a family association meeting to have all attending participants complete the survey during the meeting to ensure that all will answer the questions. Of course, this speeds up responses and makes it easy to gather information, but it is possible that family members will not have given adequate thought to their responses or will be absent from the meeting.

Focus Groups

Sometimes a family council just needs to have a general idea of the kinds of concerns or issues that are on people's minds or to get some quick feedback from a smaller group. In order to accomplish this, focus groups can be used to gain feedback.

Announcement

Date: March 20, 2012
Time: 9:30 A.M.—11:30 A.M.
Location: Sandy's home
Purpose: Gain insight into the family's thinking about collectively owned family properties.

Questions to Address

- How do we view benefits of the shared properties?
- Are the shared properties helping us achieve our family's mission?

How will the information be used?

- A summary of key discussion points will be shared with the family association during the next meeting. You will not be identified as having made any specific statements in this summary.
- Refreshments will be provided

Figure 7.3   Focus Group Announcement

A focus group is essentially a gathering of a small group of individuals, usually not more than three to six, who will respond to a question from the person calling the focus group together. For example, this could be a family council leader. In the focus group session, individuals respond to a variety of questions and document their thinking about the issue under consideration. Focus groups are particularly effective when the leader can capture everybody's thoughts on a flipchart for all to see. The advantage of this method is that it brings a small group of people together in one place, and the resources of the overall family are not taxed too heavily as most families can usually find individuals within a limited geographical range who could participate. In addition, focus groups can utilize phone calls for people who live far away. This guiding information can then be used to provide valuable input for the family council as it makes decisions. Figure 7.3 presents an announcement that was sent by the family council to family association members who were selected based on the following criteria:

- Family council member to serve as focus group chair
- One member from each of the generations involved in the family enterprise as employees

- One member of the senior generation who is a shareholder but does not work in the business
- One member of the junior generation who is a spouse of a shareholder and does not own stock
- One member of the junior generation who is a lineal descendant and also owns stock.

As you can see, the organization of the focus group is much easier than organizing a questionnaire that will go out to all family members. The obvious downside is that there is a limited group of contributors to the discussion, but this is offset by the advantage of a more efficient way to gather input from a subgroup of family members.

Subgroups

Sometimes a particular group in the family needs to give input on a certain matter. The most common subgroups that you will likely utilize in data collection are defined by generational divides, such as first, second, and third generations. Those who work in the business form another subgroup as do those who are not employed there. You could possibly have subgroups of in-laws and subgroups of those who seek the future presidency of the company or future leadership positions. The purpose of utilizing subgroups is not to divide the family association but to gather one subgroup's input on a matter that will primarily influence that subgroup. This is done with an understanding that a summary of the subgroup's decisions and/or outcomes of the meeting processes will be shared with the broader family council and possibly even the family association. Please note that the family council is itself a subgroup, and any other committee that the family association has at any given time is also considered a subgroup.

Formats for Subgroup Meetings

Let's say that you are interested in gathering the opinions of family members in the next generation who are involved in the family enterprise; you want to know their thoughts on ways to improve their first work experience. If the family is located in geographic proximity, then it is quite possible to establish a meeting time for the subgroup and allow it to meet on its own. When this happens, we highly advise the family council to make sure that one subgroup member is assigned to coordinate the meeting and lead the dialogue and that another member (or perhaps the same one if that is the only option) is assigned to take notes and bring them to the family council. If a family council member is part of a subgroup, then that family council member can assume these responsibilities, but some subgroups will likely have to form without a family council member present.

Planning Family Association Meetings

There are five key steps to achieve success when planning a family association meeting:

1. Advance notification
2. Securing the facilities
3. Arranging transportation
4. Securing housing for family association members (and guests)
5. Soliciting the agenda

Let's look at each of these steps you will need to take to help the meetings run smoothly.

Advance Notification

Even in families where communication tends to be informal, the need for advance notification of family association meetings is critical. Family members frequently schedule calendars a year or more in advance (larger families often schedule two to three years in advance as booking hotels is more of a challenge for them), and trying to find a date when all family association members are able to make the meeting can be a very challenging task, especially as the family grows over time. The meeting planner needs to identify the dates and clearly communicate them at least one year in advance. If this is a new meeting process for the family and there is momentum to move faster, a shorter time frame may be used.

Some family association members will prefer to meet on weekends for family association purposes. Other family members, especially those who work in the business, may prefer to hold meetings during the week when they have already allotted time for business. An obvious resolution to meeting everyone's needs is to hold a weekend meeting that begins on a Friday morning so that workers only need to take off a day and a half to accommodate travel and meeting time. Asking all family members what dates they would prefer allows family association members to feel included in the planning. However, it should be made clear that no perfect date will likely be found for a larger family, but every effort will be made to accommodate the attendance of as many group members as possible.

We highly recommend communicating the date several times and in several ways. For example, mention the next family association meeting date in a family newsletter, send by an e-mail reminder a week later and then another e-mail reminder 30 days later. Assuming that everyone will process and record a single message is not realistic, and even after a set of initial reminders more reminders are needed as plans become known (i.e., a special family dinner or a tour of a facility) to increase the likelihood of everyone keeping the date. We often see family association leaders make the mistake of announcing a date and then taking it personally when others do not record the date on their calendars. Given the volume of phone calls, e-mails, and regular mail family members must deal with and their fast-paced lifestyles, several reminders will help family association members to take action and keep the dates.

There are web services that can provide efficiencies in scheduling, such as www.noodle.com. These work well for smaller groups to pin down a date, but in a larger group the date will just need to be set or negotiated.

In addition, meeting planners can help the group by stating when the meetings will begin (i.e., dinner at 6:00 p.m. on arrival day) and when they will end (i.e., the meeting will adjourn at noon to allow those traveling to make flights and start their journeys home). This will allow all attendees to start visualizing the commitment they need to make in order to participate, including travel time. Figure 7.4 shows a sample announcement. A follow-up can be sent 30 days later.

Securing the Facilities

Either before advance notification or shortly after, it is critical to secure the meeting location. In order to secure the location, meeting planners

---

Email 1: Initial Reminder sent as soon as meeting dates are determined.

Dear Family—Save the Date!!!

We will be holding a family association meeting on August 3, 4, and 5, 2013. The first event will be dinner on August 3 at 7:00 P.M. We will meet all day on the fourth and until noon on the fifth. A closing meal is planned from noon until 1:00 p.m., allowing plenty of time for everyone to fly out that afternoon.

More information will be forthcoming, but be sure to mark your calendars now to save the date.

Thanks,

The Planning Committee

Figure 7.4   First Reminder

will need to know what is being budgeted for housing because down payments will likely be needed.

Choosing the Site

Families can choose meeting sites informally ("Where do you all want to hold our next family association meeting?") or in a highly structured way. It is helpful for families to identify several key criteria the locations must meet. Figure 7.5 shows sample criteria for selecting a meeting facility and can be used to compare three site options.

Once the planning group has agreed on the criteria, a facility should be chosen with those criteria in mind. We find it helpful to brainstorm possible cities as potential sites and then work backward to find locations within them that are well suited to the group's requirements. It helps if the family is clear on a budget for the hotel and meeting room expenses.

In choosing a site, consideration should be given to physical limitations of family association members. This could include family members who are unable to walk up or down hills and steps, family members who are allergic to certain environments, family members who have difficulty with altitude, etc. Please see the previous section on gathering the family's opinions and consider the example survey questions that were used as a means of determining where the family would like to meet.

Family Criteria	Site 1	Site 2	Site 3
Childcare available on-site			
Multiple restaurants on-site for a variety of options			
Comfortable meeting room chairs to accommodate a day's work			
Located near numerous options for a fun time or family downtime			
Can be reached with no more than one half-day travel			
Will cost no more than $250 per night/per room double occupancy			
Can accommodate rooms for families with up to four children			
Can accommodate family members with special needs			
Sleeping room costs			
Meeting room costs			
Total package costs			
Rank order preference			

Figure 7.5   Sample Criteria for Site Selection

Figure 7.6 presents a process that one family has used to select a meeting location.

It should be noted that announcing the next meeting while everybody is together in person allows the committee to hear immediate support and/or concerns expressed about the location. But the committee is wise to remember that no choice will make everybody happy, so unless a strong objection is made regarding the meeting location, it is best to just try and build excitement for the chosen site and proceed.

Meeting Room Layout

Once you have selected the site for the family association meeting, be sure to secure a meeting room that will adequately seat all involved. For small families, a round table giving everybody plenty of elbow room

Steps	Action Items
1.	Email the meeting dates to all and ask if family members have any recommendations for meeting locations that meet the family meeting criteria. Provide a deadline for family input.
2.	The day after the family deadline, the location committee identifies potential sites, divides responsibility, and begins to fill out the selection criteria sheet, provided above. Two weeks is allotted for research on the various locations. Date is assembled by the committee chair as it is received by each committee member.
3.	Two weeks later, the committee meets (by phone) to compare information and makes the selection.
4.	The person(s) making funding decisions is asked to verify that the amount is acceptable.
5.	Once approved, an email is sent out again to remind everyone of the date and announce the location.
6.	Information on those sites not chosen is stored for use in future years (and will be passed on to the planning committee for the following year's meeting.)

Figure 7.6 Action Items

can work well. As the family grows, we recommend a horseshoe-shaped seating arrangement, which allows everybody to focus on the facilitator who will be leading the meetings. Sometimes a facilitator is called a coordinator or a meeting planner. Once the family numbers about 30 people, it is difficult to find horseshoe–shaped arrangements that will work for all. A large board table will sometimes accommodate a larger family group, but at this point it is likely that several round tables will be needed to accommodate all.

Smaller families may also choose to meet in an informal setting such as a person's living room or family room or a casually organized hotel sitting room. When using this arrangement, answering "yes" to the following five questions will ensure optimal meeting dynamics.

Question 1:   Can everybody see each other without having to lean and/or turn around in uncomfortable positions?

Question 2:   Can the seats be arranged so as to approximately create a circle or rectangle, allowing each person to feel they are part of the group and ensuring that nobody is in a second row or feeling detached from the group?

Question 3:   Is the room free from excessive noise (families complain about noisy air conditioners and heaters) and free from distractions, such as loud noises and/or commotion outside the meeting room?

Question 4:   Does the room provide adequate temperature control? Rooms that are too hot or too cold will make work groups less productive.

Question 5:   Are the chairs comfortable? If the family association meeting is going to last for most of the day, the needs of those who may not be used to sitting that long must be considered.

Snacks, Beverages, and Meals

Participating in family association meetings can be fun, challenging, exciting, and also intimidating and intense. When engaged in such an event, brain energy gets depleted, and family association members will require fuel to remain effective throughout the day. While arrangements may vary based on a family's preferences, we find that most successful family association gatherings include the following for an all day meeting:

- Coffee and some type of breakfast food in the morning.
- Beverages available first thing in the morning and throughout the day. Water on the tables and a variety of sodas and bottled water on the side or in the back of the room on a separate table.
- A lunch meal either in the room (brought in) or at a nearby location that can be reached and the meal ordered and consumed within an hour to 75 minutes. We know of many family association meetings where meals are taken at outside restaurants. While it is appealing to get outside the meeting room to relax and just enjoy each other's company, sometimes the outside restaurant may not be ready for the group upon arrival, and the decision to eat at a restaurant also decreases the group's flexibility to delay lunch for a few minutes should a particular topic need extra time. If the agenda looks full, it is preferable to bring in the meal and/or have the meal prepared buffet-style at a set time.
- Coffee and beverages refreshed at lunchtime.

- Some type of late afternoon snack to give energy to those who will be meeting past three o'clock.
- A break before dinner.
- Meals together at dinner are a special way to connect the group. On family association meetings that last several days, allowing one of the dinner meals to be unplanned allows everyone to explore the location and its culinary delights.
- Those planning the food to be provided should be sensitive to the many individuals who have special dietary needs. It is worth asking the family to determine if anyone has food allergies, requirements for a low-carb or vegetarian diet, etc.

Even if family members are going to be on their own for meals, this should be clearly stated in the agenda and a list of options should be provided by the person securing the facilities.

Audiovisual (AV) and Communication Needs

Holding a good meeting is like fixing a car; the job is easy when you have the right tools, but it is incredibly difficult if the tools are missing or broken. During the meeting, it is likely that there will be individual presentations, group dialogue and discussion about items, and possibly group decision making. For presentations, presenters will likely utilize a PowerPoint or computer-generated presentation that will need to be projected onto a screen. Most likely, a laptop and a projector along with a projection screen will need to be reserved in the meeting location. Many families bring their own projectors and laptops and simply order a screen from the hotel. In addition, if there is going to be a group discussion and decisions will be made about actions to take, it is helpful to have a flip chart with markers nearby. The flip chart can be used to gather input from the family, to identify points of agreement, and/or to list the next steps the group will take.

If a particular topic is important enough to include family members who are unable to be present through a conference call, a speakerphone can be rented. If you are going to utilize this service, be sure to ask the hotel or facility about whether conference calling equipment has been used there before and how effective it has been. Make sure that you are absolutely clear on what the dial-in number is and test the dial-in site before the meeting. Groups get quite frustrated when simple tasks like conference calling with several family members are made impossible by failed connections and missing extension cords.

Some tips about AV needs:
- Test all of the equipment before the meeting begins.
- Situate flip charts and screens in a way that will not cause people to have to look directly into sunlight or bright lights.
- Situate projection screens, projectors, and flip charts in a way that allows the facilitator and/or others to walk freely about the room.
- Make sure before the start of the meeting that you have an adequate supply of flip chart paper and markers that work.
- Having paper and pens at each person's place will assure that all can record their thoughts during the meeting.

Special Circumstance: Audiotaping or Videotaping a Meeting

We frequently are asked by family members unable to attend meetings whether it would be possible to have an audiotape or videotape of the meeting. As a general rule, if there is an outside presenter at a family association meeting we find that videotaping is an effective tool to allow those who are not present to view the presentation. When facts and data are key to the discussion, this allows absent family members to gain the knowledge they need. However, when rich dialogue is desired on the part of the facilitator leading the discussion, audiotaping and videotaping can reduce group members' comfort in speaking candidly. While everybody may have trust in each other as family members, once something is recorded, each family association member loses control as to who may hear or see that information in the future. Therefore, we caution against the use of any kind of recording devices during sensitive discussions as they impede the free flow of information.

Videoconferencing

While most of our experience with families suggests face-to-face meetings or teleconferencing are the primary ways for groups to meet, it is possible that the venue of your family association meeting will have the capability to do videoconferencing. Videoconferencing is an excellent tool, and we urge you to consider it. The person doing the videoconferencing must be flexible because not all dialogue may be audible, especially when members with soft voices are speaking.

Transportation

The site selection committee must be clear about the availability of transportation to and from the meeting location. Sometimes that resort nestled in the mountains sounds like a great idea, but when you get there on January 20 and it's covered in two feet of snow, you may end up losing 50 percent or more of attendees because they are unable to reach the location. Moreover, if it takes a four-hour trip to reach the nearby airport and then a three-hour drive to get to the meeting facility even in good weather, travelers may be weary and less effective as family association members. Total transportation time and transportation costs should be considered by the site selection committee.

Who Pays for Transportation?

Family associations usually have a general fund or the family enterprise pay for the travel to and from the family association meetings. If reimbursement is to be made by the company and/or some type of family fund, a centralized travel agent (either a professional firm or someone employed by the enterprise or family office) may be an effective way to control costs. If each person will be booking his or her own travel, you may wish to consider the following criteria to ensure that the family association members are good stewards of the funds available. Such criteria might include statements such as the following:

- We will pay for all airline travel booked 30 days prior to departure date, which will keep airline expenses under control. A maximum of $X of airline reimbursement will be made for those who book flights within 30 days of the trip.
- We will fund coach class travel. If you wish to upgrade to first class or business class, you are responsible for amounts above the economy rate.
- Mileage will be reimbursed according to IRS guidelines.

- Include a statement such as, "As a family, we strive to be good stewards of the resources we hold. We ask that all family members seek economical travel as a way to preserve our resources for other uses that we as a family find important."

Housing

By now, you have already secured the meeting location and simultaneously should have assured that the meeting facility will provide enough lodging for all those who will attend. Keep in mind that lodging costs will likely be higher than merely for the family association members who attend. We find that family association members commonly bring boyfriends, girlfriends, fiancées, or perhaps the in-laws to take care of young children. After all, the meetings are often held in nice locations with things to do nearby.

Some questions to consider as you scout hotels, lodges, or other housing facilities in planning for a meeting:

- Do we have families coming that will require rooms of a special size, such as rooms for six, seven, or more persons and can the facility accommodate them?
- Do some family members have special physical needs that require a special type of housing? For example, a room located close to the meeting site or rooms for the disabled?
- Are there nearby restaurants and/or places to get an evening snack if family members are hungry, or is room service available?
- Are the rooms supplied with wireless Internet?
- Will the meeting planners block the hotels and, if so, what is the process for assigning a specific person's name to the hotel room from the meeting block?
- Will individuals be required to book their own reservation directly and, if so, is there a discount code that will allow them a discounted rate?

Sales departments within hotels can generally answer all of your questions about accommodations and catering. Some travel agents can arrange all the housing and meeting locations for you. Essentially, they can do the administration work. If you are to utilize this service, we recommend that you be clear about what kinds of fees and expenses will be associated with the services provides. It may be cheaper to have a member of the administrative staff in the family office or family business handle all of the travel arrangements or to assign this task to a family member.

Budget

We recommend creating a budget before the meeting that indicates likely expenses. Actual expenditures can then be compared to the budget, and over time the family will gain a clear understanding of how much it costs to hold a family assembly or association meeting. A sample budget is presented in figure 7.7.

Family association meetings take time and resources to plan and conduct. Even if the cost of the meeting is to be borne by a company, we recommend creating a budget and making clear to the family the source of funding.

Cavanaugh Family Meeting Budget–2011

Category	2010 Actual	2011 Budgeted	2011 Actual	2011 Variance Budget to Actual
Transportation (airfare, parking, shuttles/taxis, mileage reimbursement, rental cars & fuel)				
Hotel/lodging				
Meeting room fees				
Beverage & snack fees				
Meals while traveling				
Meals on site				
AV rentals				
Special activity expense (night flight)				
Fees for advisors/ speakers at the meeting				
Handouts/reproduction costs				

Figure 7.7 Sample Budget

The Agenda

The Benefits of an Agenda

The difference between a gripe session and a productive meeting often is the use of an agenda. Successful family meetings revolve around an agenda to create an atmosphere of productivity and fun. Prior to bringing the family together, it is important that everybody receive the agenda to get focused on the productive tasks at hand. This also creates positive expectations for the upcoming event.

It's important to put out a message to all attendees that agenda items can be discussed and submitted prior to the meeting. This gives people a sense of inclusion, along with an opportunity to contribute to important matters coming before the family. This also allows for the possibility of addressing important questions or concerns that the person setting the agenda may not have known about.

Three Primary Steps for Building an Agenda

Step 1: Determine who will be part of the agenda committee. If this is your first family association meeting, it is best to assign two or three individuals to work on the agenda. For ongoing meetings, the agenda committee will ideally be made up of several family members assigned at the previous year's meeting. Some families will have a standing agenda committee whose membership rotates every two to three years to allow greater participation by family association members. In families with a representative family council, the leader of the family council will usually head the agenda committee, and the family council itself will often round out the committee.

Step 2: Identify potential agenda items and offer a deadline for submitting agenda items. In this step, the goal is to determine the needs of the family, making sure to include relevant topics and questions. The potential agenda items should aim at helping the family achieve its overall goals. If the family is not clear on what its overall goals are, a question about purposes and goals would be a great first agenda item for the family to work on.

Step 3: Prioritize the agenda items. Once the deadline for allowing agenda input has expired, the agenda planners can determine the topics of the meeting, the order of the agenda, the time allotted for each agenda item, and the meeting schedule. The agenda planning committee needs to work in conjunction with the meals coordinator to assure that meals are scheduled at the appropriate times. Moreover, dealing with difficult issues is an important aspect of prioritizing agenda items (see also chapter 5). For example, if a family needs to discuss the grandparents' estate planning, and the agenda committee has ascertained that these are the most critical tasks before the family, then prior to filling in all other aspects of the agenda, the team setting the agenda should consider how much time will be needed to adequately address the estate planning issues. The team should also consider exactly what is to be accomplished within the agenda item that deals with estate planning and what desired outcomes would look like.

Not every potential agenda item needs to be (or can be) addressed in one meeting, so keep a list of potential future agenda items that didn't make the current agenda and pass these on to the planners of next year's agenda.

Successful Meeting Agendas: A Creative Mix

Regarding the needs of family groups, we know from families who have held successful family meetings that key lessons include setting aside time for a mix of education, development, connection, and fun. These topics have been dealt with elsewhere[3] and can be summarized as follows:

Learning and Development

Learning and developing together includes time spent enhancing the knowledge of the group by having a shared educational session. Educational sessions can be informative sessions about the state of the business, the state of the market in which the business competes, estate planning, communication techniques, or about the dynamics of family wealth, and so forth. A good meeting will include some time for the entire group to become more educated about areas of common interest or to develop new skills.

Accomplishing, Planning, or Deciding

Family groups often find that their time is spent most meaningfully if they feel that they are getting something done. This occurs when the family is resolving some question or producing some type of output, where family members can see that progress is being made. Some examples would include creating and approving a family vision statement or a family employment policy, creating guidelines for conflict resolution, deciding on a new board composition structure, or establishing estate planning expectations.

Fun and Social

Even family groups who are together frequently find that reconnecting during meeting time is very valuable. Many families set aside time for family members to give an update about what is new in their life and what pursuits they are engaged in. Family members are encouraged to share recent or upcoming changes. It is unusual for families to have this type of communication during their normal times of interaction. Devoting meeting time to reconnecting clearly establishes the value of family connectedness and unity. We recommend that each person be given two to three minutes to provide an update and perhaps respond to a prompted question or two, such as, "One thing you may not know about me is...."

When families gather, they usually feel an urgency to have learning or decision-making sessions. They want to feel productive, and they want to manage their resources well. However, our experience shows that working through difficult issues can occasionally open up some minor wounds that require downtime to heal. By including time for fun in the family's agenda, the family can demonstrate to itself that even after a session in which some tussling occurred, the family can enjoy its time together, for example, at a cookout or volleyball game. In the long run, it is this willingness to set aside time to enjoy each other's company that makes the effort of working together as a family association worthwhile. It also serves to insulate the family from obsession about bruises and scars that are created during the working sessions.

At any given meeting, a perfect mix of these components may not be possible, but over time, balancing these four areas will help the family association function optimally.

Agenda Segment Leader

Additionally, each agenda segment should identify who will lead the agenda segment and be responsible for explaining the goals that have been outlined for that segment. This is critical because most topics cannot be easily understood from the topic heading alone. For example, if the agenda includes an estate planning session, it may be unclear what should be done during that segment. Some may think there will be individual estate planning in the meeting while others may interpret it to mean that an estate plan will be handed out for review. Another person may believe that there will be education about estate planning. The segment leader can clear up any misunderstandings by succinctly stating the purpose for the session and the desired outcomes. These can be reiterated during the meeting.

Often, the segment topic leader is the family association member who initially brought the item to the family, usually through the agenda committee. Theoretically, the leader could be any person in the family or even a professional advisor or board member. The agenda committee then puts the topic on the agenda, and the facilitator will generally introduce the new topic to the group, but the topic leader will usually open the discussion by framing the topic for the family and identifying the reason for asking the family to spend time on it.

Prioritizing the Agenda

The agenda is prioritized based on the agenda setter's knowledge of the family's needs. Specific issues should not take priority, but the well-being of the overall family should be the one top priority that is considered when planning the agenda. For example, let's suppose that the agenda committee is made up of two people, Bridget and William. Bridget and William will consider the list of potential topics and identify those topics that they feel must get addressed at the upcoming family association meeting. The content of the meeting begins to take form.

Alternative Model for Prioritizing the Agenda

If the family association is considering an ongoing agenda that family members would like to pursue, family association members can meet to brainstorm possible agenda items, putting them up on flip charts for all to see. Some families will create five or six flip charts full of potential agenda items. Families will then take about ten minutes to consider the different agenda items, ranking them in order of importance. Some will indicate their top three by numbering their first, second, or third priority. Others will use stickers, such as brightly colored dots, to indicate which items are of greatest importance. The family can then see in the present moment which agenda items are of greatest interest to the entire family group. Again, this method of agenda prioritization should be used as a guide and not as a final draft. The family's needs may require adding other topics or priorities by the time of the next meeting.

Presenting Agenda Items

Clearly identifying the content of the agenda item and the goal of each agenda segment will help the family stay focused and minimize frustrations that are often caused when different family members try to accomplish different goals during a discussion. For example, a family agenda setter lists on an agenda for a family association meeting the following:

10:00 a.m.–11:30 a.m.   Succession issues discussed

It is easy to see how this can become volatile for a family to address. The senior patriarch sees this item and assumes that the group will discuss who is going to replace him, which is a discussion that makes him anxious. Cousin Judy is glad the family will finally be discussing estate planning, and her brothers Todd and Gerry read this and believe that their father is going to finally choose between them who is in line to be the next family enterprise chairman. If the family ruminates on these topics for a few weeks before the meeting, assumptions will proliferate and potentially create frustration and possibly even conflicts.

Outlining the purpose and goals of each agenda segment can greatly improve communication. Our example above could be rewritten as follows:

10:00 a.m.–11:30 a.m.   Succession issues discussed
    Background: Our Chairman is at least five years from retirement but wishes the family to explore his eventual stepping down from this position. The goal of this agenda segment is to visualize the potential issues involved and consider the family association's role in the succession process.

This gives clarity to the family association and allows all to prepare for the discussion, including the chairman.

During the meeting, when the facilitator introduces each new item on the agenda, he or she will review the purpose of the agenda segment and desired outcomes. This brings both purpose and focus to every minute of the family association's meeting and reinforces the value of the discussion.

The following are examples of some purposes that might be included along with an agenda item:

- This next section is for education only. We are here to learn, and not to make any decisions about the matter. There are no planned action items to come from this section of our agenda.
- We are going to spend the next hour learning about our own group decision-making processes and building trust in our processes. The purpose of this discussion is to develop teamwork so we can be more effective in the future.
- Our job in the next hour is to brainstorm our initial thinking on this topic. The outcome of this discussion will be the creation of a task force to draft an initial statement of our beliefs about the topic.
- We have previously discussed this topic, and now we need to clarify our beliefs about it. At the end of this discussion, we need to articulate a position on the topic.
- We have a decision to make about something, and here is the decision. The outcome of this dialogue is to present our decision to our board.

Figure 7.8 provides a useful organizing tool for the master facilitator when preparing an agenda. An example has been provided. If the facilitator can't answer these questions for each segment, chances are that the group will not be clear about the task, and some chaos may ensue.

Exploration. Some topics are designed for exploration only. If a topic has never been discussed in a family meeting, the agenda setter will usually present a question the answer to which could benefit the family association. For example:

- What do we envision our board doing for us over the next ten years?
- What key topics would we want our family employment policy to address, given the ages of the younger generation?
- What opportunities and challenges would a family foundation provide for our family, today and in the future?

Date of Family Association Meeting	Time Needed	Agenda Segment Description	Purpose for Inclusion on the Agenda	Desired Outcome of Meeting Time Allotted	Agenda Segment Leader	Notes:
March 2012	90 minutes	End of Aunt Sarah's Trust	Discuss implications of the termination of Aunt Sarah's trust, which terminates in July 2012	Identify issues impacting G3 and G4, and create action plans needed	Scott Farkus, family attorney	Contact Scott and verify his availability for meeting.

Figure 7.8   Organizing Tool

Straw man. After a family has had a chance to discuss an item, such as a policy, someone needs to create a first draft. A straw man is simply an initial proposal that a person or subgroup will present to the group with the purpose of having the group poke holes in the concept. For example, after a discussion of the appropriateness of using company equipment for the family's private purposes, the topic leader suggests the following:

> "We believe that company equipment may be used by family members for private use, but the equipment must be checked out for a designated time period and must be returned immediately if the equipment is needed for business purposes. Business purposes always come before family needs in using business equipment."

Bringing this straw man before the group allows the group to determine if members are aligned in their thinking about a policy, and group members can shoot holes in the straw man without causing damage to the person who drafted the statement. The topic leader assures the group that he/she will not be hurt by the "damage" caused to the straw man, and this allows the group to question items without fearing conflict. Bringing a straw man for the group requires the person or persons creating the proposal to realize that this helps the group move forward because it gives people something to react against or affirm. Thus, those creating the straw man must detach emotionally from the concepts they present.

Disseminating the Agenda

After the agenda has been structured and the family's priorities have been considered, the agenda must be disseminated to the appropriate members who will be taking leadership roles during the meeting. The first step is to verify that each agenda segment leader is clear on what he or she is being asked to do. Once the agenda segment leaders have accepted responsibility for their segments, it is time to send the agenda to everyone else. We recommend mailing the agenda to the family at least four weeks prior to the meeting (unless there are any reading assignments associated with the agenda segments that require more time). Figure 7.9 presents a complete family assembly meeting agenda with family association and family council meeting segments. This would be presented to all family association members. A shorter version might be sent to family assembly members who are not part of the family association, so they understand the schedule and where they fit in. Take note that the second morning of the meeting is devoted to a shareholders assembly meeting. The Kolecki family separates all shareholder-related issues from family issues. In practice, both family association and family assembly meetings include the same people, but they are segmented to help the family keep separate the roles of family membership and shareholder membership.

In practice, many families struggle to meet the four-week deadline and often end up handing the agenda out only a week or so in advance. This is especially inadequate when there are housing and travel logistics to be addressed. In general, families are not frustrated because agenda items arrived too early, but there are many frustrations caused and logistical nightmares created when the agenda arrives too late. The most effective families send out notices a year or two in advance, followed by logistical information (when to arrive, housing arrangements, etc.) from three to six months in advance, and then they get the agenda out at least four weeks before the meeting.

Moving Through an Agenda During the Meeting

The purpose of the agenda is to guide the meeting and to give organization to what otherwise could be an open discussion that fails to accomplish its goals. With this in mind, care should be taken in creating the agenda so that it reflects the purposes of the meeting, and each

The Kolecki Family Assembly Summer Meeting

The Hidden Cove in Outer Banks, NC

Thursday August 1

Family assembly invited to all of Thursday's events

2:00 P.M.	**Early Bird Golf Outing for those who have signed up.** Meet in lobby for shuttle at 1:30 P.M.
6:30 P.M.	**Family Cocktail Party on the Lower Patio**
7:30 P.M.	**Welcome Dinner in the Great Room**

Friday August 2

7:30 A.M.	**Family Assembly Breakfast**
8:50 A.M.	**Kids participating in activities program to meet staff in lobby**
9:00 A.M.	**Family Association Meeting Begins in the Great Room Welcome & Prayer**
9:15 A.M.	**The Kolecki Family Constitution**
	The Family Council is proposing a family constitution to guide our family as we continue to grow. Brittany will lead a discussion about family constitutions and what this could mean to our family. A sample is provided in your premeeting handout.
10:30 A.M.	**Break**
10:45 A.M.	**Constitution Discussion Forward Planning**
	Assuming family support for the constitution initiative, we will lay out next steps to move toward its creation. If the initiative is not supported, we will consider constitution components that would help our family.
12:00 P.M.	**Lunch (in the meeting room)**
1:15 P.M.	**Internship Roundup**
	Chuck will share an update on the family internship program, and the three third-generation interns will report on their experiences.
2:00 P.M.	**Education Session: Personal Branding**
	Branding expert Ellen Roemke will teach the family about the personal brands we have each created through our presentation of information to the outside world, and she will share tips on how to manage our brands effectively.
3:30 P.M.	**End of Family Association Meeting—Break for Afternoon**
	Afternoon spa visits are available for those interested. Call the concierge to schedule a visit
6:30 P.M.	**The Founders' Fiftieth Celebration**
	Family assembly meets in Salon A for cocktails. We will then move to Salons B & C for Bob and Inger's 50th Anniversary celebration dinner. Bring your stories of them as we will have open mike time after the meal to show our appreciation.

Figure 7.9 Continued

Saturday August 3

7:30 A.M.	**Family Assembly Breakfast**
	[Note: The family council will hold a brief meeting over breakfast. Please arrive promptly at 7:30.]
9:00 A.M.	**Shareholders Assembly (all family association members invited)**
9:10 A.M.	**CEO Presentation and Expansion Discussion**
	Eric will present the state of the enterprise and share an expansion proposal that was discussed at the last board meeting. Our goal for this session is to learn and ask questions. Eric will be excused at the end of the discussion.
10:30 A.M.	**Break**
10:45 A.M.	**Reactions to Expansion Discussion**
	The family association will share reactions to the expansion proposal and prepare feedback to the board on the proposal.
12:00 P.M.	**Working Lunch (in the meeting room)**
12:30 P.M.	**End Shareholder Assembly**
1:00 P.M.	**Beach Party**
	The entire family assembly is invited to meet by the family flag on the beach out front for family games and downtime. Ron and Sally have prepared some surprise activities for the little ones. There will be light food and drinks available.
7:00 P.M.	**Family Assembly Closing Dinner at the Clubhouse**
	Music provided by a surprise guest.

Figure 7.9   Sample Family Assembly Agenda

section on the agenda should accomplish its respective goals within a set amount of time.

Time Limits

Time limits for agenda segments create boundaries that help the family to stay focused. As family associations are generally large, getting off schedule can create significant logistics problems that decrease the perceived value of the meeting. Therefore, we encourage leaders and members make every effort to keep to the time limits noted on the agenda.

Using Purpose Statements for Agenda Segments to Manage an Unruly Mob

Including the segment's purpose on the agenda allows family members who experience distrust or tend to jump to conclusions to see that the agenda segment is focused. During the meeting, the facilitator of each agenda segment will have a platform to guide the group by sticking to that particular agenda item's purpose in order to achieve the stated goal. An example follows.

The Mettler family assembly's agenda included the following item:

1:00 p.m.–2:00 p.m.   Review family risk tolerance and discuss implications

Alex will present the results of a family assembly survey that explored the family's perceived comfort level with risk in the enterprise. The desired outcome is to reaffirm our current risk profile or discuss a possible task force to propose a new risk profile.

During the meeting, when Alex began to present the survey's findings, several family members began to assert their beliefs that the company should pay out more dividends, and this then escalated into others commenting that greater reinvestment was needed. Clearly, the meeting was wandering away from risk profiles to liquidity and capital allocation matters. By stopping the discussion and restating that this part of the meeting was devoted to understanding the family's risk profile and reaffirming or modifying it, Alex was able to regain control of the group, and other family association members appreciated this. A note was also made to revisit the other topics at a future meeting.

One of the biggest mistakes eager families make in addressing topics is to start the discussion prior to the actual family meeting. In other words, the agenda item becomes so wrought with confusion or instills so much fear that members feel they need to rush out and speak to each other ahead of time about what they will be talking about at the meeting. This can become unproductive if it creates coalitions of subgroups, and diminishes open dialogue and effective decision making during the meeting. Showing agenda items and desired outcomes on the agenda, allows family members to feel more respected and less fearful or defensive.

Managing an Unruly Mob : Clear Leadership

The leader of a family association meeting needs to clearly own each agenda segment. The family council president will often be the master coordinator of the meeting and will introduce the leader of each agenda segment. For example, the Schenkel family council determined that the family needed to have a dialogue about the family's policy on spouses working in the enterprise. Sally Schenkel, the president of the family council, introduced Tom as facilitator for the next segment. Tom then introduced the purpose of the agenda segment and the desired outcomes of the session. As a result, the family had a greater sense of safety in addressing the issue with positive results. In this example, everyone now knows that Tom will be in charge of the group during the session, and he has the legitimate authority to guide the discussion and pursue the group's goals.

In our view, every segment on the agenda should have a leader who will take charge of that segment. Even if an individual is only to lead one segment during a multiday family retreat, there will still be continuity of leadership presence throughout. This promotes an increased sense of common purpose to achieve family goals.

Meeting Length

Another challenge for eager family enterprise owners occurs when the same aggressiveness that is displayed in the business world is applied to a family process. When this occurs, the family falls into the trap of feeling a strong need to utilize every waking hour to be engaged in dialogue with each other to justify the cost of the family meeting process. For example, it's not unusual for a family to draw together on a Saturday morning after having arrived on late-night flights, begin the meeting at eight in the morning and plan on meeting until five or six in the afternoon. After all, this appears to be the way to achieve the most productivity.

However, our experience has shown that family process time is very draining for those in the business and also for those who are not currently employed in the business. When family energy levels run low due to long hours around a conference table or in a meeting room, miscommunication and emotional volatility become more likely. Many families have found that the productivity of their meetings declines substantially after three thirty or four in the afternoon. Families need to find their own balance in productivity versus downtime for their family gatherings, and we encourage families to plan for enough downtime so that the time the family does spend in session is of the highest quality. Moreover, family bonds can be nurtured and celebrated during the downtimes.

Role of Facilitators

It is rewarding to attend a meeting that is moved along by someone who has great clarity about what is to be accomplished. This person should not be a dictator whose purpose is to make all the decisions for the group. Rather, he or she should serve as a guide and leader. This position is also known as facilitator, and it is the facilitator's job to make sure that everyone in the group is heard, that the dialogue follows a set of common expectations (otherwise known as the ground rules), and that the purposes of each agenda segment are identified and pursued with vigor.

In addition, the facilitator of the family association meetings helps connect agenda segments and helps the group understand what will occur next. We often refer to this role as the master facilitator role. Whether it's time to take a break during a segment or for lunch, explain where lunch will be, explain what the next segment is about, announce what the segment's purposes are, or introduce who will be leading the dialogue, the master facilitator serves a tremendously helpful role for a group that is trying to do something productive together.

Another task of both the agenda segment facilitator and the master facilitator is to ensure the safety of all association members. The facilitators have the primary responsibility of keeping the discussion productive in accordance with the ground rules. The entire association has a secondary responsibility for keeping the discussion productive and safe. Thus, the association must work with the facilitator to assure that each family member is heard and that an environment of respectful mutual dialogue exists.

Who Should Facilitate?

Many business families choose those who have demonstrated a long history of leadership in the family to facilitate meetings. This decision is usually based on considering their success in leading the enterprise, and it is thus an easy solution for families to have the CEO or chairperson of the company lead family meetings.

In some cases this may be a good choice or perhaps the only choice for initial meetings, but we strongly encourage families to utilize the family meeting process to provide an opportunity for those who are not currently leaders in the business. The CEO is already endowed with so much power and responsibility on behalf of the family that it is inappropriate to expect him or her to simultaneously lead the family process. But if not the CEO, who should lead family meetings? To choose a facilitator, we generally ask families to identify those who rank high in the characteristics listed in figure 7.10.

It is not likely that any family member possesses perfect marks on all categories. This list is a guide to identify potential candidates. It is important to understand the impact of selecting a facilitator who does not have at least some level of these qualifications. If a person is strongly positioned in favor of a particular outcome, he or she will likely be seen by the group as manipulative during the process, and this can reduce the progress of the family's decision making and cause conflicts. A facilitator must be able to focus on the group's input and suppress his or her own preferred outcome. A well-chosen facilitator gains strength by encouraging dialogue and possible alternative solutions to whatever issue the group may be wrestling with during the meeting.

For this reason, the most demanding and dominant personalities of the family are generally not good choices as facilitators of family association meetings. While they may be able to lead an agenda segment that is not controversial, the outwardly dominant leaders of the group will often do more harm as facilitators than they help the group move forward.

Ideal Family Facilitator Qualities
<ul><li>Open to new ideas</li><li>Has the ability to hold multiple positions at once</li><li>Is trusted by a high percentage of family association members</li><li>Is seen as neutral in dialogue and does not have any hidden agendas</li><li>Is not afraid to confront group members who are negatively influencing the meeting process</li><li>Is seen as a champion of the family</li><li>Is courageous enough to lead the strongest of family members in a dialogue</li><li>Is respected by the family</li></ul>

Figure 7.10   Ideal Family Facilitator Qualities

Facilitator Training

Facilitating family meetings is an art that is learned over time. There are a two main ways to gain this skill. The first is to learn in current volunteer roles. We find that family members who lead volunteer organizations are already experiencing particularly effective training for the facilitator role. When family members lead volunteer organizations or task forces, they are generally responsible for motivating everyone around the table to respond to good ideas. Having to coordinate a group of volunteers also teaches how to gain the respect of individuals with different personality types. Thus, volunteer leaders also have experience in achieving group goals.

Training programs are the second path toward sharpening the skills needed for effective facilitating. We have observed family leaders enlist the help of coaches to develop effectiveness. Others seek professors in communication or psychology departments of colleges and universities who specialize in group dynamics. While this training does have a cost, it can prepare someone more quickly than might happen through trial and error.

Of course, hiring a coach or attending a training program will be an investment, but it can be worthwhile if the individual has a personal passion to learn and if the group desires to invest in its future. Many enterprise leaders have a clear vision to invest in training for a business manager to become a more effective supervisor or manager of people. Strong facilitation can result in the group experiencing much better communication and more trust—both critical elements in a well-functioning family.

Roles of Attendees

In a family meeting process, it is not only the discussion facilitator who has a responsibility to the group. In addition, attendees share responsibility for the meeting's success. By participating as family association members, each member of the group is committing himself or herself to a process with a shared set of rules and expectations that help the family function effectively. Each is committed to building camaraderie, mutual respect, and trust and work toward the goal of making effective decisions. In our view, association members must have a set of productive skills to foster a successful group outcome. The following is an example of a pledge that each family association member commits to when becoming a member of the association.

Family Association Member Pledge

- I will remain focused on the topic at hand.
- I will support one person speaking at a time and wait until it is my turn to speak.
- I will not monopolize the discussion.
- I will allow others to express contrary points of view.
- I will articulate my positions respectfully.
- I will disclose hidden agendas and known conflicts of interest to promote transparency in the group.

Each group member has to take responsibility to help the group function properly. Each person must help the group create a safe environment for dialogue to take place. If a person engages in behaviors that are accusing, attacking, or avoiding, it is likely that the trust felt in the group will decline. As a result, the ability to make decisions and agree on common goals will also decline. It is especially important for family assembly members to commit to a process before joining the family association and hold themselves accountable to the group for productive behavior. In the next section we will address one format for creating those common expectations.

Attendee Training

Family members who have become part of the association can gain the skills necessary for participating in meetings through reading, interaction, and self-exploration. Many business families utilize readings on basic communications as a method for preparing the association for group dialogue.

The preparation for group dialogue would include lessons in communication skills such as:

- How to make a presentation of a topic
- How to make a proposal
- How to listen using active listening techniques
- How to give feedback in a concrete and effective manner

However, it can be beneficial for the entire group to practice effective communication behaviors together. Many families utilize segments of their family association meetings, especially when the family association is still new, to practice these skills. Through the use of exercises and behavioral training, the group becomes more aware of the communication skills needed to effectively hold meetings.

The combination of reading and behavioral training can lead to impressive results for many groups. However, occasionally family members find the intensity of a family meeting process so great that their capacity for functioning in the group is compromised. This often reveals itself when association members experience anxiety, hurt, or anger during group meetings, and in these cases we have found therapeutic assistance to be helpful. A therapist who understands family dynamics can provide needed support to allow troubled association members to contribute positively to the group's goals.

Ground Rules

When families come together for initial family association meetings, family members may naturally behave as they do when they are in family mode. In family mode, the senior members of the family typically are considered leaders and the junior family members are thought of as followers. This fits with the typical family structure, and it usually takes only a few minutes for adult family members to drop into well-worn family roles they played as children. For example, a forty-one-year-old daughter may be a highly confident executive but still defer to others when confronted in a family association meeting by her dominant parents. However, for a family meeting to be productive, the group needs to behave as a group of adults (or soon-to-be adults) who agree to interact with each other on more equal footing.

For example, in large families sometimes family members wishing to speak at the dinner table must assert themselves with loud voices and interruptions in order to be heard. When this dynamic occurs, it requires that a number of family members fail to assert themselves or seek to avoid the dialogue in order to allow the group to function. These roles often emerge without conscious awareness by family members, and usually several family members dominate the discussion. While this is not a problem during family dinners, it does not help a group of adults make decisions together. Thus, each member of the group must be responsible for adapting to more professional interactions and stepping outside of comfortable family roles, the person who interrupts just as much as the person who usually remains silent.

It is up to the facilitator to make sure that each person is heard or at least has a chance to be heard. The facilitator can help the quiet people be heard, but the quiet members of the group must help by asserting themselves. Conversely, the talkative members of the group must help the group and themselves by refraining from talking so much and dominating the group. That is, every member of the family association should have equal opportunity to participate, contribute, assume responsibility, and rise to leadership.

Moving the Family Toward Shared Expectations

How do we undo dozens of years of family history and roles and create a new set of communication rules to operate in the family during family meeting time? One method to move in this direction is to use shared expectations, which are also called ground rules. The shared expectations serve as a focal point to move a family's communication in a positive direction. For example, families whose members interrupt each other frequently may adopt a shared expectation that only one person will speak at a time. By adopting this expectation and agreeing to it, the facilitator will be empowered to stop a person who interrupts in order to help the family achieve its shared expectation of one person speaking at a time. Similarly, families whose members tend to wander off the topic during discussions may adopt the ground rule of sticking to the topic under discussion as a goal all can strive for. When family members start changing subjects or get sidetracked into other topics, having the group's agreement that everyone should stick to the subject will guide both the facilitator and group members in pursuing that goal. A sample list of shared expectations is presented in appendix 5 ("Examples of Shared Expectations").

Creating Accountability Regarding the Shared Expectations

Many family association groups evaluate their own behaviors every time they have a meeting. This serves as a constant reminder that the

Forming Shared Expectations: 5 Helpful Hints
1. Discuss the purpose of expectations and get the group to agree that expectations could help the group.
2. Ask the family to consider, based on their knowledge of their family, what expectations would help them become especially effective as a group.
3. List all suggestions on a blank sheet of paper without judgment as to whether any suggestion is valid.
4. Look for commonalities and compress the suggestions.
5. Affirm the final list.

Figure 7.11   Forming Shared Expectations

expectations are important and also allows for correcting behaviors that don't match the expectations set forth.

Such evaluations allow the group to discuss how well it is communicating and can reveal gaps between the family's preferred and actual behavior. Just having awareness of this gap is often enough to bring about changes, but continuing struggles may require other remedies.

We caution families against creating a list of expectations that is too long to remember. When families try to have fifteen shared expectations about their family meeting process, it is unlikely that more than one or two can be recalled at any given time. Having between five and eight expectations will be most effective. Figure 7.11 provides a guideline for setting shared expectations.

It may take 30 to 60 minutes of group time to agree on a set of shared expectations. But this time is well worth it because the dialogue around productive expectations can help the family focus. Individuals presenting an expectation for the group to consider should also explain how they think it will help the group move forward. On the whole, an hour or two spent getting the group aligned may save dozens of hours of unproductive dialogue down the road.

Disagreements over the Expectations

When family members disagree about the common expectations, chances are high that conflict will emerge during later discussions. That is why ground rules are so valuable. If there is disagreement about the expectations, family members should take time to discuss why they think a particular expectation would be valuable for the functioning of the group. We find that some disagreements are merely a question of semantics, and the members realize they agree upon the fundamental purpose of the proposed ground rule. It is important that the group take time to understand where each person is coming from so the expectations don't become another source of conflict.

Timekeeper

Because it is important to draw boundaries around every family association discussion, we have recommended that the agenda committee clearly set a time limit for each agenda item as well as for the entire meeting. In addition, we recommend appointing a member as timekeeper whose purpose during the family association meeting is to clarify how much time will be allotted for a segment and to let the group know when that time limit has been reached. For example, letting the group know when half of its allotted time has elapsed can help everyone stay on task. A five-minute warning is also helpful and allows the segment leader to bring the discussion to a conclusion. The timekeeper's job is to keep everyone aware of how much time has elapsed.

Secretary

Another productive role belongs to the secretary who takes notes during the meeting. The secretary is responsible capturing the essence of the discussion in the notes and for recording any agreements reached by the group. Notes should not include individuals' comments but should capture only the highlights of the discussion and the resulting action steps or agreements. Therefore, notes should not say, "Susie said this, and Joe said that." Instead, notes should read as follows: "The group discussed use of the family vacation home. It was agreed that Cheryl will be the scheduler for those wishing to use the home, and everyone would give a week's notice when making a request." In this way, the essence of the discussion is captured, and specific outcomes and action steps that will guide the family are identified. Whether one person objected or somebody spoke up during the discussion is not relevant; only the outcome is relevant.

At the end of the meeting, the secretary includes in the notes the date and location of the next meeting as well as the names of the facilitator, timekeeper, secretary, and persons responsible for creating the next meeting's agenda. In many families the same individuals keep these roles from one meeting to the next, and in some families they are rotated every 24 or 36 months to ensure continuity for the meetings.

Identification of Action Steps

To move toward achieving their mission and purpose, families need a system of accountability and follow-up. For this reason, the master facilitator will identify the next steps at the end of each meeting.

The first step includes setting up future meetings. Families may wish to schedule one or two meetings in order to help family association members plan their schedules. Some families meet on a quarterly basis and schedule meetings two years in advance to accommodate those who have busy schedules or travel from far distances. Other families may meet twice a year and only schedule the upcoming meeting. Whatever system is chosen, before the current meeting adjourns, the group reviews its schedule and family members write dates on their calendars.

The second element of follow-up includes an accountability component. In the notes, the secretary identifies all follow-up actions that will occur and who is responsible for leadership of the follow-up actions. Figure 7.12 shows one family's action item list as an example.

The master facilitator for the next meeting will be responsible for summarizing all action items that are due by the following meeting. The facilitator will typically ask for a report regarding each of the action

Action	Action owner	Due Date
Assemble family history documents for archiving	Tom and Katie	July 2012
Propose changes to family internship policy	Ann and Dave	December 2011
Secure resources to discuss group access to insurance products	Bill and Kathleen	March 2012
Research potential resource to educate next generation on dealing with wealth effectively	Tony and Lora	March 2012

Figure 7.12   Family Action List

items and will schedule a time to contact each member who has taken responsibility for an item before the due date to discuss his or her progress. By doing this, the family holds itself accountable to the agreements that were made and the actions that were agreed upon. Furthermore, the person who committed to an item will give an account of his or her contribution. Obviously, if a family develops a pattern of failure to act, this lack of accountability will become an unfortunate pattern. When members publicly take responsibility for an item, their respect for the group and the well-being of the group will motivate them to complete the item or at least make progress in that direction. Each commitment made and successful completion of the action item will increase the trust and confidence the family association holds in that person.

Conclusion

The first half of this book has focused on initiating family meetings and developing family councils and family assemblies. In the next chapter, we will explore additional structures that are important but are used less frequently in family governance. The final chapters will focus exclusively on the transition, development, and maintenance of family governance structures once the family council and family assembly are up and running.

8

Special Family Governance Structures: Owners Councils and Executive Committees

Two family governance structures have not yet been discussed, namely, owners councils and executive committees. These structures appear in many different forms tailored to the specific business families they serve, but they also have some common elements.

An owners council is useful for larger business families and businesses where it might be good to keep the affairs of the family council separate from the owner group. Privacy, the organizational needs of a large family, and a family council focused primarily on developing family relationships may be reasons for a separate forum for owners. Another structure is used in business families where all of the owners work in the business. A regular management meeting, which we refer to as an executive committee, is used not only for business management but also for addressing owner topics and decisions and planning on family matters. In business families that do not yet have a family council, these two structures may serve as the primary family governance structures.

Owners Councils

One of the competitive advantages available to business families is that members know each other, share similar values, and, given the opportunity, are likely to find a way to agree on the capital priorities of the business. A forum for coordination is a way to take full advantage of owner alignment. An owners council is either a representative group acting on behalf of all of the owners, or, in smaller families, it is a forum for all owners to gather and coordinate with one another.

Owners councils are valuable for large business families with several branches and generations. The purpose of the family assembly/association and family council is to represent the entire family, when some of the members are not yet owners or owners in name only with control still in the hands of a few. For the purposes of coordinating with one another and seeking alignment on shareholder matters, the annual shareholders' meeting may be insufficient for the desired level of coordination. An owners council can fill a need when no other structure, including a family council, can do so effectively. Our partner and cofounder Craig Aronoff[1] has identified three distinct responsibilities of an owners council:

- Forge the owners' goals, vision, and values for the enterprise. The vision includes the owners' views on family ownership and the role they hope family members can play in the business. The goals include positions on growth, profitability, risk, and liquidity.
- Design the governance system. Owners must determine the size, composition, and charter of the board. They must also define the relationships between board and owners and management. Part of the governance system is to decide how owners can be helpful to management and to regulate the owners' behavior that affects the business.
- Plan for ownership continuity. It's the owners' responsibility to assure that the estate plans and share transfer plans assure that their vision and goals can be realized into the future. Owners need to agree on their plans and need to understand each other's plans.

If the owners council is a subset of all owners, they will represent and efficiently work for the benefit of the entire group of owners, yet will need support and ratification for their direction and decision making. As with other governance functions, one way for a representative group to communicate its goals, vision, governance structure, and function is to put them into a written document, a charter. According to our other cofounder, John Ward, an owners council charter would include answers to the following questions:

1. Why are we committed?
2. What are our expectations as owners?
3. How do we add value as owners?
4. What is our structure of ownership?
5. How do we make decisions as owners?
6. What is our vision for our enterprises?
7. What are our roles and responsibilities as owners/ beneficiaries?
8. How do we hold ourselves accountable?
9. How do we prepare ourselves and the next generation for ownership?

Owners councils can serve all owners or can be representative of just one generation, and in that case there can be more than one, an owners council for the senior generation for the assets it controls and one for the younger generation for its separate assets. Before a senior generation is ready to turn over control of the larger core business(es), new acquisitions, vertically integrated support businesses, or real estate might be put under the sole ownership of the younger generation. This is a way to let family wealth appreciate in value in a younger generation, and it also provides a developmental opportunity for that generation to practice being a team of owners before ultimate control of the core business is transferred. To make capital allocation decisions, establish and maintain governance functions for assets, and plan for the next generation, an owners council of representative shareholders has been shown to be an effective forum. Such a council does not replace the shareholders and does not usurp authority and rights of shareholders, and does not replace the board, but it offers increased efficiency and the option to retain entrepreneurial agility for larger family groups. Finally, in such a larger family scenario, a family council would add considerable value and coordinate with the owners councils in both generations.[2]

Owners councils have also been developed in smaller families. For example, the Evans family business is a manufacturer serving the auto industry. When control of the shares was in the third generation, there were two brothers and three cousins representing the five branches of the family, and they met once per year. Ostensibly, the main purpose of their meeting was to discuss family liquidity and business capital needs; practically, this meant negotiating cross-purchases of shares if desired and communicating one message to the board regarding their desires for company distributions. This informal meeting always took place in December, and it was something the whole family looked forward to as a part of the holiday season.

The Evans family never referred to their meeting as an owners council or a family council, but it functioned as a combination of the two. Looking back, the five family members recalled that their informal discussions often went beyond liquidity and capital; they recalled the following developments:

> *The board was significantly enhanced.* Early in the third generation's period of control, the board was dominated by family members. Realizing that they needed more independence and perspective, the Evans owner group agreed to implement a reconfiguration of the board. Moreover, they decided that independent directors should dominate the board in terms of number. They made difficult decisions, including who among them would resign their seats in order to make room for more independents.
>
> *Rules for family members working in the business.* At the time that the third generation's oldest children were becoming eligible for employment in the business, the discussions at one Evans holiday owner meeting centered on the possible family relationship disasters that might accompany unfairly providing or not providing employment opportunities for their kids. The next year the owners asked the CEO to meet with them to discuss this issue, and the outcome was a policy and procedures for hiring and employing fourth-generation family members.
>
> *Formation of a family council.* After several years of effectively functioning as an owner group, the Evans family proudly recognized that its alignment and harmony had been greatly supported by the annual holiday meeting and the many informal conversations family members enjoyed as the controlling owners. The company had prospered, but they also realized that while they were very capable and the entire family was benefitting, they were not teaching anything to the next generation. In an effort to make changes, the family decided to get the younger generation involved, beginning with a task force to study what was needed. The task force included members of the fourth generation for the first

time. Ultimately, the task force recommended a first ever meeting of the entire family with opportunities for family members to become educated about what other family firms had done regarding continuity and to talk about what they wanted. The meeting resulted in the formation of a family council.

After these developments, the fourth generation became much more involved and has taken on significant responsibility for the family contribution to the success of the business. The Evans family owners' "group of five" continues to meet annually as it did in the past, but there are no plans to find successors for the members. The family members find that they are honoring a tradition and enjoying a holiday dinner together. The board of directors, the family council, and the annual family assembly have assumed much of their former informal functions and contributions. From the perspective of family owners, they look ahead, they coordinate to produce an aligned message of many owners to the board, and they anticipate their changing needs and plan adjustments accordingly.

Regular Family Management Meetings: Executive Committees

Often referred to as an executive committee meeting, a regular family management meeting is a special kind of family governance function. When all of the family owners are working in the business, a weekly meeting is common. Its scope will likely go beyond coordination of management decision making and also incorporate many items that might go to a family council if there were one.

The Lamberti Foods Executive Committee

Three brothers and a sister work in the food processing business that was first owned by their parents. The business was acquired late in the parent's careers, and the four siblings, all in their twenties at the time, began working with their parents just after the business was purchased. There are two other younger children in the Lamberti family who have never worked in the business and are not owners.

Several years later, the founders are still interested in the business, but they are not considered owners by their children and don't see themselves as such either because they have received payment for over 90 percent of their shares and have long ago relinquished all operational involvement. Once in a while Mike Lamberti Sr. visits the office, always calling ahead two or three days in advance. He is careful not to intrude; employees who know him jest that he makes appointments to see his children.

All of the Lamberti sibling owners have spouses and their children range in age from one to fourteen. The siblings are Mike Jr. (48 years old), the president, Maria (46 years old) is sales manager, and the twin brothers Joseph and Tony (both 42 years old) are also in sales reporting to Maria.

The business has two very valuable senior managers who are not family members: Alex Hettinger is plant manager and Roberta Rodriguez is the CFO. The human resources and quality control positions are also viewed as very valuable to the company. The business is strong; it has been a steady performer, often through adapting and adjusting its business model over the years.

The siblings follow a tailored "first among equals" leadership format, which means for them that Mike is the president and leader, but he is more of a consensus builder rather than merely "boss." While Mike Jr. has only one family member direct report in Maria, his influence extends equally to his two brothers and sister when they assemble as a group. Mike leads the discussion and guides the group to a consensus decision. He also obtains consent from the group to act independently and follow through on issues in accordance with their discussions, such as when he approached their corporate attorney to make changes to the employment agreements for their two top non-family managers, Alex and Roberta.

The four siblings meet once a week for two hours and then are joined by Alex and Roberta; when all are assembled, they are called the executive committee. Internally, they distinguish between the two portions of the executive committee meeting as the owners segment and the management segment. Mike sets the agenda and runs both portions of the meeting, but he is quite responsive to all others' recommendations for agenda items. Among the topics discusses during the owners-only portion of the meeting in the past two years were the following:

- Growth expectations for the business and the expected distributions for the next two years

- Policy for family members working in the business (Whether to offer summer internships for high school children in the third generation was also discussed and how to communicate this decision and policy. This led to planning the first meeting with the family.)
- The potential for inviting their youngest brother, who has excelled in a rival company, to join and whether to offer him stock at some point (What his first job would be and who might supervise him were also discussed.)
- The role of the siblings in caring for parents who are beginning to show their age
- Planning their own expected retirement schedules and discussion of the adequacy of their retirement benefits and their relationship to the shareholder agreement
- Challenging work expectations and strained relationships for Maria with Joe and Tony, who report to her

As is clear from the list above, there is a combination of family, owner, and management issues among the topics that were addressed. All are common for business families like the Lambertis. The Lambertis do not have a family council; even though they have a board on paper, it consists of the owners and meets as a formality only. Everything of any importance to the family and its business, whether management roles, ownership issues, or matters concerning them as siblings, is covered in these executive committee meetings. This represents a typical family council/board/management meeting in many family firms.

While the way the Lambertis work is practical and effective for them, there are some indicators to be aware of for making adjustments. As the family grows and changes, it will become important for the Lambertis to adjust their family governance. They must remain alert to the need to develop more clarity about the boundaries between family, ownership, and management. They are already separating topics concerning the family owners only from those also concerning management by holding the executive committee meetings in two portions. Next, they will want to be clear about what topics they bring up that might also be relevant for a meeting of the entire family.

Two years after the executive committee meetings were adequately handling the topics above, the Lamberti siblings have adjusted a little and now hold four distinct meetings. They still hold weekly executive committee meetings, just as they have for years; a one-hour meeting of the sibling owners followed by a one-and-a-half-hour meeting with Alex and Roberta joining them. They frequently invite others, particularly the human resource and quality managers, to join them for part of these meetings. The Lamberti family also has a family meeting once per year during which the members discuss many topics related to continuity of the family business. Spouses and children above the age of thirteen attend. Finally, the Lambertis hold a shareholder/board meeting once per year and invite their corporate attorney to attend. This last development has been a bit of a challenge to distinguish what should be reserved for the shareholder meeting and why they should hold one separate from the executive committee, and the attorney's involvement has been helpful in this respect.

While the Lambertis have a structure that works for four siblings and will work for other sibling teams in similar circumstances, it should be noted that other family configurations will be candidates for the same executive committee arrangement particularly if family members and owners all work in the business. We know of several first- and second-generation and second- and third-generation business families who use the same executive committee structure with great satisfaction. In most cases, the businesses employ several family members, and they use the convenient structure of business management meetings for all issues, family and business, because all the relevant players are present.

Ling Industrial Products Executive Committee

The Ling family business is a national distributor of institutional cleaning products. Martin and David are brothers who are in their late sixties and are both very active in the business with daily operational responsibilities. Martin has four children working in the business and David has three, and all are in positions that fit their skills and outside work experience prior to joining the family business. However, not all of them, especially some who have joined only recently, are in management roles. Like the Lambertis, this family has managers who are not family members but contemporaries of the brothers; these managers hold key leadership roles. Long before any of the brothers' children joined, the two brothers and three senior managers ran the company as a team and grew the business from a regional to national supplier.

Martin and David have shared the same goal since the second of their children entered the business, namely, that of teaching them everything about the business with the expectation that their children will some day own and operate the business together. The Lings are not formal and resist efforts to establish a formal structure, especially formal meetings. However, they have a structure that is clearly understood by anyone who works there and certainly by all family members. Every Monday morning the Ling brothers are in the company cafeteria at six for coffee. They have met this way with their three non-family managers for years. Things changed only slightly after the younger generation became involved. After Martin's oldest son had worked in the business for a while, David's oldest child joined. Soon thereafter, the two cousins started showing up for coffee at six without ever having been asked. Somehow they knew they were welcome. Early on they listened a lot, and then they gradually started to participate. It has been the same for each cousin thereafter.

Monday coffee discussions for the Lings are always about gaining new customers, servicing existing customers, and managing operations. Departmental decisions are coordinated, expectations are set, and commitments are verbalized. Yet, the Monday morning discussions have sometimes also been about compensation, disagreements between the cousins over how best to serve customers, and changes to the roles of the cousins to manage both personal tensions and personal development. The non-family managers join in the discussions without restraint and fulfill the combined roles of teachers of the younger generation and managers of their areas of responsibility. They do not refer to their meeting with a name; it is certainly not an executive committee to them. However, they function as part executive committee and part family council.

While the Lamberti and Ling families and their structures are different, they cover a lot of ground that other families would reserve for family councils and family assemblies or associations. In fact, executive committees composed of family members working in the business often evolve into separate structures. For the Lamberti family, they will discuss more and more the question of what part of the meeting should be communicated to the rest of the family. For the Ling family, the cousins will begin to hold their own meetings separate from the Monday morning coffee meetings. And then, at some point, they will hold a special meeting and invite their spouses to attend—this will be their first family assembly. Both the Lamberti and Ling families will have the option of creating a separate family council some day, just as they will both consider the timing and the value of a more formal board of directors.

Evolving structure of the Lambertis' governance. For business families that use executive committees for business planning and for family business relationship maintenance and planning, it is a challenge to remain clear on what is covered where when they begin to develop further separate governance structures. For the Lamberti family, two years after they developed the structure of two family meetings per year, one annual shareholders meeting, and their weekly executive committee meetings, their attorney provided the following descriptions of the four forums:

1. Executive committee A: Family owners who work in the business to discuss all owner, business, and family topics, and repeatedly identify valuable issues to reserve for the other forums.
2. Executive committee B: Owners with non-family management to "get on the same page" about short-term and long-range management issues and to communicate the family owners' decisions and plans that affect the senior leadership and company.
3. Family meeting: All members of the owning siblings and families above the age of thirteen plus the founder parents for family business issues affecting the owning family and for general family topics affecting the extended family.
4. Annual shareholder meeting: All shareholders including the founding parents for legal and shareholder responsibilities, such as setting liquidity, risk, growth and profit expectations and to elect the board members.

The Lamberti family formed a family council several years later when their children in the third generation were graduating from college. They wanted to give the spouses and the next generation more of a forum and responsibility for family and planning leadership. They realized the family would all leave everything to the siblings led by Mike Jr. and while all family and business matters would be handled, they would lose the commitment and learning that might take place through broader involvement. The twice annual family meetings were inefficient for decision making and planning, and therefore a family council was formed. It included two shareholder siblings, Maria and Tony, Joe's spouse who does not work in the company and two cousins from the third generation. The Lamberti siblings continue to meet as an executive committee, but they actively restrict their discussions about family matters to allow the family council to become more relevant and influential, to better define its scope and objectives, and ultimately to make a greater contribution to the unity and alignment of all members of the owning family.

9

Family Leadership

Leadership in a family requires courage, optimism, persistence, and a focus on serving. It requires doing the right thing for the family even when there may be some family members showing apathy, resistance, or opposition. This is challenging enough when working in a paid position, but many family leadership positions are unpaid, making family leaders susceptible to questioning the value of their work when appreciation is ambivalent. On the other hand, strong family leadership can make an enormous difference in the life of the family and in the family's ability to function as a cohesive, supportive, and caring group. Seeing the impact on the overall family and its members can be incredibly rewarding and is a lasting legacy for family leaders. This chapter will focus on how family leaders can excel at their role, whether leading the family council, a committee, or a task force. We use the term "family group" when referring to these various leadership bodies of the family. These concepts are especially relevant for family members who wish to assume stronger leadership positions in the family though we recommend all family members read this chapter so they can develop a greater empathy for those who assume leadership roles on behalf of everyone. We encourage family leaders to review chapters 5 and 7 of this book, as there are many additional insights that can be gained when leading a family group. In addition, excellent resources on the topic can be found in the books *Preparing Successors for Leadership: Another Kind of Hero* and *Effective Leadership in the Family Business*.[1]

Clarity of Purpose

Regardless of what family leadership position you hold, you will do the family a great favor if you clarify the purpose of the group you are leading. One of the leading causes of family conflict is the frustration about family members' unmet expectations. When a family council, committee, or task force is formed, group members' expectations about the group's purpose typically vary widely and often are unspoken. If subsequent actions are not consistent with each member's expectations, the result can be mistrust and poor communication. When beginning any family group, effective leaders forge the group into a team by first gaining alignment on the purpose of the group even if this takes time and requires a challenging discussion. The case of Andrew James illustrates this point well.

> Upon being named the chair of the family education committee of the James family council, Andrew James first called a face-to-face meeting of all members to discuss the nature of the committee and to prepare a purpose statement. The council had given limited direction, and Andrew wanted clarity for his team. When they gathered, they spent almost two hours just focusing on what the education committee could be doing for the family and talking about their highest aspirations. There were many different ideas expressed, and they were all captured on a large white board in the meeting room. As the group members talked, they realized that they had three primary purposes the education committee could fulfill that would most benefit the family.
>
> 1. Champion each family member's passions and interests, regardless of what field they are in and link those passions and interests to the James family mission.
> 2. Foster excellence in interpersonal and group communication, presentation of ideas, conflict management, and decision making.
> 3. Educate family members on the roles, rights, and responsibilities of effective shareholders and governors of the enterprise.

The desire to be productive often pushes leaders to jump right into problem solving mode or action planning. Imagine, however, if Andrew James had started the meeting with a proposal to work on bringing in a speaker for the next family meeting that focused on shareholder rights. It is quite possible that another education committee member held a view that the committee should focus on the family's conflict management skills. This could easily lead to a rough start to the first meeting; rather than motivating members, the resulting disagreements might lead to negative feelings. By clarifying the purpose of the group, the leader gets everyone focused on a context in which decision making and action planning makes sense for all involved.

Developing a Plan

Creating a plan to achieve the family group's purpose will help align everyone toward a common direction. The leader who can guide the group in this endeavor will generate confidence in his or her abilities to guide the group and will give the group clarity of direction.

At the previous meeting of the James family council, Andrew James received support to pursue the purposes developed by the education committee, then scheduled a committee meeting to begin working on a three-year plan. A month later during the education committee's planning meeting, the committee members brainstormed how they could help the family achieve the purposes spelled out in their first meeting, categorizing possible education offerings according to each of the primary purposes. The group then selected two offerings for each purpose statement, giving them a total of six offerings. Andrew had everyone rank the six offerings and those receiving the most votes were given priority on the family calendar. By the end of the meeting, they knew which educational offerings would be presented at each family meeting for the next three years (the James family met twice per year and wanted to offer two or three hours of education at each meeting) and had assigned a member of the education committee to begin working on each offering, determining whether a family member, current advisor, or outside resource would be most effective in providing their learning needs.

When a family group forms, there is often high energy among its members and optimism about all that the committee can accomplish. If this energy is harnessed in a plan, it helps the leader pace the work

Purpose of Group:		
Primary Goals:		
Plans Year 1:	Plans Year 2:	Plans Year 3:
a._____ b._____ c._____ d._____	a._____ b._____ c._____ d._____	a._____ b._____ c._____ d._____

Figure 9.1   Family Group Planning Sheet

of the group, avoiding the mistake many leaders make by trying to do too much too soon. This latter approach leads to burnout and family frustration as the family struggles to keep up with the actions of the committee. Families like to see progress, and a plan that lays out goals that are consistent with the purpose of the family group and identifies plans for achieving those goals will help the family understand how each activity fits into the overall plan, and this reduces anxiety. A family leader who recognizes this will better earn the respect of even those family members who have the highest performance expectations. The planning sheet shown in figure 9.1 is a tool a leader of a family group can use to help focus the group.

Prioritizing to Gain Alignment on Important Issues

Regardless of what family group you are leading, it is important that you help the group prioritize its goals. Prioritizing helps in several ways. First, it focuses the group's efforts so that it can accomplish something rather than spend valuable time deciding what to do. A leader is well advised to write down lower priority items on a list we often term the "Parking Lot" for ideas that are important to remember for later attention. This allows the group member identifying the lower priority concept to feel heard and allows the leader to get the group back on task.

A second way prioritizing helps is to avoid "flooding the table," which happens when multiple issues come before a family group all at once, and different people are responding intellectually and emotionally to too many concerns, leading to dissonance and frustration. When the table gets "flooded," people begin to feel that they are in crisis mode and start reacting accordingly. The following example highlights this common phenomenon and describes how excellent leadership helped regain stability.

Don Hatke, the chair of the Hatke family council, was leading the family through a discussion about long-term liquidity planning, assisted by the family's primary CPA, who was presenting general concepts of liquidity planning. Don had started the discussion with a clear focus, which was to help the family think through the liquidity needs of the senior generation and discuss the implications.

During the discussion, a family shareholder who was not employed in the business proposed that the family should focus on short-term liquidity and suggested an increased dividend. A family member working in the business quickly complained that the family should not raise the dividend because the company cannot afford to pay out additional distributions and stated, "Besides, I don't want junior generation shareholders getting dependent on dividends when they should be learning how to earn a living!"

Recognizing that the group was quickly getting offtrack, Don asked everyone to pause for a moment, and he refocused the group on the primary purpose of the discussion, which was to explore long-term liquidity planning options. He acknowledged the importance of the family having a discussion about dividends and company reinvestment, and stated that it is well worth some family meeting time to discuss how best to teach a work ethic to the next generation, but he emphasized, "Those discussions are not today. Today we are learning about long-term liquidity planning and discussing the implications."

Had Don not acted to refocus the group on the priority of the day, family members could have quickly attached themselves to a secondary issue that was flooding the table. Don's quick action cleared the table of the distracting issues and got the group focused on the single issue that had been identified as the top priority of the day.

Pacing Your Family Group

Pacing the work of any group is an art. Leaders have to be sensitive to balance the needs of the overall family with the needs of individuals. Push the family too hard in a direction, and individuals my respond by increasing their resistance, which increases the risk of unproductive conflict. Expect too little of the family, and individuals will get bored, frustrated, and apathetic towards the family's work.

An effective leader begins meetings by stating the goals and then moves the group toward those goals. If members become agitated, it's up to the leader to slow the process down. If members seem comfortable, the leader can push the group forward. At the end of the meeting leaders need to restate the meeting's goals, summarize what has been discussed to move toward those goals, and read aloud any action steps that have been agreed to by the group. This helps align group members on what they have agreed to and reminds them what they have accomplished. Finally, the leader outlines the next steps and what may be on the agenda for future meetings.

Pacing within meetings is also an art. When a meeting is scheduled for two hours and there are three topics to address, it is the leader's role to help the group address the desired issues. Many family groups engage in repeating issues over and over, raising distracting issues, storytelling that is related to the topic but slows the process down, and other time consuming behaviors. Depending on the needs of the family, some tools that a leader may employ in helping the group stay on task include the following:

- State the amount of time that will be allotted to the agenda and either set a timer or assign a timekeeper to let the group know when the amount of time is nearing an end.
- Read the goals of the meeting up front and when the group gets off track, remind the group of the meeting's goals.
- When group members are repeating issues, interrupt the discussion and summarize the points that the group agrees on. Or ask a member of the group to summarize the points he or she hears the group agreeing on.
- When a person is telling a story, summarize what you hear him or her say and state that given the short amount of time, you want to

make sure you hear from others. Then call on quieter members of the group to share their ideas.

- Write down points of agreement on a flip chart or white board so all can see that agreement has been reached, then move on. This avoids the tendency of many families who fall into the pattern of "beating a dead horse."
- Interrupt discussion of a side issue that is not directly applicable to the full group and ask those participating in the side discussion if they can talk about the issue "off-line."

Balancing Process with Results

Another art for family leaders to develop involves balancing the need for family members to be heard and to discuss and process matters with the need to achieve something tangible (like an agreement or action step). Setting goals and achieving them is important, but there are times when the family group you are leading needs to take time to share ideas and talk issues through without the pressure of accomplishing a goal. In fact, taking time to process an issue can actually result in quicker implementation of a goal, as the group will typically be more supportive if members believe they were heard and contributed to the outcome of the meeting. Recognizing when to push toward results or taking additional time to process can be aided by looking for the following signs when you are leading the group.

Six signs that you need to slow the group down and let members process issues:

1. Tensions are rising over differences in ideas related to the discussion.
2. Group members are verbalizing that they are not being heard.
3. Quiet members of the group appear concerned or upset, but are not speaking.
4. Despite efforts to focus the group on the designated issue, the group keeps going back to a seemingly unrelated issue.
5. When summarizing a discussion to help the group move on to the next topic, there are reactions about the accuracy of the summary.

6. When stating the agreements of the group, individual members do not verbally affirm the agreements.

Six signs that you need to speed up the group toward accomplishing more results:

1. Group members are verbalizing frustration that things are not being accomplished.
2. Group members make statements such as "We have already done this!" or "Where are we going with this?"
3. Family members are questioning the value of meetings.
4. Family members are not able to verbalize the accomplishments of the group.
5. Side discussions are becoming more frequent.
6. An individual group member is dominating the discussion and engaging in storytelling while other members are tuning out (eyes aiming down or away from the person speaking, checking emails, etc.).

Self-Empowerment through Role Descriptions

When taking on a position as family leader, one of your first actions after clarifying the purpose of the family group will be to assure that a clear role or job description is in place for you. If there is an existing role description, you will benefit by reviewing it and making sure that it is helpful in guiding you toward accomplishing the group's purpose. If it is not, or if you have suggestions on how it might be improved, preparing a modified version and presenting it to the body that oversees your group (for example, a committee chair would take the proposed modifications to the family council for approval) will assure that you have the authority to proceed in that area. This affirmation of empowerment will be essential later on if the family begins to struggle with an issue and your leadership is needed to guide the family through the issue. By avoiding a question of your leadership authority or role's purpose in the middle of an emerging hot issue, you are helping the family to maintain clarity on who will lead them forward. Of course, if there is not a role description, you will need to create one yourself, ideally with some input from other family members. A sample role description for a committee chair is presented in figure 9.2.

The family employment committee chair reports to the Rahrig Family Council and is charged with carrying out the development, maintenance, interpretation, and enforcement of the Rahrig family employment policy.

Role of the chair

- Keeping the family employment policy current and regularly reviewing its effectiveness
- Leading the family employment policy committee and ensuring that the committee meets its goals
- Keeping abreast of family employment trends through reading or speaking with other family businesses
- Educating the Rahrig family about the family employment policy and how it impacts the family
- Ensuring that the company board is educated about the policy and is clear on its their role in policy interpretation and enforcement
- Orienting young family members to the policy when they reach the age of 15, with the support of their parents
- Report on the state of the family employment policy to the family council at least annually

Figure 9.2   Chair Role Description: Family Employment Policy Committee

The role description states the position held, who the position reports to, and the primary role expectations for the person holding the position. Every formal family leadership position (chair of the family council, chair of a family committee, or chair of a family task force) deserves the clarity of a role description to empower the person serving as a family leader. However, we have found that many families go beyond just creating role descriptions for family leaders. It is sometimes very confusing to be a member of a family group (such as a shareholder or member of one of the family groups described above), and many families find it quite useful to clarify the roles of family group members, which further empowers the family leader by reinforcing the meaningful roles of those who follow the family leaders.

Delegating

We commonly see family members who are quite adept at accomplishing tasks and may enjoy doing the work of a family group. These individuals often see what needs to be done and simply add those items to their "To Do" lists. Before long, they can easily become so scheduled with tasks that they lose sight of their primary role, which is to lead the group. In fact, by taking on all of the tasks themselves, these leaders can actually deprive the family group of a sense of teamwork, commitment, and shared responsibility.

Delegating responsibilities is a primary task of being a family leader. A family task force leader is responsible for making sure that notes are taken at each family task force meeting, but does not need to take notes himself. The task force leader is responsible for making sure the work of the task force gets accomplished, but he or she does not need to do all of the work. Successful family group leaders are not afraid to roll up their sleeves and do the work, which is excellent modeling. However, they spend more time in a coordinating or facilitating role, asking for volunteers to complete required tasks or assigning tasks to group members. In this sense, it is true that the work of the family group gets accomplished *through* the effective family leader, but it is not a good practice to have the work of the family group be done *by* the family leader.

Coping with Loneliness at the Top

Family leaders face unique challenges when assuming positions of leadership. First, there is the challenge of coordinating a volunteer work force. Most family groups do not compensate group members, and some members may find it easy to prioritize their day jobs or driving kids to ball games above the family group. For this reason, we often recommend that family members interested in family leadership prepare themselves by seeking positions in volunteer organizations (chambers of commerce, nonprofit organizations, churches) where they can learn skills in leading a volunteer task force or committee. A second significant challenge faced by the leader is raising tough issues that need to be addressed for the family's well being but also bring resistance from family members who seek to avoid changing behaviors or making tough decisions. Family reactions can range from aggressive (argumentation, verbal attacks questioning the decision to raise the issue) to passive (refusal to respond, ignoring requests to speak or meet) and, of course, include the passive-aggressive (saying negative things about the matter behind the leader's back or trying to build a coalition against a concept rather than holding the discussion out in the open for the family to address). It is not unusual for leaders experiencing these reactions to begin questioning their own abilities and wondering whether it is worth the difficulty to try to help the family move forward. We'll talk about ways to get support later in this section, but for now we can say that family leaders will be more likely to avoid these concerns if they have clarity about what they are trying to accomplish, have garnered support for the group's purpose and roles, and have the courage to stay on the path even when they meet resistance.

Another challenge involves the difficulty of being both a family leader and a family member. This can result in role confusion as the leader tries to balance a sense of neutrality on issues (so as not to be seen as taking a side if an issue becomes divisive) with his or her own feelings about what is best for the family or his or her own interests. To be able to take multiple positions at one time, subordinating one's own personal desires for the sake of leading the group in considering multiple options is a skill that must be developed. We know of family council leaders who while facilitating their family meetings will step to the side and say, "I am now speaking as an individual family member" and provide their individual perspective on an issue, then step back to the center spotlight and say, "I am now speaking as the family council chair again, and I think we should proceed as follows" and continue leading the discussion. This act of literally stepping out of one role (family leader) and into another role (family member) helps the leader differentiate his or her own feelings, and helps the family see that this leader is able to hold an opinion and also continue serving the family as leader.

Probably the biggest challenge a family leader will experience is when a close family member shows emotional heat toward the leader because of a decision made. For example, Lisa King knew that putting the issue of selling the business on the agenda would be difficult for her brother Philip, who was the CEO. Nevertheless, as family council chair she had become aware of increased family ambivalence about shareholders' commitment to the enterprise, and she wanted to get the issue on the table and resolved. She envisioned the family coming together and just hearing each other's hopes and goals as owners, and she saw herself then leading the family through the discussion about what to do to either reaffirm commitment to keep ownership in family hands, buy some family members out, or explore options to sell the business. She believed the family's inability to hold this discussion was a greater threat to family harmony than dealing with the issue directly.

When Philip saw that Lisa put the issue on the agenda for the next family council meeting, he was crushed. He had always believed Lisa was his loyal supporter, and he felt hurt that someone so close to him would hold a family discussion that threatened all of the hard work he was doing in the business. He called Lisa in a fit, and his first comment was, "How could you do this!" He vented his frustrations that she was putting him in an impossible position and questioned whether she had any idea how hard he was working to build the business back up after a few difficult years caused by the recession.

Lisa knew it would be hard for Philip, but she had no idea he would respond the way he did. She had approached him in advance and had heard him say it was "probably not a good idea," but she had not detected the emotional force that was so clearly behind his most recent call. She began to question whether she had made the right decision and was full of anxiety and fear that her relationship with Philip was irrevocably harmed. She felt awful. Luckily, her husband Migi was home and he was able to help her see that the family's needs required the decision she had made. He was also able to help her see that Philip was just venting and would not allow their loving sibling relationship to be destroyed over this. She just needed to let Philip calm down. Though still anxious, Lisa was more hopeful after speaking to Migi and was thankful for his loving support.

Leading a family group, particularly through a difficult issue (and there will always be difficult issues), can be lonely, but as Lisa experienced, having a partner to go to for support and perspective is a valuable resource. We see two primary sources for family leaders who wish to develop a support resource: a trusted family member or an outside agent.

When a family leader turns to a family member as a source of support, several factors should be considered. The most obvious factor is whether the family member can offer support without becoming entangled in the issue or overly involved emotionally. Turning to a spouse for support can be highly effective—with the spousal relationship usually being the most trusting relationship among family members—but this is not a good option if the spouse becomes overly protective of the family leader and builds resentment or anger toward others in the family that are "causing" their family leader any distress. This is a classic family business dilemma—for example, a husband comes home from work and angrily vents to his wife about what his sister did at work today, then feels better after he vents to his wife, who now feels bitter toward the sister for the pain her husband experienced. Then the wife may give the sister the cold shoulder the next day at cousin Jimmy's birthday party. In this case, the wife is not able to remain emotionally neutral as a listening resource, and her inability to do so becomes a net loss to the overall family functioning. Instead of keeping the problem between her husband and his sister at work, the wife has now become part of the problem because of her newfound anger toward her sister-in-law. The husband will soon learn that his relationship with his sister has now become more complex (and troubled) as she tries to understand the bitterness coming from her brother's wife.

A family member can serve as a resource if he or she is able to remain emotionally independent of the challenges being discussed and can take the position of champion of overall family health even if this means confronting the family leader about ways in which he or she might be playing into family dysfunction. As a resource, a family member must also be able to remain neutral as a listener, being careful not to espouse a divisive position or to champion one part of the family against another part of the family. And, of course, such a family member must be trustworthy, keeping the nature of the discussions confidential, not sharing information received in private from other family members or advisors. We have seen family leaders use a senior generation mentor, a sibling, a cousin, or a spouse to serve as either a formal or informal support resource when leading a family group. But not every family leader feels comfortable using a family member as a support resource. Some turn to agents outside the family.

An outside agent is a family advisor, consultant, or colleague who is not attached to the family but is a capable listener and can offer insights. Sometimes, for example, a family council leader might establish a relationship with a family business consultant, industrial psychologist, or business coach with expertise serving entrepreneurial families. While some family council leaders might meet regularly (monthly or quarterly), it is not uncommon to hold an initial meeting and then schedule meetings as situations arise where perspective is needed. In addition to neutrality, based on training and experience, the outside professional (if well trained) is able to see how emerging issues fit in with the overall needs of the family. As long as the professional is able to provide wisdom, neutrality (especially free of conflicts of interest), and confidentiality, the relationship can be very helpful to the family leader as he or she navigates family business dynamics in the leadership role.

We also know of family leaders who have met with counterparts from other family businesses, often through association groups, and the two leaders then mutually support each other. These relationships can be quite fruitful as long as the person providing support does not allow his or her own family situation to influence the counsel given to the family leader needing support. This happens when the person in the supportive role tries to push his or her own family's solutions on the person needing support. Every family is different, and while there are commonalities among families and relationships between family groups, championing a position for someone else's family is likely to be unhealthy. Rather, the supportive listener is most useful when playing the role of listener, helping the family leader see different perspectives or alternatives, and supporting that person in defining his or her own path forward.

Of course, some family leaders may start out at the formation of a group anticipating the potential for loneliness and propose a solution that seems an obvious way to solve the issue: co-leadership.

Co-leadership

Family leadership can be made less isolated by employing coleaders in a family council, family committee, or family task force. This is most often used when a group is forming for the first time, and workload and role descriptions have yet to be determined. Co-leadership can be a source of great support for family leaders, or an additional burden, depending on a variety of factors we will discuss below.

When two leaders (we do not recommend more than two family members serving as coleaders) have high communication skills and a strong working relationship, they have a higher probability of enjoying and succeeding at the co-leadership experience. The odds of successful co-leadership are further advanced when the leaders structure their roles so there is always clear accountability. If they are not clear about who is responsible for what, the group they are leading will also be unclear as will the family they serve. Clarifying accountability helps each person know what they must do and avoids situations in which something does not get done because everyone dropped the ball. In fact, if coleaders ever use the words, "I thought you were doing that!" it is a signal that they are being ineffective in defining responsibilities.

We see a number of ways that accountability is shared in co-leadership models. Each can be successful or unsuccessful based on how well it is executed.

1. **Permanent hierarchy model.** In this model, the leaders are called coleaders, but it is assumed that one of the persons will be the point person, so to speak, on all matters. That person will be in charge of setting up meetings, setting direction, bringing new resources to the table, and making sure that the family group is a success. The coleaders agree beforehand on these arrangements, and the person serving as the subordinate leader is supportive when the other person assumes leadership. They also understand that in the event that the primary leader is unavailable to serve, the secondary leader will step into that role. This model works especially well when the primary leader is a strong leader and the secondary leader is comfortable playing the steady force behind the primary leader. Conversely, it starts to break down if the secondary leader shirks responsibility or becomes resentful of the primary leader's directive behavior.

2. **Rotating hierarchy model.** The rotating hierarchy model is similar to the permanent rotating model, except that the person occupying the primary leadership role alternates based on an event, responsibility, or time period. For example, Dean and Sheila are coleaders of the site selection & logistics committee for their family council. They agreed that they would rotate leadership of the committee every other meeting. Dean lead all committee activities and communications related to the October family meeting that was held Boston, then Sheila took over and lead all committee activities and communications for the April family meeting that was held in San Diego, and then they rotated back and forth until their terms expired. This model works well when neither person has an inherent psychological need to be the sole leader and when both leaders are willing to accept responsibility for the outcomes equally.

3. **Division of labor model.** Some coleaders use a division of labor model, in which one family leader assumes all responsibility for one area, while the other assumes responsibility for a different area that is clearly distinct in terms of requirements to fulfill the need. For example, Tom and Katie assumed co-leadership of the family education committee of their family council. They agreed that Tom would be responsible for the overall committee leadership, but Katie would be responsible for researching, planning, and logistics related to bringing in outside resources. In family education committee meetings, Tom led the meetings up to the point where discussion turned to outside resources, at which time Katie would take over. Once Katie's segment was over, Tom resumed control. This model works especially well when one person has a passion or unique skill for a specific part of the leadership responsibility and neither wants nor needs to be the overall leader.

4. **Equal coleader model.** Infrequently, we see a co-leadership model in which both parties try to be perfectly equal in all decisions, including the leadership of the family group and in communications. This is a difficult model to carry out, as inefficiencies in trying to make every decision and plan for every communication to the family cause a high work burden for both coleaders. More than likely, two co-leaders who attempt this will default into one of the other models to become more productive. In addition to requiring added time, it is not unusual for all but the most patient of family leaders to experience some resentment towards the other, as the constant need to be aligned with each other will eventually be experienced as a restrictive shackle. We favor one of the other models of co-leadership.

In truth, co-leadership is not as easy to carry out as it might seem, and many family groups have found that one of the coleaders emerges as the primary leader. For this reason, we encourage coleaders to clarify how they see the relationship working and who will hold the primary accountability for results prior to initiating the work of the family group. In addition, family leaders should be honest about their abilities to share leadership. Some leaders are simply much more comfortable being in charge and do not want to share the responsibilities of the job. Stating this at the outset will avoid much unhappiness later, as this preference will no doubt emerge later in group activities and may be accompanied by a fellow coleader who feels not respected due to the partner always wanting to be in charge.

For the following situations, in particular, we recommend considering co-leadership:

- Periods of family leader transition, when a long-standing family leader is leaving a position and a new leader is going to be taking over. This allows a mentoring period and a smoother transition of authority.
- Two individuals wishing to improve their working relationship when they and the family view the situation as a learning opportunity. By viewing it as a learning and relationship development opportunity, inefficiencies and communication challenges may be allowed by family members who support the learning effort.
- When one of the co-leaders who otherwise would have been considered the primary leader has health or career complications that make it uncertain as to whether he or she will be able to fulfill the leadership responsibilities to the family.

Preparing Family Leaders

Family members who wish to move into leadership positions will do well to seek experiences that prepare them for taking on responsibility. Working with a non-family agent (described above) can help a family leader work through leadership issues as they arise, thus enhancing the leader's skills. Some leaders will even videotape a meeting segment (with the family's permission) and review the tape with the non-family agent. Each of these methods is available to the individual who seeks to become a more skilled leader. Finally, serving as a loyal member of a family group will provide a platform from which a young leader can contribute to a group and learn how to be an effective group member, a skill needed to become an effective leader. Figure 9.3 presents an excellent summary of the requirements for earning a voice in family matters and should be read periodically by all family members, especially those who wish to become leaders.

Many families realize that they can increase the odds of having strong leaders by taking more of an active stance in developing new family

Guidelines from the book *Family Business Governance: Maximizing Family and Business Potential*[1] (Palgrave 2010) are as follows:

1. **Excellence** at your vocation, from homemaking to investment banking. Excellence at any vocation requires hard work, high standards, expertise, and education. Excellence earns respect.
2. **Flexibility** in your views of difficult issues. That means you have the ability and desire to listen to other points of view, an ability to empathize, and an understanding that you aren't always right. Open-mindedness reduces defensiveness.
3. **Literacy** in business language and the characteristics of your industry. Family members who are willing to hold themselves accountable to the business will learn how to interpret financial statements, judge competitors, and keep up with business trends. Literacy eases communication.
4. **Preparedness** to understand business concerns. This means a willingness to do your homework and to study and understand the information you are given by management.
5. **Trust** in management. Family members' trust in experienced, talented managers makes it easier for management to institute constructive changes, innovate, and take the risks necessary to running a successful business. The more trusting family shareholders are, the greater is their capacity to strengthen the business. Trust makes teamwork possible.

Craig E. Aronoff and John L. Ward, *Family Business Governance: Maximizing family and business potential* (New York: Palgrave Macmillan, 2011) p.10.

Figure 9.3   Qualifications for Earning a Voice in Family Business Governance

leaders, rather than just leaving it up to family members to develop themselves. Some family councils will even set up a committee to identify and prepare family leaders. These families use a variety of approaches to develop family leaders, among them the following:

- Families will orient new family members (those who marry in or those who become of age) to the family process and help them identify a path to move from being a rookie toward ever greater involvement.
- Families will invite members of the junior generation to sit in on a family group meeting to see what that group is about. This helps the younger family members decide if they might have interest in that group.
- Families will ask potential family leaders to lead a small segment of a family meeting, preparing the family at the beginning of the

session that this is an opportunity to give the potential family leader experience in leading the family group. This works best in families with well-developed communication skills and when the issue being discussed is noncontroversial.

- Families either bring in someone to teach the family group leadership and facilitation skills, or they send family members to workshops on effective leadership. The focus is on individual skill development and each person practices with those in attendance.
- Families send members of the junior generation to multiday programs that focus on owning, governing, or managing a family business, family office, or family foundation. The focus here is on learning from other families and developing tools for thinking about and leading an enterprising family.
- Psychological assessment will be used to help potential family leaders identify both strengths and areas to develop in their new role as leaders.

The success of a family leader is not dependent solely on his or her skills and experiences, but the rest of the family also has a hand in helping family leaders be successful. We encourage families to spend time developing role descriptions for those who are family assembly or family council members, including codes of conduct that will guide group members in how to relate to each other. Just because a family member assumed a leadership position does not give the rest of the family permission to become ineffective family or group members. Role descriptions and a code of conduct will reinforce the important role of followers.

Leadership Feedback

Leaders who adopt a continuous improvement mindset are much more likely to improve their skills than those who are not interested in feedback. In fact, family leaders who avoid feedback on their performance may actually harm the group's performance because group members see ways to improve but are met with resistance when offering helpful insights and then begin detaching from the leader. Fortunately, we find that most family leaders are keenly interested in learning how they can be more effective. They employ many different tools to get the feedback they need to achieve that improvement.

The easiest way to get feedback is to ask for it. A common way to do this is to allow an extra five minutes at the end of the meeting and ask the group to offer feedback on how to become a more effective leader. If there is enough trust among members so that all will respond candidly, this can be enough to bring valuable insights for the open-minded leader. However, not all group members may be comfortable speaking openly. Some may prefer a less public means of providing feedback. In that case, leaders may seek out individual feedback from group members in a confidential setting or can end a meeting by asking group members to complete a brief feedback form about their leadership. A simple form is shown in figure 9.4.

As you can see in the form in figure 9.4, it is simple and quick to complete and offers immediate feedback to help with improvement. Furthermore, note that the feedback is couched in the language of how the family leader is performing in regard to the goals of the family group being lead. By wording questions in this way, the leader avoids getting general feedback that may be interesting but not directly relevant to the achievement of goals. Moreover, the member giving the feedback can focus on skills that are most related to achieving the group's goals. In this way, the member is simultaneously thinking about helping the group achieve its goals and his or her concurrent learning is an added benefit for the family's improvement.

In addition to immediate feedback, families may wish to perform periodic leadership assessments of key family leadership positions as a means of improving family leadership skills. They reason that while immediate feedback is useful, a longer time horizon can be helpful in

---

I have a personal goal of improving my family leadership skills. Please help me improve my leadership skills by answering the following:

1. What actions or behaviors do I perform that are most helpful in guiding us to achieve our goals?
2. What actions could I take to improve our progress toward the goals we have?
3. Please offer any other suggestions on how I can improve my family leadership skills.

Figure 9.4 Family Leader Feedback Form

giving the leaders feedback about their overall leadership endeavors. Figure 9.5 (Family Council Chair Leadership Assessment) shows a tool that the Arnold family used to provide feedback to the family council chair, who also completed the form and compared her answers with the input of the group. In this case, an outside consultant gathered the data and summarized it so as to provide anonymity to those responding in the hope that family members would then be more candid in their responses.

The Family Business Consulting Group, Inc.ˢᵐ

Arnold Family Council Chair Leadership Assessment
Anonymous Questionnaire

August 3, 2011

Dear Arnold Family Members,

In an effort to provide feedback to the Arnold Family Council Chair (Ann Arnold), your valuable input is being sought. Each of the following questions is designed to gather your perspectives on the Ann's performance relative to the Role Description currently in place for the Family Council Chair.

Please respond with your ratings and comments to Chris Eckrich by Friday at 5:00 p.m.

If you have any questions, you can also reach me at by email or phone.

Thank you,
Chris Eckrich

Instructions: For each statement on the following pages, circle the number from the rating scale that corresponds to your own view of Ann Arnold's performance in the **PAST 12 MONTHS ONLY**. Then, in the boxes below, you can elaborate or add additional comments.

Figure 9.5 Continued

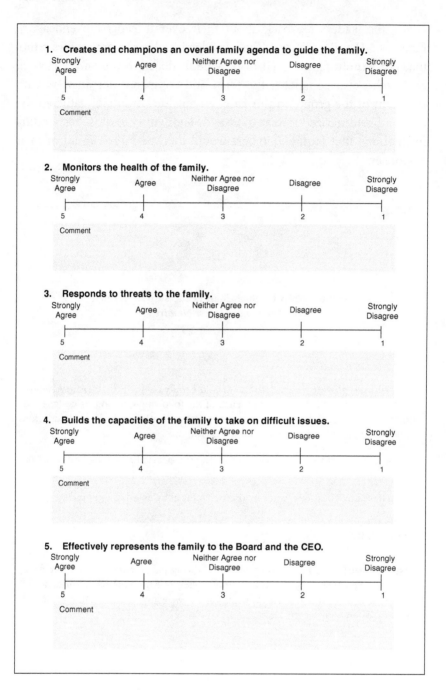

1. Creates and champions an overall family agenda to guide the family.

Strongly Agree	Agree	Neither Agree nor Disagree	Disagree	Strongly Disagree
5	4	3	2	1

Comment

2. Monitors the health of the family.

Strongly Agree	Agree	Neither Agree nor Disagree	Disagree	Strongly Disagree
5	4	3	2	1

Comment

3. Responds to threats to the family.

Strongly Agree	Agree	Neither Agree nor Disagree	Disagree	Strongly Disagree
5	4	3	2	1

Comment

4. Builds the capacities of the family to take on difficult issues.

Strongly Agree	Agree	Neither Agree nor Disagree	Disagree	Strongly Disagree
5	4	3	2	1

Comment

5. Effectively represents the family to the Board and the CEO.

Strongly Agree	Agree	Neither Agree nor Disagree	Disagree	Strongly Disagree
5	4	3	2	1

Comment

Figure 9.5 Continued

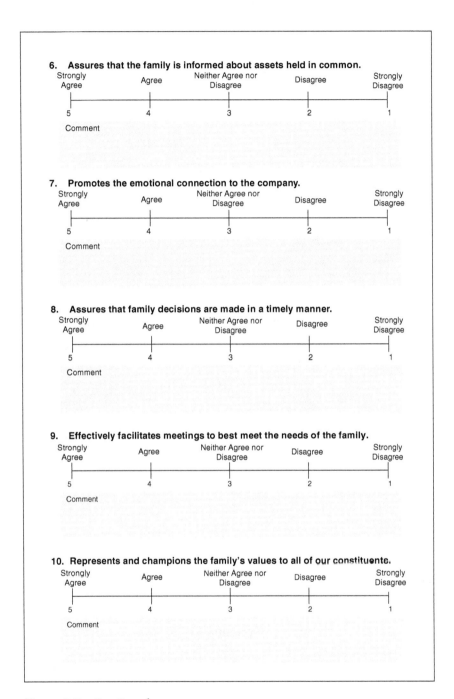

6. Assures that the family is informed about assets held in common.

Strongly Agree	Agree	Neither Agree nor Disagree	Disagree	Strongly Disagree
5	4	3	2	1

Comment

7. Promotes the emotional connection to the company.

Strongly Agree	Agree	Neither Agree nor Disagree	Disagree	Strongly Disagree
5	4	3	2	1

Comment

8. Assures that family decisions are made in a timely manner.

Strongly Agree	Agree	Neither Agree nor Disagree	Disagree	Strongly Disagree
5	4	3	2	1

Comment

9. Effectively facilitates meetings to best meet the needs of the family.

Strongly Agree	Agree	Neither Agree nor Disagree	Disagree	Strongly Disagree
5	4	3	2	1

Comment

10. Represents and champions the family's values to all of our constituents.

Strongly Agree	Agree	Neither Agree nor Disagree	Disagree	Strongly Disagree
5	4	3	2	1

Comment

Figure 9.5 Continued

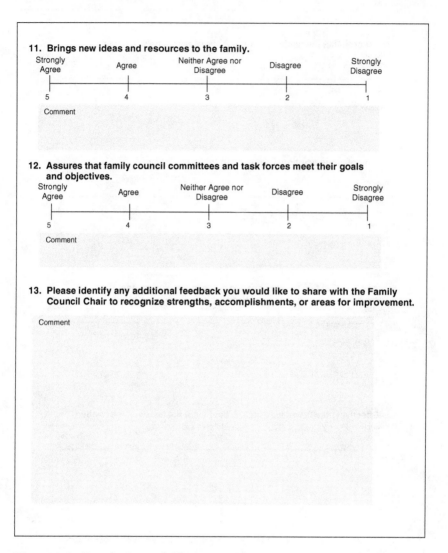

11. Brings new ideas and resources to the family.

Strongly Agree	Agree	Neither Agree nor Disagree	Disagree	Strongly Disagree
5	4	3	2	1

Comment

12. Assures that family council committees and task forces meet their goals and objectives.

Strongly Agree	Agree	Neither Agree nor Disagree	Disagree	Strongly Disagree
5	4	3	2	1

Comment

13. Please identify any additional feedback you would like to share with the Family Council Chair to recognize strengths, accomplishments, or areas for improvement.

Comment

Figure 9.5   Family Council Chair Assessment

Conclusion

Leading a family group is an excellent way to contribute to the family's well-being. Learning to deal with the ups and downs of family leadership further develops leadership skills that can be easily transferred to leadership roles outside the family. In this sense, the family becomes an excellent training ground for leaders who can strengthen any organizations they are part of outside the family and the immediate community. Many families recognize this development of human capital as a deeply meaningful pursuit in improving the world they live in.

Still, there are times or situations in the life of a family when a family may prefer to have a professional who is not a family member lead meetings. This will be the focus of chapter 10.

10

Using a Professional Facilitator

Introduction

The previous chapters have given many suggestions on how to facilitate family council and family assembly meetings. As the story below describes, there are times and reasons why a family may choose to use an outside facilitator to achieve its goals. This chapter will address why families consider outside facilitators, how to best utilize an outside facilitator, and what to look for when selecting one.

The Steinacker family council meetings had been effective, but family leaders were increasingly finding that when they facilitated their own meetings, the need to maintain a neutral role kept them from weighing in on important family issues. Cathi, the current chair of the family council, proposed that they begin using an outside facilitator to free up family members for full group participation. After weighing the potential advantages against the added cost, the family council supported Cathi's recommendation, and a search for an outside facilitator was initiated. Cathi and her brother Steve were assigned the task of finding someone who could serve in this role.

Philosophies on Using Outside Facilitators

Families that use outside facilitators believe that they can accomplish more, and in a more productive manner, by using a facilitator who is not a family member. They reason that having a family member facilitate meetings does not allow that person to fully participate as a group member, and they wish to allow each family member an equal opportunity for participation. Additionally, it is often difficult for even the most neutral family member to remain, or be perceived as remaining, neutral on all family matters. An outside facilitator who has no other connections to the family than being hired to foster excellent communication can be seen as neutral, and through that neutrality can foster the belief that the discussion leader will not take a particular side as the family discusses important concepts or makes big decisions. This belief allows the family to focus on the issue at hand, rather than worry about family politics.

Bringing the family together is a significant investment in time (and often financial resources), and family members see the added expense as a worthy investment. Especially when the family has experienced difficulty functioning, with meetings marred by hurt feelings and conflict, an outside facilitator is seen as either a temporary or permanent resource that will improve the group's functioning.

While there are philosophical reasons to use an outside facilitator, some families hold philosophies that lead them in the direction of not using outsiders as facilitators. A belief that keeping meeting costs low is better for the family is a primary belief for many families. This can be true even for families who have the resources to pay for most expensive advisors. Similarly, a family may hold the philosophy that outsiders should be used only when the family does not have the necessary skills, and family members may believe they can facilitate meetings by using family talent.

When the Middleton family was forming its family council, the family held the belief that leading family council meetings would develop group leadership skills among family members. The family therefore decided to facilitate their meetings themselves. In order to provide the experience for all family members, the Middletons chose to rotate meeting leadership among all of those who wished to have the opportunity to lead a family meeting. Because the family understood that each meeting facilitator was in the process of developing skills, the other family members were patient when a family facilitator struggled to keep the group focused or did not keep the group on schedule. In fact, at the end of each meeting, the group gave constructive input to the person who facilitated that day.

Clearly, the Middletons were willing to sacrifice some meeting efficiency for the chance to teach its members. The Middletons are an example of a family who believe that facilitation is a useful tool for the family's development.

Facilitators, Family Business Consultants, and Traditional Business Advisors

There are numerous professionals who are skilled at group process, and many of these individuals are capable of facilitating family meetings. We will use the term facilitator to describe these skilled professionals. Typically, a facilitator is brought in to lead a meeting, and is usually briefed by a family leader prior to the meeting about the goals of each agenda segment and time allotted for discussion. The facilitator may or may not meet each individual family member prior to the meeting and often has only modest input regarding the agenda. Facilitators are being hired for their group process skills and may know little about the topics being discussed. They are not being asked to give expert advice but merely to manage the dialogue of the group.

By contrast, a family business consultant is a professional who studies the unique issues families owning a business encounter and specializes in working with asset-owning families. Typically, a family business consultant will interview the individual family members to understand their hopes, goals, and perspective and have a more consultative role in meeting planning and execution. In an early meeting, family business consultants usually will provide feedback to the family and work with the family to establish goals and action steps that will guide the consulting process. In addition to meeting facilitation, they will have a substantial knowledge of best practices in owning and operating a family enterprise, family office, or family foundation. During the process of planning the meeting, family business consultants are generally very active in setting the agenda and guide the family leader on how best to arrange an agenda; they may even create the first draft of the agenda for the family leader's review. They guide the agenda creation and meeting facilitation to meet the needs of the overall family group. They may even propose agenda segments designed to teach the family some aspect of owning or operating a business together, or they may lend their expertise based on either research or their experience in working with other asset-owning families.

Whether to hire a meeting facilitator rather than a consultant with specialized expertise is a decision the family council typically makes when identifying resources to serve the family. Families with high communication skills and clear roles and responsibilities often find that a facilitator without specialized training is adequate. Families with a highly complex asset structure, more difficult communication concerning the enterprise, their roles, or succession matters often seek a family business consultant if they want to use an outside facilitator.

We should note that in some families, their current advisors (accountant, attorney, financial advisor) may facilitate all or part of their meetings. While many specialists do not have the skills to effectively facilitate groups, there are talented business advisors who can fulfill this role. When making a decision to use a current advisor, the following key questions should be asked regarding that person's ability to carry out this important role on behalf of the family.

1. Is this person perceived by all family members to have our family's best interest at heart?
2. Is this person perceived as neutral and not favoring one or more family members (i.e., the family CEO) over others?
3. Is this person replaceable if the facilitation is not successful and the family loses trust in this person?

Many families have asked their business advisors to facilitate sensitive family discussions only to end up having that person be perceived as favoring one side over another when an issue emerged that polarized the family. From the business advisor's perspective, he or she is merely trying to help the situation and often is not actively favoring one side versus another. However, perceptions are often more important than facts, and the loss of trust can lead to advisors being replaced, causing a double loss to the family—the loss of their facilitator and the loss of a previously trusted business advisor.

Skills and Qualifications of a Professional Facilitator

Professional facilitators have a wide variety of backgrounds and training, all potentially bringing useful skills to serve the family. If the family has identified its goals in using an outside facilitator, the goals can help the family narrow in on the most useful skills needed in a facilitator. For instance, if the family is having significant anxiety or conflict regarding the direction of the business, a facilitator with training in strategic planning or substantial experience in consulting business-owning families may be necessary. If the family is experiencing difficulty in communicating with each other and if emotions are prone to escalate to the family's detriment, a facilitator with training in psychology, family systems, or communications may be a better fit.

Regardless of a family's goals and the more technical training and experience desired by the family, any facilitator should possess the following essential traits and abilities:

- Ability to create as sense of trust through effective listening to each member of the family;
- Be free of any conflict of interest (real or perceived) that might be called into question at some point during the process. If there are potential conflicts of interest, the facilitator should disclose those during the hiring process;
- Commitment to the well-being of the overall family;
- Ability to balance the need to let the group process an issue with the group's need to make progress toward accomplishing its goals and reach decisions.

Bringing in a Professional Facilitator

Once a decision to bring in an outside facilitator has been made, the family has the responsibility of deciding which family member the facilitator will work with to manage logistics and achieve the family's goals. In a first-generation business, this is usually the founder, sometimes with his or her spouse. In second-generation or third-generation families, either an individual or a committee will serve in this capacity. It is important that the family is in agreement on who will oversee the facilitator and work with him or her to make the family meeting processes a success.

In truth, a founder who serves as a benevolent dictator is the most efficient in overseeing an outside facilitator. Discussions can be quick as the founder makes decisions about the family, and there may be little need to gather family support. He or she can decide how much to pay the facilitator, determine the scope of the facilitator's work, and direct the facilitator when crafting agendas and conducting family meetings. Some of this efficiency is lost when a sibling or cousin or a committee serves in this oversight capacity. The authority of this family representative is often not entirely clear, and he or she may need to keep going back and forth with the family group to make sure that a desired direction will be supported by the family. Failure to gain the support of the family results in increased tensions between the family representative and the rest of the family and may frustrate communications between the family representative and the facilitator. A brief scenario will demonstrate how this happens and show its impact on the family.

Karen Piper and her cousin Julia Noel had been selected by the Mancini family to identify a facilitator for the family and to make recommendations on how the family would work with that person to make family meetings more effective. The family's last two meetings had been quite tense, with several angry outbursts by family members who didn't feel heard or respected. It was hoped that a facilitator could guide them to more productive discussions. As much of the conflict surrounded the business and its functioning, a family business consultant was chosen by Karen and Julia after they had researched several different sources. The consultant had recommended that prior to meeting with the family, she would like to interview each of the cousins about their hopes for the enterprise and their goals and learn more about the family's communication, decision-making, and governance processes.

The day before Karen and Julia were to present their findings and forward recommendations to the family, they met and prepared their presentation. Both were excited that they had found a resource that they were quite sure could help the family. Furthermore, they felt very good about themselves for all of their efforts in serving the family though the research they had done. They were eager to share their findings with their cousins and were looking forward to starting the consulting process. In fact, they had told the consultant that they would like to start the interviews within a few weeks and then have the consultant lead the next meeting.

Unfortunately, the meeting did not go as planned. When they told the family about the consultant's request to interview each cousin, two of their cousins raised strong objections and said they would not support the costs. They had wanted someone to come in and facilitate the family meeting, but did not want to have someone know about the family's "stuff." In addition, they said they were offended that Julia and Noel had spoken on behalf of the family in setting up a more involved process than they had remembered agreeing to. The cousins could not agree on how to proceed; they decided to do nothing and revisit the issue (still without a facilitator) at their next meeting several months later. Feeling that all of their hard work on behalf of the very people who criticized it was wasted, both women went home feeling sick that their family could not agree, angry that they were criticized despite trying to do the right thing, and frustrated that the family had made no progress.

Clearly, this was a family that struggled to be aligned in its decision making. But much more is happening here that deserves mention. The goal appeared to be to hire a family advisor, but individual family members interpreted this differently. Some thought that they had agreed to an advisor who would simply help out for a day, while others thought they had agreed to bring in someone who could work more in depth with the family. This is a family struggling with false agreement, reflecting that family members were not clear with each other about their expectations regarding the decision to hire someone to help the family. Likely, this same pattern of false agreement was hurting the family in other areas.

When hiring an advisor for the family, it is important for the family to define the goals of bringing in expertise and the desired scope of help. Then, the family can empower the leadership team (the family member or members who will bring in the outside resource) to accomplish this goal. Unfortunately, the Mancinis had not clarified their goals and expectations and therefore missed out on an opportunity to bring in the right family advisor the first time. In addition, it is not uncommon for family conflict over bringing in a family advisor to polarize the family as in the Mancini's example, and an otherwise perfectly good candidate gets ruled out for no other reason than the family's inability to communicate effectively. As you can see, this then creates a lose-lose situation for the family because not only is the family still without a desired advisor, but the members feel even more hurt, frustration, and mistrust. Families do themselves a favor when they answer a few questions about how they wish to work with the new advisor.

Had the Mancinis been able to address these questions successfully, they would likely have had a new facilitator at their next meeting, rather

Question 1: What outcomes do we wish to realize from our relationship with an outside facilitator?

Question 2: Are we just exploring resources to learn about options, or are we empowering the family leadership team to make the decision and bring the new advisor on board?

Question 3: Who will serve on the leadership team bringing in the new advisor (even if just one person)?

Question 4: If the leadership team does not have the authority to bring in the new advisor, what group will have this authority and how will the decision be made?

Question 5: What individual or group of persons will work with the advisor on logistics and direction setting regarding the relationship?

Question 6: Once the relationship begins, who will oversee the family advisor on an ongoing basis?

Question 7: How will we pay for the services of our new family advisor?

Figure 10.1   Questions to Answer when Bringing in an Outside Facilitator

than prolonging a dysfunctional family dynamic. But even holding the discussions needed to answer the seven questions listed above requires a certain skill for a family. This includes the ability to sit together and enough trust to explore different opinions held by various family members. However, some families need an outside facilitator precisely because they are not healthy or functional enough to hold these types of discussions. How do you bring in a facilitator when you need the facilitator to be present to even make this decision? This is one of the many conundrums asset-owning families sometimes find themselves wrestling with. The following section will address several options for effectively bringing in new facilitators or consultants.

Bringing a Facilitator on Board during a Period of High Conflict

If your family is experiencing significant conflict in dealing with each other, and especially if that conflict concerns the family business, family office, or family foundation, answering the above seven questions may not be possible. In these cases, someone in the family must step up as a leader and guide the family toward bringing in outside help. This could be a parent, a sibling, group of siblings, or even a group of cousins. This can be a scary task, and requires a servant leader's attitude—seeking what is good for the group even though the work toward this endeavor may not be appreciated.

For example, Ferdinand could see the tensions building in the family. First, there were many expressions of hurt feelings and a general feeling of mistrust in the family. Then a rift opened up, and it felt like ice when his siblings were in the same room. There were five of them, and they had previously been pretty close, but now the tensions over both the roles people played in the business and the goals they each held as owners were spreading to the family. For the first time, his sister Maria skipped a family Christmas party she had always attended, and she seemed deeply troubled. He felt pained seeing his family struggling and no action being taken to find a better path.

Realizing that this was not just an issue of a troubled sister but concerned the entire family, Ferdinand set out to get the family back on track. First, he approached each sibling and shared his concerns, asking each sibling if they would commit to working with a family consultant on the issue in the coming year. Two siblings agreed, but his brother Domingo, who was CEO, was not in favor. Ferdinand moved forward anyway. He began to speak to other business families to inquire if they used outside help or knew of someone who helps families, careful not to share any confidential details of his own family's struggles.

Ferdinand spoke with several different consultants on the phone, each time learning more about how to think about his family's difficult situation. Finally, he identified a person he believed to be a good fit for his siblings. The consultant recommended that he visit with the five siblings to discuss their current situation and talk about how they might address the situation. Two weeks later, Ferdinand and his siblings met in his home with the consultant, and despite Domingo's reluctance all agreed to begin a consulting process to address the family's challenges in functioning and to work on common goals.

As shown in the above example, sometimes a person or group needs to push the process forward though the resistance when help is truly needed. While Ferdinand never received Domingo's full support, the latter was at least willing to come to the table. This type of resistance is quite normal in business families. There are many different individuals, generally serving in multiple roles (sibling, shareholder, executive), and fears that talking about the difficult issues will only make them worse are common. Some family members may also fear that they will not be comfortable with needed changes and may therefore hesitate to bring in an outsider. While there is some risk that things will get worse before they get better, most families who choose a well-qualified facilitator find the experience positive in the long run.

Ferdinand was able to push the process through to the point of action thanks to his persistence and personal persuasion, but not every difficult situation can be resolved this way. Below are three scenarios, each featuring a different way a conflicted family came to hire a professional facilitator.

> **Scenario 1**: Syd and Suzanne were happy when their children came into the business, but now things were very tense. They feared that family relationships, which they always valued more than the business, were being threatened. As their children were promoted in the business, the conflict seemed to be getting worse. Suzanne was frequently on the phone with her children or their spouses, listening to their frustrations. Syd, who ran the business, was not only concerned with the family, but he did not see how his children could work together in the business. When he proposed that they bring in someone to help them talk through things, two of the three siblings merely blamed each other and said they did not need help. Recognizing that time was not healing wounds, Syd and Suzanne met with a consultant who specialized in working with difficult family business situations. As a result of their discussions they decided that the family would begin a process with outside facilitation, and they met with their children to tell them of the decision. While there was grumbling, in the end their children's respect for their parental authority was strong enough to bring everyone to the table, and they began working with the consultant.
>
> **Scenario 2**: The Carmichaels' family office was owned by six cousins and had served the family since the sale of one part of their family enterprises seven years ago. In addition to a substantial investment portfolio, they still held significant investments in real estate and owned two businesses that their fathers had begun together nearly thirty years ago. The family struggled to communicate effectively and gave many mixed messages to the president of the Carmichael family office, who was not a family member. There seemed to be confusion or conflict between the two family branches and also within one of the branches. Last week

during the annual meeting, the family office president approached the cousins about the need to "get everyone on the same page" and suggested the family work with an outside facilitator to reach clarity on the overall direction of the family office and on the relationship between the family and the family office. The cousins agreed to the idea of hiring an outside facilitator and authorized the president to bring them a recommendation of a family advisor to serve this purpose.

Scenario 3: The Moran family enterprise consisted of numerous manufacturing, technology, and distribution firms as well as other holdings, owned by 58 different cousins. Nearing its seventy-fifth anniversary since the founder Daniel Moran began the enterprise, the family was experiencing difficulties in holding family association meetings, despite their years of operating with a family council that had always been able to lead the family. Family members had strong and different opinions about whether to keep the business or sell some or all of it. The current family council (consisting of nine family members), recognizing the need for help, approached the family and explained that the family needed to hire a neutral party who could facilitate productive discussions to help the family determine the best path forward. A vote was held on whether to hire a professional facilitator, and the family agreed through a vote of a significant majority of the family members. The family council asked for approval to create a Request for Proposal (RFP) document that would be sent to three or four potential facilitators, asking each to outline the process they would use to help the family resolve its current challenges. Then the family council would rank the candidates and interview the top two candidates. The family council would then select the candidate it felt could best meet the needs of the family. The family approved this process.

In each of these scenarios, there was a person, persons, or formal body of the family willing to step up and lead the family toward use of an outside resource. While this is not effective in all situations and should be approached with the greatest of respect for the feelings of family members, when the family is not functioning properly, someone will need to initiate the effort to bring in a professional facilitator.

Sometimes, when the family members who see the need for outside facilitation are members of the junior generation minor stockholders, the senior generation or major stockholders may need to be introduced to the concept. Some ways that these family members in more powerful positions can be oriented to the concept of using an outside facilitator include:

- Sharing an article or book that focuses on planning in a family enterprise and requesting a discussion of the concept after the senior family members have finished the reading.
- Having a current trusted family or business advisor approach the senior family members and present the concept; the recommendation would thus come from a neutral party.
- Invite the senior family members to a presentation, seminar, or workshop that focuses on how enterprising families can address both family and business needs.
- If you are aware of other families who have used professional facilitation successfully, ask the senior family members to meet with a representative of a family who has had positive experiences.

Professional Facilitation versus Therapy

There may come a time when the difficulties a family experiences are so significant that you may be unsure whether a professional facilitator or psychological assistance is needed. Indeed, it is not uncommon for the professional facilitator to have a background in either psychology or family therapy. And there can be much emotional healing if the facilitation helps resolve the causes of family stress. Nevertheless, there are times when psychological help should be considered.

When an individual family member is experiencing significant emotional turmoil that has resulted in increased stress, ailments such as depression or anxiety, suicidal thinking, or destructive drug and alcohol use, a trained therapist can provide support and help strengthen coping skills. Especially if the family is resistant to the use of outside facilitation and if the individual seeing the family dysfunction is experiencing any of the above symptoms, the perspective and support gained from a therapeutic relationship can strengthen the individual. As the individual gains strength, he or she may learn how to detach from the family conflict. In this process, the individual's improved health will help stimulate change in the family. However, changing the family should not be the primary motivation. Instead, gaining support and clarity and functioning capacity for the individual should be the motivating factor.

We know of many families that use a family business consultant to address the family's business needs and use psychologists, couples counselors, and family therapists to address the needs of individuals in the family or those of family subgroups, especially on issues that are separate from the business enterprise. This added support can help the individual family members gain strength to be again full participants in working through the family business matters before them. Thus, it can be very helpful to request that the family business consultant and therapist speak to each other to make sure that they are not working at cross-purposes. When making this request, the therapist and family business consultant will ask for a release of information that allows the therapist to speak about the situation to another party.

Locating and Vetting a Professional Facilitator or Family Business Consultant

There are many consultants and business advisors serving the needs of business-owning families. Unless you are familiar with the facilitators and family business consultants used by other satisfied enterprising families, finding the right one for you may seem like a daunting task. Most families assign one or more persons as the search committee to locate a professional facilitator. When the search committee begins exploring hiring a professional facilitator or family business consultant, you should feel comfortable asking the family business advisor a number of questions to make sure the person is properly qualified to serve your family's needs. What follows is a list of twenty questions to help you vet a potential facilitator. It is not necessary to ask all the questions, and often responsibility for certain key questions is assigned to various members of the committee.

Twenty Questions to Ask Family Advisor Candidates

1. Do you offer family business advising exclusively? If not, what other products or services do you provide?
2. How long have you been a family business advisor?
3. How are you different from others in your fields?
4. Describe your experience with multigenerational families.

5. What is your highest level of academic training?
6. What steps have you taken to be considered qualified to do this work?
7. How do you stay abreast of the latest developments in your fields, for example, business strategy and family dynamics?
8. What are your values and beliefs about working with clients? Why do you do this work?
9. Can you provide examples of situations you have encountered that might relate to ours? What were your goals, what did you do, and what was accomplished by the business family?
10. Can you provide an example of when you were not successful?
11. Describe how you have helped successfully engage members who have become more distant or are reluctant participants.
12. Please provide an example of where you encountered a very sensitive family issue that you had not anticipated.
13. Who will you go to if you are working with our family and you need additional insight to help us?
14. How long do you usually work with business families?
15. What makes your approach and experience uniquely suited to our needs?
16. How do you verify quality control in your practice?
17. How often do you open yourself up for peer review, and who does the review?
18. Do you carry professional liability insurance?
19. How many books or articles have you written on relevant matters?
20. If you are unable to continue your work with our family, what is your succession plan? Who would we work with in that situation?

Answers to these questions will help you determine whether the candidate you are considering is a good fit for your family. Once the search committee has interviewed the family advisor or several potential advisors, we recommend that you take the time to review reactions to the interviews, then meet to discuss the results and make a decision on how best to proceed.

Appendix 6 (Family Advisor Candidate Rating Form) presents a rating system, developed by The Family Business Consulting Group that you can use to record your reactions after each interview. It may be helpful if each member of the search committee is given a blank rating form for each candidate to be interviewed; then each can take five to ten minutes after each interview to complete the rating sheet while the information is still fresh.

11

Transitions in the Family Council

Ronaldo had done a great job as the first chairman of Garcia family's family council. Not only had he built trust among his large family, but they were doing things that even a few years ago would not have been possible. Among the group's accomplishments under his leadership were the support and staffing of a strong independent board to govern the company, the start of annual family meetings to strengthen relationships among cousins previously distant from each other, and clarity around the family's employment expectations for those interested in working in the business. In addition, the family council was in the process of beginning to gain unity around the concept of a formal family office instead of the current informal family office that was run out of the main operating company. Ronaldo had much to show for his efforts over the past three years. But the Garcia family had initially adopted a policy that the family council chair should be replaced every three years to allow fresh ideas and new energy to emerge. Ronaldo was concerned that the new family council chair may not share his vision for the family office and feared that the family's progress could be stunted if the new leader was ineffective. Tomorrow morning at the family association meeting, the family would elect a new family council chair and his term would end.

Building momentum in a family council takes passion and energy. Once a council is up and running, the task of the family is to keep productive energy levels high and momentum moving forward. At any given time, a family council or one of its bodies (committees or task forces) has numerous routine activities in play (such as setting up the next meeting) as well as several core initiatives that it is implementing (for example, establishing a family office). Current leaders may feel quite comfortable with the group's activities, but progress may be threatened if the family council group is facing a leadership transition or even a significant transition in its membership. In this chapter we will consider ways to prepare for and conduct smooth transitions in the family council.

Preparing the Family for Transition

Most of the literature on leadership transition focuses on the role of the incoming and outgoing leaders, but in a family council the family itself is often the key to a successful transition. If the family is unclear on the timing, process, and qualifications that will be used to bring new members into family council membership or leadership, missteps can result that are at a minimum frustrating and could lead to rifts in the family. For example, if the family is electing a new family council chair, and one of the in-laws volunteers to be the next chair, sudden discussion about whether or not a spouse can chair the family council will likely cause hurt for the in-law who may feel devalued and perhaps singled out. It can take years for a family to recover from such an incident.

Well in advance of key transitions on the family council, the prepared family will take time either at a family council meeting or through a task force meeting to define the role of both its leaders and members (see also chapter 9). After gaining clarity on the roles, the family approaching transition will clearly specify qualifications for individuals who wish to hold the role or roles concerned. For example, the following is a list of qualifications agreed upon by members of the Shank family.

By agreeing up front as to what the qualifications are, potential Shank family leaders have a clearer picture of whether they are qualified, and the family has criteria with which to assess whether a candidate is ready

---

- An active member of the Shank Family Association for at least four years
- Effectively chaired at least one family committee or task force
- Demonstrates commitment to the betterment of the Shank family
- Can take multiple perspectives on an issue and is willing to subordinate his or her own self-interest for the well-being of the family
- Champions the Shank family's values

Figure 11.1   Chair Role Qualifications: Shank Family Council

and qualified to serve in the position concerned. More important, the criteria serve as a means of unifying expectations about what is required of the family's leaders. The value of having the family aligned on expectations cannot be overstated. Alignment regarding expectations is like a lubricant that helps family transitions move forward with minimal friction.

Families also need to understand how a transition is to occur. Knowing the process that is going to be used to bring a new member into leadership or membership reduces anxiety and allows each family member to mentally prepare for the shift that is being planned. If a family meets every six months, as many families do, then at the meeting before a significant transition, the family council chair can prepare the family by identifying upcoming transitions, reminding the family about the process that will be used to make the transition, and sharing any applicable qualifications and role descriptions. John Shank, the Shank family's family council chairman, helped his family make a smooth transition when it came time to begin thinking about his replacement. Here are excerpts from his encouraging talk to the family association:

> As you know, I will be stepping down as the chair of our family council at our family meeting next October in Naples. Now is the time for those of you interested in serving as the next family council chair to begin thinking about the opportunity. I'm available to answer any questions you have today or anytime about the role of the chair and the things I have been working on. Just give me a call.
>
> Here is a quick reminder of the job qualifications we agreed to last year (shows PowerPoint slide of figure 11.1 and reads the qualifications). In our family council charter, we ask those interested in serving as chair to notify the outgoing chair within two weeks of the upcoming meeting so we can get your names on the ballot.
>
> During the October meeting, we will give each person interested in the position an opportunity to tell the family why they would like to serve as chair, remind the family of different leadership positions they may have held, and answer questions from association members.
>
> Then we will have the vote, with each family association member having one vote, which we will cast on ballots. The new chair will be announced at the end of the meeting and will assume the role of chair after the October meeting is over. I will stay on as an advisor to the new chair for the first few months to help with the transition.
>
> "Does anyone have any questions or concerns about the process?"

While it might seem that John was just informing the family about the process being used, what he was really doing was getting out in front of the process and making sure that everyone is clear on how the transition would occur. He knew that elections aren't something the family did at every meeting, and he wanted to make sure that everyone got a chance to speak up about differing views regarding the election process for his very large family of three generations. If anyone raised a concern, it would be much better for the family to have it sorted out well in advance of the election.

The Shank family was a large family that needed a formal process, but many smaller families may not need quite so much formality for a leadership transition. In a small family leaders may simply say that their leadership term ends at the next family council meeting and ask if anyone is interested in filling the role. Leaders may also ask for nominations, so potential candidates have a chance to be affirmed by other family members. Still, we recommend talking the group through the selection or election process to ensure a smooth transition.

Many family members grow quite accustomed to letting others lead and may not even be thinking about serving on a family council or other family group. Rarely is this simply a matter of being too busy to serve, as everyone is busy with jobs, volunteer work, social lives, and other family events. Often, people simply do not see themselves in a leadership role and cannot envision a more active level of participation. However, this is truly lost family potential; even the quietest or least experienced family member has something valuable to contribute. Family leaders prepare the family for upcoming transitions when they identify underutilized potential in the family and begin a dialogue about serving. Inviting family members to observe a meeting is an excellent way to start this process, but sometimes a simple recognition of a person's value and a little encouragement will engage a family member who has mostly been on the sidelines.

Astute family council leaders will keep track of each family group leader's intentions to either continue serving or transition. For a small family group, this is likely clarified in a quick call or discussion. In a larger family, one with a formal charter stipulating qualifications and more formal voting, the family council leader will at least know when leaders are up for reelection and should prepare for the transitions. Just as important is verifying periodically—at least annually—that each family committee and task force is being lead as well as possible and that the current leaders and members are willing to continue serving the family in this capacity. While the entire family is responsible for making sure that family leadership positions are filled, the family council chair should assume leadership for reinforcing or changing leaders of subgroups as needed. This is all part of preparing the family for transition. Imagine the potential turmoil if everyone showed up at a meeting and an entire committee tendered its resignation. The loss in continuity would be a blow to the family process. While such things sometimes happen, preparing the family in advance will at least ease anxieties.

Preparing New Leaders for Transition

Often a family group has already decided who will be its next leader well in advance of the transition. When this is the case, there is ample time to make the transition smooth for the person taking on the new responsibility. For significant leadership changes, we recommend a time period when both leaders share responsibilities if this is possible. The current leader assumes primary responsibility, and the incoming leader assumes secondary responsibility until the day of the official transition, becoming oriented to the position. Pictorially, the transition would look as shown in figure 11.2.

This approach helps the new leader to learn many of the so-called secrets about upcoming job responsibilities, and the family begins gradually seeing the new leader as someone who will lead the family even before that person takes on actual responsibility. This orientation period could take as little as a few short meetings or could last for a period of months.

The areas usually addressed during the orientation period are highlighted in the following checklist (see figure 11.3), which is designed for the orientation of a family council chair but can be modified to fit any family council leadership transition. This is a systematic way to ensure that key areas are discussed.

We recommend an orientation period before the new leader standing before the group and begins leading any initiatives, which will occur later during the transition period. This is to allow the family's first experience with the new leader to be one of confidence in the new leader's

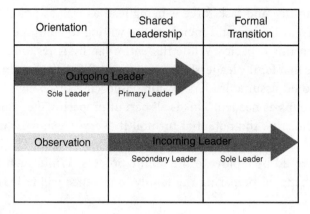

Figure 11.2   Sample Leadership Transition

- Review significant accomplishments during the past two years
- Review current projects underway, including progress on all committees and task forces
- Review direct reports to the position and note any concerns
- Discuss best methods for communicating with family council members, the greater family, the board chair, and the CEO
- Review of all guiding documents and document management processes, including passwords
- Discuss all repeating responsibilities of the position
- Review budget procedures and process for addressing funding and expenditures
- Share key contact information of the family and other important contacts

Figure 11.3   New Family Council Chair Orientation Checklist

abilities, rather than one of doubt, which might result if the incoming leader steps up before understanding the role and its intricacies.

The second stage is a transition period in which leadership will be shared between incoming and outgoing leader, with primary responsibility falling on the outgoing leader until the actual transition date. During this period, the new leader will begin leading in communications with the family and may also facilitate a portion or portions of family meetings. These first few segments facilitated by the new leader should not be highly controversial or polarizing discussions but only those most likely to lead to successful resolution. The new leader may also provide directions to the family regarding logistics matters during meetings. This gives the incoming leader an opportunity to earn family members' respect as a leader by taking on ever greater responsibilities with the encouragement and under the supervision of the outgoing family leader. A shared leadership stage is especially useful in family council chair transitions.

While not every leadership transition will require this formal approach, especially in situations where a family leader has held the role for a significant period of time and has performed well, the successor can gain much from a thoughtful approach to orientation (see also chapter 9).

Managing Elections

Small families are likely to approach elections rather informally, simply asking who would like to be considered as the next family leader and using a simple consensus procedure to affirm a candidate as leader. When more than one individual is interested in leading, it is not unusual for the interested parties to agree on either rotating the position (thus making sure that there will be someone to step up after the first person has finished his or her term) or to consider co-leadership (see chapter 9 for a discussion of co-leadership). As long as the family can agree on a new candidate, consensus decision making is generally transparent and effective.

In larger families, especially those that have representative family councils, elections can become quite cumbersome and even thorny. Misunderstandings and ambiguity can lead to resentment when someone feels hurt by an unorganized process that is deemed unfair. Hanging chads and uncounted ballots cause upset and anger among the masses in national political elections. The effect is more personal when a family election becomes chaotic because all involved are members of the same family and will see each other at future family events. Thus, large families need clear election rules to provide a stable platform for the transition of family leaders.

Before the meetings at which elections will take place, the current family council chair typically conducts a mock election to make sure that all nuances have been prepared for adequately. He or she will answer several questions to guarantee a smooth election, for example:

1. What positions will we be voting on at this upcoming meeting?
2. Have I made family members aware of the positions that will be voted upon?

3. Is the family clear on the qualifications for available positions?
4. How will individual names be submitted for consideration; if a slate of nominees will be used, who will determine the slate?
5. Will we allow nominations from the floor, or must a person be nominated in advance (and by when)?
6. Will candidates be required or invited to share biographical or other information, and when will they do this?
7. How will the ballots be produced and introduced to the family, and who will do this?
8. Will proxies be used, and how will they be produced and collected?
9. What will be the method of tallying ballots, and what will we do if there is a tie or a ballot that is not filled out correctly?
10. How will we announce the results, and when?

Figure 11.4 shows voting rules for a large family; these rules are part of this family's governance documents.

Votes before the family assembly will be made according to the following principles and procedures:

- Active family assembly members who have attended at least one previous family assembly meeting are entitled to one vote
- The family council chair will run all elections, except in cases where the current family council chair is being considered for a position. In this case, a different member of the family council will run the election
- Candidates will be identified for the specific office they are seeking
- Terms will be identified by the person running the election
- Candidates will be given an opportunity to make a brief statement before the family assembly if they desire
- Candidates will be assumed to be voting for themselves and will not participate in the vote
- All candidates will step outside of the room during the actual vote
- Votes will be cast by a show of hands, unless a member of the family requests an anonymous vote, in which case each voting family member will receive one ballot on which to vote
- Votes will be tallied by the person running the election, with at least one witness to the counting of ballots
- In the event of a tie, the standing family council chair will cast the deciding vote with the stipulation that candidates under consideration will recuse themselves from the family council vote

---

Figure 11.4   Rules for Voting in Elections

You are voting on the three people you would like to sit on the family council for the term running from August 2011 to August 2014. Place an "X" next to three (3) of the following individuals to serve as your family council representatives. The three candidates receiving the highest number of votes will begin their terms upon the conclusion of today's meeting.

__John Anthony   __Laura Thomas   __Sam Thomas

__Alyssa Williams   __Blake Williams   __Josh Williams

__Ryan Williams

Figure 11.5 Ballot

While the family council chair is generally the person in charge of elections, he or she may delegate this task to an individual or family group either on a permanent basis or on a one-time basis, such as when the election involves the current family council chair and he or she must recuse himself or herself from overseeing the process.

Earlier in this chapter, we considered the excellent job John Shank had done to prepare his family for the upcoming elections. We support family leaders spelling out the process for everyone to understand, as John did. Furthermore, in large families the ballot itself can serve as a tool for clarifying the election process. Consider the example of the ballot one family used (see figure 11.5).

Including some process definition on the actual ballot will further anchor the family in the processes to which they have agreed.

Continuity of Projects When Passions Differ

Frequently, the undertakings of family leaders are a reflection not only of their interests for the family's well being but also of their own personal passions and interests. It is natural for incoming leaders to have differing passions and interests that will fuel their initiatives. This is not a problem but provides an opportunity for the family as a whole to benefit from the passions of its leaders. It does, however, present challenges during times of transition. Projects that fizzle out lead to disappointment and apathy among family members. Completed projects lead to feelings of accomplishment and confidence in the family.

Planning for project completion is important for the family's sense of success.

We have already discussed the need for new leaders to understand roles, responsibilities, and projects that are under way. New leaders have a responsibility to see projects already begun through to completion. Projects are under way when they have been identified as a need by the family or family group, when a plan has been developed to achieve a specific outcome, when financial resources have been allocated, or when a family group or individual has been assigned to complete the task. Initiatives meeting all these criteria should be continued unless the family agrees to move in a different direction. If only a few of these criteria are met, the incoming and outgoing leaders can discuss the matter and decide how best to proceed.

When the outgoing leader is personally passionate about a project, one possible resolution is to have that leader continue on as project leader. The incoming leader then assumes all other responsibilities of the family council leader role. The outgoing leader would then report to the incoming leader or an appropriate family group until the project is completed. For example, prior to stepping down as the family council chair, Bill had initiated an effort to teach personal financial management skills to the family. His own background in education fueled his desire to make sure that all family members—including the younger generation—were educated on how best to manage their personal finances. He believed that it would lead to becoming more effective owners in the future and would lessen unrealistic demands for continuously increasing dividends. The incoming chair, Kathleen, was equally passionate about many new initiatives she hoped to include in the family's agenda. They agreed that Bill would continue with the financial education initiative and report directly to the family council (they did not have a formal education committee; otherwise, his activities would have fallen under the auspices of the family education committee).

Sometimes the initiative that is under way might deserve an ongoing committee that reports to the family council. Had Bill and Kathleen determined to expand the financial education effort to a more broadly defined ongoing effort to educate the family on many topics, a formal family education committee of the family council could have been formed to address this need. The family education committee would then need to develop a charter and establish roles and goals for its members. This would be a means to establish a permanent functioning committee, and Bill could have even been elected to membership or leadership of that committee.

But let's assume that Bill and a few family members were interested in the financial education component only, and Kathleen did not wish to pursue a more general education platform. In this case, the family council could have agreed to have Bill lead a financial education task force together with other interested family members, and this task force would then identify goals and objectives, including a schedule for the project. Kathleen could have presented the concept to the family and empowered Bill and his task force to continue the effort. After the task force had delivered the education and met its goals—thus contributing one more achievement to the family council—it could then be disbanded.

The above-mentioned methods are all legitimate and are based on nourishing family passions and creating a sense of continuity from one family leader to the next. Unless the family has changed priorities and chosen together to stop an initiative, completing the project is the best path forward.

Special Transitions

Up to this point, we have focused on transitions involving family group leaders and members. There are several special types of transitions that every family encounters and that require attention: including new family members in the family process and recognizing outgoing family leaders.

Including newcomers. Most business families do not think much about how to include new family members. Typically, most families bring in new family members through birth (or through adoption) and raise their offspring over time; in addition, family members bring in spouses and relationship partners gradually over time. In this way, young children, new spouses, and partners slowly get used to the family's beliefs, culture, and mores. If we compare this type of introduction to exposure to a steady drip, then coming into strong enterprising family for the first time without adequate preparation is more like standing in the path of a fire hose. Sensitivity and preparation are both needed.

In enterprising families, younger family members are typically shielded from the entire family process until they reach a certain age—often as young as fourteen or sixteen or even late teens or early twenties. Though young family members may be present at the meeting location (after all, some resorts have many activities for young family members to bond) before this time, they are not usually exposed to what happens in family meetings. They don't understand the terms used by the family; financial statements and concepts would be daunting or even terrifying to them, and family disagreements may be interpreted as threatening. While they may know the beliefs, culture, and mores of the family from having grown up as family members, when entering into the formal meeting process, the environment may seem unfamiliar and produce feelings of anxiety or incompetence.

New spouses and partners face an even steeper learning curve. Most likely they have grown up in families that do not meet formally, and the family meeting process may be very unnerving as they struggle to figure out the intricacies of their roles (wondering if they have a voice in the meeting) and often complex family dynamics. This is a time when bad initial experiences can lead to years, even decades, of bitter feelings. We believe there is a better option and favor a more systematic and educational approach to introducing new members to the family process.

Spencer Valpora, the Valpora family's family council chair, had decided that the family needed a way to successfully integrate new family members into the family council. There were seven members of his generation on the family council, and they were approaching the age when marriage proposals would be most likely to occur. As the oldest member of the second generation—his three uncles had started the business together many years earlier—his own experience of bringing his wife into the process was cumbersome and disorganized. He was committed to avoid repeating this experience with his younger siblings and cousins in the second generation.

The Valpora family's orientation process was developed by the family council in Spencer's first year as chair of the family council. The first person to utilize the orientation process happened to be his younger brother's new wife, Maggie. First, a member of the senior generation met with Maggie to talk with her about the values of the family and the goals of family council meetings and to learn more about Maggie. This was helpful as the senior family member assigned to Maggie was a spouse who had entered the family as a new member several years earlier. Next, Spencer—the family council chair—met with Maggie to orient her to the meeting process and familiarize her with the family's guiding documents. She asked lots of questions and felt she understood what the family was trying to accomplish. She was also given an overview of the business so she would better understand discussions at the upcoming family council meeting next month. Then, at her first meeting, the senior family member she had met with stood before the family council and shared what she had learned and appreciated about Maggie, thus formally introducing Maggie and welcoming her into the family council.

The last component of the family orientation process involved meeting with a member of her generation who had been assigned to mentor Maggie by showing her the ropes. While they met only twice in the first year and mostly just got to know each other, Maggie felt deeply valued by the family because it had made this support available.

Most families do not have this much formality when welcoming newcomers. Spencer's decision to create such a formal process grew out of his own frustrations and the complexity of his growing family. More commonly, we see families adopt a simple orientation to the family process by just assigning a mentor, offering training in how to read financial statements, reinforcing confidentiality, providing a brief orientation to the family's meeting processes, or merely having the newcomer's spouse introduce the newcomer to the family's way of doing things. The need for additional structure will be determined by a number of variables. We favor a more structured approach under the following conditions:

- when the family is large and the asset structures are complex;
- when the family council is highly active with numerous committees and/or task forces;
- when the newcomer is from a family that did not own a business and thus may not be familiar with the need to meet and deliberate on decisions;
- when the family meetings frequently include conflictual interactions that may be confusing to the new member; and
- when the family has many underlying family dynamics it struggles to manage effectively.

In our experience, there is no one right way that will work for every newcomer. A very private newcomer may be uncomfortable standing before the group to introduce herself and may prefer to just observe for a few meetings. A new spouse who is a financial advisor would likely not appreciate sitting in on an session entitled "Introduction to Financial Statements." The most effective orientations are welcoming, flexible to meet the needs of the newcomer, and conducive to two-way learning. On this latter point, enterprising families can have powerful cultures, and many families focus so much on the newcomer learning their culture and values that they forget to learn about the newcomer's family and heritage. Asking the incoming family member about his or her background creates a feeling of being valued by the family.

Approaches to farewells. Just as welcoming a new member is an important transition, recognizing outgoing family council leaders and members is an important transition to manage well. When a family council leader has served the family for many years, honoring that person reinforces the value of family leadership to the rest of the family and provides a clear transition that can further empower successors to the position. Gifts of appreciation are often presented by the new family leader in front of a family council or family association meeting along with heartfelt thanks for the exiting leader's service. This gives the exiting leader a chance to speak before the family one last time and marks an official end to his or her leadership term.

Some creative ways of saying goodbye include a fun song or poem presented in front of the family association, a round of toasts to the outgoing leader at a celebratory family meal, or a donation from the family's foundation in the name of the outgoing leader to a cause he or she is passionate about.

Perhaps the most significant transition in a family council is the formal exit of a senior family member. While most families do not have an official retirement date for serving on a family council or participating in family association activities, sometimes a senior leader wishes to step down officially from active participation in formal family activities. In managing these departures, families wrestle with two competing schools of thought: fading away slowly versus going out with a bang.

Families opting for a strategy of fading away believe that the family is better off if the exiting senior family member just slowly reduces involvement so that his or her exit is hardly noticeable. New family members assume more and more leadership and the senior member essentially "sneaks out the back door," letting the rest of the family carry on with little fanfare. This decision often just emerges as new life pursuits or limited energy lead to the decreased involvement. At other times, the exiting family member may plan this type of exit with the family council leadership so as to limit any anxieties or fears the collective family may have about going forward without the senior member and minimize feelings of loss. After the time of fading out, the exiting family member will usually continue to be present at family events but no longer be part of formal family meetings.

Families opting for a strategy of "going out with a bang" believe that celebrating the family's accomplishments, including the many years of senior members' family service, is best for the family. These families typically set aside time at the exiting member's last meeting to celebrate him or her and share their respect for the years of participation and personal contributions. They will usually present a gift that is meaningful to the person (for example, a picture signed by everyone, a donation made in that person's name, a piece of art, or an item to add to a collection held by the person exiting) and spend time telling stories of the senior member's accomplishments. While there may be some roasting, most comments will focus on all that the person has done for the family, and individuals will share stories about how they were positively influenced by the person. Emphasizing the person's legacy in the family is the primary focus of the send-off.

Regardless of the method, or mixture of methods, you choose, the choice should be made with the exiting person's input and the best interests of the family in mind.

12

Connecting the Family Council with the Board and the Business

For the family council to be effective, it must be a viable and constructive resource for the family. To achieve its full potential, however, the family council should also work effectively with other structures and functions, notably with the owners and managers of the business. In this chapter we describe the different ways a family council integrates, supports, and adds overall value to the entire system of family, owners, and the enterprise.

Family Council's Coordination with Owners and Management

We have previously discussed how the family council connects to, serves, and is held accountable to the broader family. What follows below is a description of how the family council coordinates with and connects to the owners and their board and to management. This is not just a one-way process; that is, the family council not only coordinates with the other two bodies, but they in turn are responsible for coordinating with the family council. For example, if issues come up, such as a family conflict or an interest on the part of the owners to increase dividends or distributions from the company, what is the role of the family council, the board, and management? Two cases are provided to illustrate the distinct responsibilities of each entity, and also highlight where there is confusing overlap. Detailed accounts of the Tate and the DuBois family councils introduce how family councils and their leaders establish proactive policy and procedures and then how they behave with all the other entities when the policies are tested by conflict.

A Family Conflict: The Tate Family Council Case

Advance preparation. The Tates, for example, have a Harvest Table family council (see chapter 3): a representative group of five family members from the second and third generations, one from each branch of the family. Each year they hold one family assembly meeting attended by all spouses and children and offering planned sessions for all age groups. When the family needs to make decisions affecting the entire family, the family members convene the family association, consisting of all family members over the age of fourteen and their spouses, to ratify policies and agreements and to elect family council members. They also use this time for the shareholders to meet, which happens usually on the day after the family assembly and association meetings. They have a board of directors, which is chaired by a family member, Sarah Tate, and includes three independent directors; the company's CEO is a member of the second generation. It is a close family centered on the five second-generation siblings, and they are also a trusting family.

The Tate Family Council anticipated that family conflicts would need to be managed well and long ago adopted procedures and policy. The family began by establishing a philosophy on conflict that ran counter to its usual style of dealing with differences, which was to avoid them and act as if they did not exist.

The Tates' adopted conflict philosophy was to recognize that legitimate conflicts and mistakes will occur and will produce unavoidable emotional reactions. Furthermore, they established an overall expectation that conflicts would not go unaddressed but would be resolved by those involved and that it was the family's responsibility to see that resolutions were pursued and achieved.

Of course, the Tates also realized that it would not be enough for everyone agreeing to the new philosophy, and thus they proceeded to create policy and procedures for conflict resolution and identified educational and developmental resources to provide the skills and confidence needed. Finally, they circulated their drafts to all family members who were eligible to participate in the family association. After discussion and modifications, a code of conduct and the philosophy, policy, and procedures for conflict resolution were adopted in a family association meeting.

One step that was especially helpful during the process was a surprise to both the chair of the board and the CEO. The family council chair, Melissa Tate, contacted them independently and asked if they would each review copies of the draft policy and of the code of conduct. Both responded with a question of why they should be involved in something that was a family matter. Melissa persisted and was able to get two valuable ideas. The chair of the board pointed out that the independent directors on the board might be a source for objectivity if needed in a significant family dispute, and the CEO offered ideas about where the family might get access to training on conflict, negotiation, and communication skills. Furthermore, the CEO invited the human resource manager to the discussion, who made suggestions about how training programs could be conducted during family association meetings and what might be available to individuals and groups outside the meetings. Not only were good ideas the result, the family council chair reasoned that these interactions also set the stage for a shared interest and investment in family harmony, unity, and continuity.

A second step on the part of the family council was to ask themselves about the owners, specifically, "Do they have a good agreement among themselves that supports the conflict resolution philosophy the family wants to adopt?" This question seemed a little beyond the scope of the family council when it was first discussed, but family council members realized that an unfair or outdated shareholder agreement would not support resolution of ownership disputes, and could even fuel them. The board chair was asked to understand the family's interest in productively dealing with conflicts and to consider the offer to review the shareholder agreement and provide suggestions.

The family council's offer was turned down, and they were informed that recently the lead shareholders in the five families had discussed the shareholder agreement and come to the conclusion that it was good enough. No one was interested in getting it out again and making changes. The message from Sarah, the chair of the board, to her sister Melissa, the family council chair, was that it would be too much work for too little gain: "If we open that can of worms, we might not be able to reseal it." Melissa's words to the family council before they moved on to a new topic were, "We gave it a good try, and, who knows, they may be right."

Conflict arises. Robert Tate's family branch had come to the conclusion among each other that the business performance was below potential, and these family members were critical of the CEO's direction of the company. The fact that the CEO was Robert's brother led to a tense atmosphere between the two family branches. Discussions extended throughout the family, with some members taking a neutral position, some offering solutions, some trying to sweep the conflict under the carpet, and some siding with the CEO's branch while others sided with Robert's branch.

Fortunately, one of the recommendations circulating in informal family discussions was that the family council ought to get involved, and it did. The family council chair called a meeting that included the following agenda items:

1. Do we have agreement that it is appropriate for the family council to become involved?
2. Are we as a family following the code of conduct, policy, and procedures we had agreed on?
3. Where there are inconsistencies between behavior in the family and policy, how might we encourage compliance and hold individuals and branches accountable for following policy?
4. Do we need any help? What resources are available to us?
5. What action do we agree to and how might we follow up?

The family council agreed that for various family members to be holding informal discussions as advocates of positions, curious listeners, advice givers, or judges was not productive and ran counter to the "no triangulation" section of the family's code of conduct. The backchannel discussions would escalate the conflict. Furthermore, the family council determined that the initial steps of their conflict resolution policy, "for two family members with a conflict to first discuss it directly," while generally a good first step, was not an appropriate step now, and so they wisely did not recommend it for this particular conflict. Finally, their initial view was that this conflict was between two family members and their respective family branches and thus a matter concerning the family council, but they came to the conclusion that the solution was to be found in the boardroom. They agreed on the following three actions:

1. Write a letter to the family reminding everyone of the code of conduct and policy and of the responsibility of the family assembly, which had debated and ratified the policies, to uphold them, and

encourage each other to comply. Even more important, remind each individual to be accountable for adhering to procedures. The rest of the letter described what the family council's next steps were and when the family might be expected to hear of progress. Finally, the letter indicated that since this matter involved a potential performance issue, family members should not expect to know all the details because privacy had to be respected, but they should anticipate learning enough about the fairness of the procedures and details about the processes used to trust any conclusion. Thus, the implication was that family members should remain at arm's length to the process, yet expect to be very well informed about the steps.

2. The family council chair made a call to her brother Robert and asked that he personally speak to his family members and to reinforce among them adherence to the code of conduct and conflict resolution policies. She also indicated what she would pursue the matter with the board and asked for his patience.

3. Melissa's next call was to the board chair to confirm her knowledge of procedures used by the board to evaluate the performance of the CEO and to gain support for a plan she hoped would involve the independent directors.

When Melissa Tate was elected family council chair she had not anticipated making a call to her sister, the board chair, regarding a conflict of such magnitude between two brothers. Her sister Sarah was equally uncomfortable with the situation but was aware of it before getting the call from Melissa. She had known that the family council was meeting to discuss the topic and was anxious to hear of results. Melissa and Sarah agreed to the plan outlined below even though Melissa as family council chair understood that while they were coordinating, the plans were mainly in Sarah's area of responsibility, namely, the board.

1. Sarah would speak with their brother and inform him that the matter would be addressed by the board. Furthermore, she asked that he not take it personally, that he remain patient, and that he, like Robert, lead his family branch in respecting the family's communication guidelines set forth in the code of conduct and conflict resolution policies. She also assured him that his performance was not to be put into "family court" as she was committed

to following and respecting board protocols for performance reviews and privacy of confidential information.

2. Sarah would speak with the three independent directors to explore their perspectives on two options and perhaps identify other alternatives as a result. The two options she presented were to reinforce the existing performance review and metrics for company performance currently in place and used by the board to evaluate the CEO or to introduce an extra step, namely, a special, more thorough review of the company's performance and an associated special assessment of the CEO.

3. Sarah would also communicate with her brother Robert to reinforce adherence to the procedures and policies agreed to, basically reinforcing Melissa's earlier message to him, but let him know that the matter was the responsibility of the board.

4. Finally, Sarah sent an additional message to the family owners indicating that the issue of an owner being concerned about the management of an important asset was nothing unusual, and that it could be addressed in a way that would promote confidence. Furthermore, she stressed that the owners should do everything possible to limit the potential for this issue to become a threat to their solidarity as an owner group.

Based on the advice of the independent directors, Sarah's recommendation was that a special assessment be conducted of the performance of the business compared to goals and benchmarks and that they review the CEO's performance as well. This would be a recommendation to the full board for their consideration and discussion leading to a decision on a process. Moreover, the family council chair and the chair of the board agreed on a way of updating the family and the owners and the two brothers with appropriate information and news as the process unfolded.

The point of this example is to highlight how a family council can work with its constituency, primarily the family, and also interact and make contributions by working with the board. Even if this conflict had been initially acted on by the board, the family council and its chair could have coordinated much in the same way as described above with very similar steps and results. The key to coordination was the respect the board chair had for the responsibilities of the family council and the family council's deference to the board. The family council chair could have gone directly to the independent directors for advice, without involving the board chair, and in this case that would have been a mistake. Instead, the family council chair worked with the board chair to align their purposes and activities.

Granted, trust among family members plays a role in getting everyone to cooperate with procedures. The family council was influential with the family, first by leading the family members through a "what if" process that allowed them to agree on what they would do and how they expected to behave when a conflict occurs. Then, the family council reminded the family and individuals of their responsibilities to follow the procedures agreed upon. The family council had little involvement with management in this process and respected the role of the board. However, through coordination between the chairs of the board and of the family council a consistent message was sent and reinforced in all directions.

The following is a summary of the areas of primary responsibility for preparation as well as the steps for finding a solution to this conflict.

Planning and Preparation: Philosophy, Policy, and Procedures for Conflict Resolution

Family Association's Responsibilities

1. Authorize the family council
2. Get sufficiently involved to internalize the principles and philosophy of managing conflicts within the family
3. Ratify and support the conflict resolution policy and code of conduct

Family Council's Responsibilities

1. Propose a family philosophy regarding conflict for consideration and adoption by the family assembly
2. Propose a code of conduct and procedures and policy for conflict resolution
3. Design and facilitate family education, including skills for successful conflict avoidance and resolution
4. Perhaps also facilitate development of a shareholder agreement or modification of it if desired by the owners

Family Council Chair's Responsibilities

1. Facilitates the work of the family council
2. Manages the boundary between family council's draft policy preparation and the responsibility of the family assembly for understanding and support then leads the process of ratification of policies

Owners' Responsibilities

1. Maintain a fair and up-to-date shareholder agreement
2. Establish and maintain lines of communication and trust to support shareholder unity

Addressing a Conflict: How Best to Handle It

Family Association Members' Responsibilities

1. When a significant conflict is detected, refer it to the family council
2. Hold the family council accountable for its role in addressing a conflict
3. Maintain discipline within the family and hold each other accountable for behavior specified in the conflict resolution policy and the code of conduct

Family Council's Responsibilities

1. Recognizes significant family conflicts within the council's domain and evaluates whether the family is following procedures agreed upon
2. Communicates to individuals and the family as a whole what is expected
3. Recognizes when a solution process needs others, i.e., the board in this case, and seeks resources, i.e., objective independent directors, as needed
4. Plays a role in procedures to maintain trust, e.g., continually and appropriately updates the family and individuals, monitors adherence to the code and policy, and keeps the issue an active part of the family council dialogue

Family Council Chair's Responsibilities

1. Liaison with individual family members and the chair of the board
2. Takes a lead role in communicating with individuals and the family assembly and appropriately involves the board chair and the CEO

Owners' Responsibilities

1. Avoid allowing the issue to become divisive among owners
2. Let the board represent them and avoid interfering in its process

Board's Responsibilities

1. Hold family council accountable for family communication and adherence to policy
2. Consider option and role of objective resources as a potential contribution to a solution, i.e., independent directors, and manage their involvement
3. Conduct a transparent process that promotes trust while appropriately respecting privacy

Board Chair's Responsibilities

1. Communicates with complaining family owners, the owner group, the family council chair, and the CEO
2. Consults the independent directors
3. Places the issue on the board's agenda suggesting two courses of action:
   a. Continue with standard vigilance and evaluation procedures; or
   b. Conduct a special assessment.
4. Coordinates with the family council chair and communicates with the owners and the family assembly to inform them about the process, its reasons, and outcomes to expect from it so that they will resist direct interference.

Management's (CEO) Responsibilities

1. Abide by the processes and policy adopted by the family assembly (just like all family members)
2. Cooperate with the board

Structural Variations

Figure 12.1 indicates that due to the overlap of family and ownership, distinguishing pure ownership functions from family governance functions is not straightforward. In addition, changes over generations mean that what works at one point will not necessarily be appropriate in the future. Family councils will differ in the degree to which they represent the owners and the family, or are primarily representatives of the family only.

In figure 12.2 the family council is primarily concerned with family governance but will also address some ownership functions, for example the education and development required to prepare future owners. In this case, owners will manage their decision making and planning separately in shareholder meetings or meetings with the board and in some cases with an owners council.

For other business families, particularly those with few members, perhaps only the founders and their adult children (Dining Room and Negotiating Table family councils), there is so much overlap between

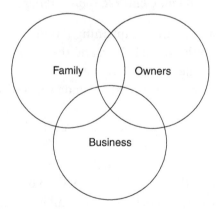

Figure 12.1 Overlap of the Roles of Family, Owners, and Business Management

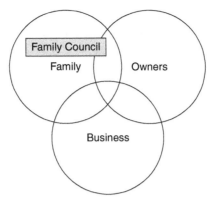

Figure 12.2 A Family Council with Responsibilities Separate from those of the Owners

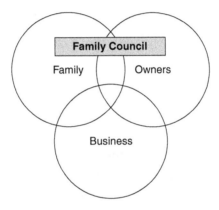

Figure 12.3 Family Council Representing Family and Owners

owners and the family that having separate functions is not practical. Figure 12.3 is an illustration of this case.

More Dividends: The Dubois Family Council Case

The Dubois Family Council is much as the one shown in figure 12.3; the family has a Negotiating Table family council (see chapter 3) consisting of the founding parents who are in their seventies, their three middle-aged children and spouses, and four third-generation college-aged grandchildren. Most Dubois family council meetings focus on business family issues, but when ownership issues emerge, they are not

immediately shut down because they belong in the domain of ownership. All of the owners are members of the family council and feel free to
discuss capital investment issues in front of everyone else; they feel this
is especially instructive for the third generation. Several family members work in the business, but the business has a non-family CEO. The
company's board consists of the three siblings, the CEO, and three independent directors who speak their mind and are valuable contributors
to business strategy sessions.

In a recent family council meeting, George Dubois, the youngest of
the three second-generation siblings, remarked, "In looking at this year's
projected profitability, I think we can double the shareholder distribution. Shall we vote on it?"

Preparation

One of the valuable contributions a family council can make even if the
owners do not manage this is to lead a process that places the owners in
alignment with one another regarding their expectations for the business's performance from the perspective of investors. A few years before
the meeting at which George made his remark, the family council had
worked through a process to produce a distribution policy. For some
families, the owners might have met separately from the family council; however, the Dubois owners discussed the issue with the rest of the
family as an observing audience. They first worked on a set of investment principles to which all owners could agree. Then they approached
the non-family CEO, shared their investment principles, and asked for
comments. They also asked for the perspective of the management team
on capital needs relative to strategic business opportunities.

In one very instructive session, the CEO presented two alternatives:
(1) slow growth without debt and minimal but dependable annual return
to shareholders or (2) aggressive growth funded with medium to high
debt and variable returns to shareholders. The CEO had an opinion about
management's preference, but recognized that the goal was an informed
decision by shareholders. The debate between the owners and the CEO
was fascinating, and a position developed that combined elements of the
two options. A draft of a distribution policy was also developed.

Next, the family council agreed that the owners needed to take the
policy to the board as a final step. It turned out that the board agreed

completely with the balance of capital costs, business strategy, and shareholder returns, and the policy was adopted. Thereafter, family council sessions included the CEO once per year and provided updates regarding initial assumptions and continuous learning on the part of all family members involved in the family council.

George Dubois Proposes Doubling the Distribution

There was no immediate reaction to George's recommendation; he had taken everyone by surprise. Some council members were thinking about the extra amount and what they might do with the money, some were wondering if the distribution policy covered George's request, others were concerned that George had brought this proposal up in the family council and thought it would have been more appropriate for a meeting of just the owners or a board meeting. Mark Fox had been chair of the family council for one year, a respected brother-in-law of George, and a successful business owner separate from the Dubois family business. He saw value in slowing the process down, getting more information for an informed decision, and determining whether the family council was the appropriate forum for the discussion. After the discussion facilitated by Mark, the following decisions and plans emerged:

1. No vote would be taken at this time.
2. The CEO would be invited to present management's views on capital deployment. Since the board chair was at the meeting, he volunteered to speak with the CEO.
3. A special family council meeting would be the forum for management's presentation so as to take advantage of the educational value of the discussion.
4. The owners would then make a decision among themselves and take the matter to the board.

The special family council meeting with the CEO was inconclusive. The management team had studied the options, and the CEO was unwavering in his opinion that any additional earnings should be applied to debt reduction. After the CEO had finished talking, George called for a meeting including just the owners so that they might make a decision, but this resulted in disagreement. Without Mark, the family council chair, facilitating, the meeting ended with George and the siblings' parents demanding a special distribution and George's two angry siblings siding with management's recommendation. Accusations were leveled in both directions, but the more personal attacks were directed at George; his siblings called him greedy and accused him of manipulating their parents.

If the question of a special distribution went to the board for a vote, George would need all three independent directors to vote with him to win; this was unlikely but he agreed that it was the appropriate next step. The family members also agreed that future discussions would be held in the family council because then they could be more productive. When Mark heard the plan, he had another suggestion: Instead of going to the board for a vote, the family council could invite the independent directors to discuss the proposal with all the owners and the members of the family council; this would be a special session. Everyone agreed, and Mark and the board chair were asked to arrange the meeting. Mark also recommended that the CEO be invited so his views could be heard in the forum, and since this constituted the entire board, the meeting was called as a special session of the family council and board of directors.

The special meeting, now involving for the first time the three independent directors, was productive and instructive. The younger third-generation family members found the discussion fascinating. The directors expanded the discussion to other ways of providing liquidity, in addition to offering their views on the question of a special distribution this year. As the discussion wound down, Mark asked each independent board member how he or she would vote if the matter was to be decided now. The independent directors were unanimous in saying that they would make a decision if and when the question comes before the board, but they preferred that the family owners make one more attempt to find unity rather than depend upon the independent directors at this time.

The meeting was adjourned, and as next step an additional meeting of the family council was planned to attempt a solution. It was suggested that the owners meet alone, but they once again reasoned that Mark's presence as well as that of spouses and children would set the stage for a more productive discussion and be educational as well. In the end, after much discussion in the last family council session and no consensus, the owners took a vote, and George's proposal was defeated. George, respecting the decision, did not put his request before the board and did not bring it up again. When the board chair proposed the standard distribution and called for a vote, George voted with the others and the proposal passed unanimously.

In the Dubois case, the family council is an integrated family council and shareholder group, so there was no liaison role for the family council chair to play. All shareholders and the chair of the board were in the room at all meetings of the family council. Meetings outside the family council were less functional, and thus the preference was for the owners to conduct their business with all family council members present. This has worked well for them. Their main challenge was to understand how best to involve others, respecting both the role of the board and that of management. In two cases, the family council served as the central forum to accommodate first management's presence and then a meeting with the full board.

Mark Fox, the family council chair, serves a valuable role as a facilitator, and he is very aware of the overall family dynamics. He understands the separate domains of different entities, plays a crucial role in connecting parts, and speeds up or slows down processes as needed. In this case Mark pursued multiple meetings, leading to frustration for George who wanted a decision, but Mark was determined to provide the younger family members and spouses with an education in how the board and management can coordinate with the family owners; he also wanted to develop their financial capabilities by exposing them to the wisdom of all available resources. Mark also made sure that the CEO was an appropriately active part of the policy development and the debate, thus avoiding any potential awkward conclusions management might adopt regarding the interests of the family owners and ensuring that the debate was based on correct information and ultimately producing alignment between all shareholders and management.

The future of the Dubois Family Council. In a few years, as the family gets larger and as ownership is transferred to the younger family members, the Dubois family will need to make changes. Because of the larger size of the family, family members will likely establish a representative family council, and at that time the scope of the family council will most likely shrink, with fewer responsibilities for ownership issues. When not all of the owners are on the family council, they may miss the organization provided by the family council, and from time to time they may enlist the family council's help to take advantage of its organized communication linkages with the family. Alternatively, the owners may enhance their level of organization by establishing an owners' council or by establishing a shareholder representative role to interact with the family council and the board.

Finally, with a representative family council, a family association will become the family's forum for getting all adult family members together. With many more members, overall alignment will become more of a challenge and impose new demands on the family council; there will be a need for new procedures and the skills and willingness on the part of individuals in leadership roles to coordinate with one another.

If the issue of a special distribution comes up again in the future with the associated greater degree of complexity, the family may not find it so easy to get the educational value from the debate. The owners could conduct the debate in shareholder meetings or special sessions and, of course, in the boardroom. The family council could again play a supporting role in developing shareholder unity, but financial and investment education and development of future owners would more likely come from institutional sources, such as seminars, presentations, workshops, and special projects.

Family Council, the Board, the Family Assembly, and Management

Family councils can informally coordinate with a board, management, the family, and the owners by taking advantage of the lines of communication afforded by common membership and family relationships. An owner is likely to be a member of the family council, of the board, and sometimes also a family member who is also part of management. Some family council charters go as far as to specify that at least one member must also be a board member and that one member should be a family member who works in the business. However, as the above examples illustrate, the interaction between entities such as the family council and the board depends upon the size of the family, the kind of family council (e.g., Dining Room versus Round Table), and the degree to which a family uses distinct, formal, organizing, and governance functions. For a family with an informal board and no formal shareholder function (i.e., shareholder meetings), there are many opportunities to facilitate family governance, business governance, and ownership alignment in

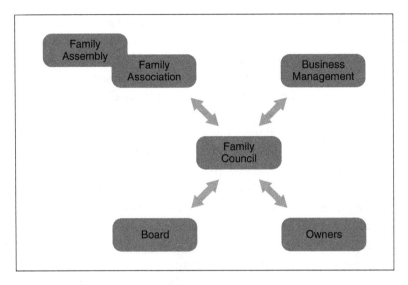

Figure 12.4   The Primary Entities with which the Family Council Interacts

the family council. More coordination is needed with larger families that have a distinct board of directors and even more so when there is an owners' council or shareholder representative to coordinate with the owners.

The Family Council and the Family Association

When a business family is large enough to have a family association and assembly, the family council represents them. Thus, their relationship is defined by how effectively the association and assembly of family members are being represented by the family council. It is a two-way street as family council members expect their constituent family members to do their part in the relationship and read materials, prepare for meetings, and support the family council in its representative governance function. That is, family members must resist all temptations to bypass or undermine the family council in any way. Maintaining a good relationship between a family council and the family association requires the family council to listen well and respond sensitively; it must pay attention to the family's explicit and implicit needs for information, explanations, involvement, education, and development and must anticipate needs arising from shifting dynamics and growth of the family. The family council formulates goals and objectives from what it has heard and provides the leadership needed for achieving goals. For example, based on its assessment of the family's needs, the family council may formulate developmental goals, such as improved understanding of financial information on the part of owners, greater family unity, integration of the younger generation into leadership roles, and increased commitment from all to continuity.

Much of the activity of a high-functioning, representative family council is to keep the family involved enough in what the council is doing so that there is not only support but sufficient commitment and involvement for the success of projects. For example, a policy on corporate assets use that has been well researched may be rendered completely worthless if the broader family has not been involved enough to own it as theirs and is not committed to following it.

Finally, the family association expects the family council to fulfill its governance function and produce results. If part of the family council's mandate is to address conflicts in the family, the family council is expected to be working on any conflicts that arise and to provide the positive outcomes expected. If a family member is having difficulty in his or her role in the business and rumors about this emerge in the community, the family council is expected to get involved. When the family council's purpose and goals are established, a good process is to conduct a periodic assessment of progress and communicate results to the family association.

The Family Council and Management

The family council is the official face of the family in interactions with management members who are not members of the family. This role of the family council is especially important if there are no family members working in the business, but even if there are, the family council should be the family's organized, unified voice. Consistent messages conveyed by the family council to management should include the family's values, its commitment to a long-term business focus, and its commitment to the continuity of responsible family ownership. Keeping management abreast of the family council's work to prepare younger family members and to manage potentially destructive conflicts contributes to management's loyalty and security.

Some family council activities call for management involvement, such as when a family employment policy is being developed or when the family first begins to play a role in corporate philanthropy.[1] Employment and the company's charitable contributions are within management's domain, but when family members become involved, collaboration is needed. Joint committees involving members of the family council and of management are a means of ensuring that necessary knowledge and perspectives are brought to a philanthropic strategy project and of laying the groundwork for effective implementation.

A family council can advance trusting and valuable relationships by inviting members of management to make presentations to the family council on new initiatives and aspects of the business the family is not familiar with. Direct exposure of management to an organized, well-functioning family council will have positive effects throughout the family and business. If there is only little exposure, this can lead to stereotyping and the formation of incorrect assumptions, but increased and direct exposure can reverse this effect. Members of the management team might be insecure during generational transition periods, and the family council can do much to communicate why and how the next generation will be responsible owners. Family councils can easily be so engrossed in preparing for and adjusting during succession that they forget about management. Just letting management know about their activities can be reassuring. An ideal but worthwhile goal of both the family council and management should be a cooperative relationship that results in the CEO genuinely regarding the family as a competitive advantage of the business.

Management also has an interest in reaching out to the family council to build a constructive relationship, to provide a source of information about the business, and to assist in other ways with family goals. For example, the management group can assist the family in reaching goals of developing future business leaders, finding ways to create developmental opportunities that do not conflict with the company's merit-based culture, and strengthening the development of passion for the business among future owners not involved in business operations. Management can also reach out to engage families in the joint goal of avoiding natural traps where management might become an unwitting accessory to a family conflict.[2] For example, management might ask to speak with the family council about the potential destructiveness of family members bringing non-family employees into their conflicts with each other. There are many traps to avoid with family employment, and these could be the basis for a valuable discussion with management members participating as guests in a family council meeting. Both the family and management members can learn together how better to work with and support one another.

Knowing when to reach out and include the family is a valuable skill on the part of the business leader. For example, when a significant change must occur to the core business, a savvy CEO will recognize the family's emotional attachment to the business the founder started and involve family members early on to inform them and lessen potentially negative reactions and also to invite their participation in any choices they might have. Management can engage with a family to find ways to capitalize on family relationships and social capital to enhance business competitiveness and the goodwill of employees and the community at large. When family members are asked to participate in these ways, they can see themselves as contributing to business problems and opportunities and seek further ways to align themselves with management on matters that benefit from both family and business perspectives. In addition to responding well to such initiatives on the part of management, family councils can indicate that such a relationship is expected and can work with management on ways to formalize it.

When management formally recognizes the purpose of the family council and seeks to utilize it, there will be pressure on the family council to improve its effectiveness. When management asks for family members' participation, this reinforces their value, and the family council will naturally want do its work well. When management brings engaging, appropriate challenges to the family council and participates with council members in working out solutions, management will be exposed to the family's values and the family in turn will be exposed to business realities. As both struggle with challenging problems and the challenges of working together, both management and the family council will get better, and each will become a more valuable in the eyes of the other.

The Family Council and the Board

Family councils that have a productive relationship with management must be clear about their relationship with the board; a direct connection to management should not bypass the board. Knowing when to go to or defer to the board is an important part of a family council's understanding of interrelationships. Just as with management, family councils performing well have a productive connection with the board.

Boards appreciate hearing one voice from a unified family on a number of issues, including the family's values, expectations about family employment and family leadership, and, in cases when the family council speaks for the owners, the family's expectations for business performance. The family council is especially valuable in its role of creating the unified family voice and communicating it to the board. Armed with clear direction, the board is then in a position to determine how best to apply a family position in its supervision of management and policy making. Though boards welcome the family's input, they are most interested in one position; the family's influence is marginalized when board members are subject to opposing positions from different family members who contact individual board members separately.

Whether a board consists of family members only or is an advisory board or a legal board of directors that includes independent directors, boards generally are more productive given when the family council provides clear statements, such as written policy recommendations. For example, a general statement that the family desires family members to occupy leadership roles is of less value to the board than a specific and complete policy recommendation with details on qualifications and compensation of family members seeking roles in the business. With a specific policy from the family council a board can listen also to management's viewpoint and then respond with an informed perspective. If there is a productive relationship between the board and the family, the board can communicate concerns about a request from the family or a recommended policy before acting on them. The family council can then reply with consideration of the board's reaction. For example, the board may ask about an ambiguous position on leadership, "The draft policy recommendation from the family council indicates a preference for a family member as a leader of the business; should it specify a preference for a qualified family member?" The family council is obliged to reply and provide greater clarity. Such dialogue between the board and family council serves to reinforce a collaborative relationship.

The board may call for unity when it hears conflicting requests from family shareholders or when unexplained impasses appear to have family dynamics at their core. An intense situation for the board is when family members not involved in business operations are in conflict with family leaders of the business, and the board finds itself in the middle. In such cases, the board may exert all its influence to persuade the family council to get involved to help manage or resolve the conflict. As in the Lamberti case described above, the family council and the board can be very effective collaborators in finding solutions to family conflict.

Like management, the board can make a contribution to its relationship with the family by reaching out to engage the family council in a discussion of goals and other issues important to the family now and in the future. For example, management initiatives that may run counter to family values may serve as triggers for engaging with the family council. A board that works well with the family council can help avoid misunderstandings on the part of the family and blunders on the part of management. Joint sessions of the board and the family council can produce a cooperative relationship of trust and respect that can go a long way toward avoiding and resolving tense situations that may emerge in the future. Other options are for the board to invite the family council chair to attend a portion of a board meeting; and it is especially helpful if the board chair and family council chair have regular dialogue.

The Family Council and the Owners

The family council's relationship with the owners could be more complex than its relationship with the board and management. While family members may or may not be on the board or be employees in the business or be on the family council, owners and future owners will in any case definitely be part of the family council. With so much potential for overlap between family governance and ownership, it is likely that the family council represents owners in some way; the question will be to what extent and on what issues. Moreover, the overlap in membership makes it difficult to form a policy on how to interact with the owners as a distinct group.

Family councils can interact with owners by including ownership and family council boundaries as part of their charter, by addressing some but not all ownership issues, for example. Family council practices may include connecting with a distinct shareholder group or shareholder representative; a designated owner who is a liaison with the family council who may even be included as a member of the family council. Some families limit membership in the family council to family owners and future owners as they anticipate that many of the issues coming before a family council will have an ownership component, and they consider this private and separate from issues concerning the rest of the family. Other family councils will have a separate owner committee.

Whatever a family council does to serve owners, it should be clear that the family council is serving a segment of the family; whether or not owners initiate a formal process to do so, the family council should ensure that owners sanction its work. A family council may define the qualifications and even handle the nomination of family members who will serve on the board, but it will be the shareholders who elect them, and it may be up to the family council to lead the shareholder process to elect or appoint family directors. The family council can determine the configuration of a board of directors, can find a consensus on significant divestitures or acquisitions, and can provide a foundation for liquidity decisions, but these tasks are a service to the owners. The Dubois case above illustrates how a family council can play a significant role in the development of a distribution policy, but it became the shareholders' policy to be communicated to their board, not the family's policy. Protecting owner sensitivities when non-owners on the family council seem to exert too much influence regarding owner issues is an important function of the family council. With clarity about when the family council is working for the whole family and when it is working for the owners only, the family council can provide tremendous value. Dealing with owners is just a little more complex than dealing with management or the board, each of which have their own forums or domains; with the owners, the domains are much more likely to overlap.

Family councils including all family members commonly handle both family and owner issues, especially if there is action to be taken, by officially stopping one meeting and immediately starting the next one. That is, a family council meeting might begin at 8:00 a.m. and adjourn at 10:00 a.m., and right after a short break the shareholder meeting might begin. Some business families depend upon this forced segmentation to help them keep matters separate enough while practically benefitting from one forum. Families differ on how they handle the transition from the family council meeting to the shareholder meeting. For those who value privacy, all family members who are not shareholders may be excused from the second segment. Other families value openness, and everyone will be invited to stay but only share-holders will vote on or decide matters concerning ownership. In larger families with a representative family council, the family council is authorized to speak on behalf of the owners, for example, conveying a request to the board.

Family owners who otherwise collaborate well can be quite dysfunctional when they are focusing on their shares and the control they have with them relative to other family members or branches. Ownership does not always provide an effective forum for developing overarching goals and resolving differences. A family council can provide the forum for shareholder unity and continue to be a service to the entire family with proper attention to the boundaries.

Family Councils with Family Offices and Family Foundations

We've addressed the family council's relationship to the family association, management, the board, and owners, but what if there is also a family office or a family foundation? Lank and Ward[3] provide a structure for the relationships a family council must maintain within a large business family with multiple business and family entities. Figure 12.5 connects the family council to the boards of both the family office and family foundation, both of which are likely to have non-family directors and other staff.

Family offices vary in purpose and scope, but the director and staff of a family office usually play a significant support role for the family council. Funding of the family council may fall within the scope of a family office, as may also logistics, communications, and the education and development of the family. Even if the family council is funded by other means, the family office may have a contract to provide the former with services. Coordination between the family office and the family council is managed by the elected chair of the family council and the director of the family office who may also participate in family council meetings. For example, a family council's education committee may be supported by the education director employed in the family office. The family education committee could be involved in establishing philosophy, vision, and goals while the professional in the family office could

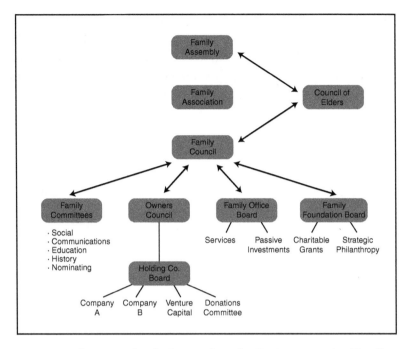

Figure 12.5   Structure for the Large, Complex Business-owning Family

work on in-house development opportunities and arrange for access to outside resources.

The family council in turn may initially be involved in establishing the scope, governance configuration, and goals of the start-up family office. In providing a resource for the family office board, the family council may play a lasting role in nominating family members to the family office board. A family council's charter may also require that one member must be a member of the family office board if a strong connection is desired.

Like the family office, the family council may be involved in nominating family directors to the family foundation's board. The foundation director would be a liaison with the family council and provide a communication conduit, but most the active philanthropic involvement on the part of the family would fall within the scope of the foundation. Like the director of the family office, the chair of the family council and the foundation director would be responsible for communication and coordination. Family members who participate on the foundation board and on the family council may be asked to aid in linking the family council's activities and direction to those of the board of the foundation. Their membership in both forums positions them to strengthen communication between the two forums and some families make communicating an explicit rather than informal role expectation.

13

Family Communications

Families thrive on quality information and choke on the perception of a lack of transparency. Making a family governance process work at a high level requires vigilance by those communicating important information to ensure that great ideas and progress and news of any kind are disseminated properly. This simple task of passing on useful information builds trust in the system, which speeds up decision making and decreases hidden and real conflict in families.

This chapter discusses the many types of communication required to make the family governance system operate properly and to promote transparency. Figure 13.1 shows a graphical representation of communication avenues between the typical standing bodies found in enterprising families. The arrows represent communication lines in this

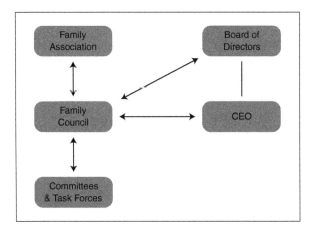

Figure 13.1 Communication Avenues in Enterprising Families

graphic, not lines of authority (these were addressed in chapter 12). As you can see, the family council is situated at the epicenter of healthy communication.

The Communications Nerve Center: The Family Council

Ensuring effective communication is one of a family council's core purposes. Knowing what to communicate and when will help family council leaders and members gain the family's support as they fulfill their roles. In each of the descriptions below, we will assume that the family has grown to the point of needing a representative family council, but the concepts are quite similar for smaller families that do not have a representative family council, and this chapter will still be useful for them too.

Communication between the Family Council Chair and Council Members

The most important information the family council chair communicates to council members is direction about where the group is heading and accurate summaries of where the group has been. Direction is established by sending out agendas well in advance of family council meetings—preferably at least two weeks before the meeting to allow adequate consideration of the ideas. Members should have an opportunity to submit agenda items to the chair before the agenda is finalized. Agendas may be accompanied by interesting articles related to an upcoming topic or family matter, drafts of documents that will be reviewed, or proposals under consideration. In this way, family council members feel respected by the chair, and the meeting will not begin with venting about having no input or receiving too little advance notice.

During family council meetings, the family council chair typically reminds the group how each topic of interest fits into the family's mission and purpose, thus reinforcing those core concepts and the direction of the family council. Some family council leaders share stories or examples illustrating how other families in business function; these examples serve to educate the council. When appropriate, a chair will bring in an expert speaker on a topic so as to educate the group sufficiently for an informed discussion on an important topic.

Family Council Communication with
Committees and Task Forces

The family council is responsible for making sure that all committees and task forces are functioning properly and pursuing the purposes they were created to address. An effective tool for accomplishing this is for each committee or task force chair to provide meeting agendas, minutes, and progress reports. Sending agendas in advance allows the family council chair to determine if the information would be useful to the group. When meetings are held, notes should be completed within a week or two, so as not to become stale. In most families, the family council should request quarterly progress reports. The progress report is a brief update of no more than one or two pages on key initiatives, progress to date on those initiatives, and next steps identified. Progress reports may also include document drafts or emerging proposals. The task force or committee chair fosters trust and demonstrates leadership by holding to this type of communication.

Periodically, the chair of a task force or committee will report orally to the family council. This is particularly valuable when new concepts are being considered by the group and when there are many nuances associated with these concepts. For example, a philanthropy committee that is for the first time considering engaging the services of a consultant to advise on foundation structure and governance may wish to speak directly to the family council about the initiative, why it is being considered, and what its goals and boundaries are. Including the concept in a written proposal may raise more questions than it answers, and the benefit to the family may be lost because of misperceptions. Attending physically assures that both the spirit and the letter of the issue are communicated effectively.

The family council also has a responsibility to the committees or task forces to communicate key initiatives that may impact their work. If a task force is developing a policy for sharing a family property, a potential decision by the family to invest in a home next door to the property that just became available should be communicated to the task force. This is all part of being transparent and allows the task force to determine how such a decision might impact its work. Finding out after months of effort that the family council has taken action to negate the task force's hard work would only foster feelings of disrespect and frustration among task force members, and this could result in distrust toward the council. Keeping everyone informed nurtures trust.

Communication Expectations between Council Members and Their Branches and Units

A family council composed of family members from different branches and generations provides an avenue for informally disseminating information to the family. It is generally an unwritten expectation that members of the family council will communicate important information to members of their own family unit that are not currently serving on the council. Especially important is being able to provide some color to the black-and-white meeting minutes the entire family has seen or to rumors about family council activities that need further elaboration.

The most common approach to this type of information dissemination is to have an individual family council member from each branch reach out to the members of their branch either through meeting in person or through phone calls to talk about specific topics needing attention. If a branch is not currently represented on the council, a member may be assigned to reach out to that branch. Typically, the council member shares an important happening at the council meeting and asks branch members to offer input or concerns regarding the topic. This is not a problem-solving session but merely an approach to information sharing designed to give those who are not council members a voice, and it allows the family council representative to take information back to the council. We emphasize that the goal of this information sharing process is to support excellent communication, not to foster branch thinking that may threaten the greater family unity. Special care should be taken to avoid perceptions that any family branch has interests separate from those espoused by the family council.

Obviously, the ability to deliver accurate information in a respectful manner is a skill that family council members should possess. Family council members should present information only when they feel they have a firm grasp on the concepts being discussed, can respond to questions in a nondefensive manner, and have the family council's support for sharing the information. This last point deserves special mention, as there are times when sharing a concept or idea under consideration would be premature and could cause strife in the family rather than build trust. For example, a family member may bring a proposal to the board chair to coinvest in his own start-up venture, but the family may not yet have any written philosophies or policies regarding the matter. In that case, the board chair can then inform the family council chair and ask for clarity on the family's philosophies regarding start-up investments of this nature. At the next family council meeting, the family council chair may then present a proposal and explain the board chair's request for clarification. At this point, sharing specific information with the broader family about the individual investment proposal would be both inappropriate and unfair because it would single out one family member's investment concept and transmit information that was likely expected to remain confidential. A better path forward would be for the family council meeting minutes to reflect the new initiative—gaining clarity on the family's beliefs and philosophies regarding venture funding—and family council members could explain that the new initiative is to help guide the family in the future as individuals demonstrate entrepreneurial spirit and may wish to access company funds to launch start-ups or buy existing businesses.

Occasionally, when engaging in this type of information sharing, family council members learn of new issues and concerns from their particular branch of the family. It is important that family council members not fall into the trap of bypassing any formalized communication channels between branch members and the family council. For example, if the family council's policy on submitting new proposals is well established, family council members should encourage member of their branch to submit a formal proposal if a new issue has been raised in informal discussions. Sharing reactions to a concept the family council has already proposed can help the broader family as the council seeks to clarify how best to implement a concept. Bypassing an established process for submitting new ideas detracts from family unity.

Communication between the Family Council and the Family Association

Continuously sharing the family council's activities is a core purpose of communications between the family council and the family association. These communications are a constant reinforcement of the family's vision, values, and mission—which are the enterprising family's core purposes and the reasons for working together as a group. Astute family councils will actively seek ways to promote this sense of purpose through a steady flow of information shared in a variety of formats, thus demonstrating transparency in the system and creating an environment of trust.

We want to briefly remind readers here that while we believe in the importance of information sharing, those receiving the information have a duty to treat it confidentially. If the family has not already had substantial discussions about the need for confidentiality, we recommend that these discussions take place before significant information dissemination begins. Everyone should understand what it means to treat information confidentially, how to recognize what types of information can be shared, what must be kept confidential, and what to do if they engage in or hear of a breach. Expectations surrounding confidentiality should be reviewed by the family association periodically—at least annually or when taking on new members.

The family's vision, values, and mission are reinforced through a variety of means, most commonly through periodic progress reports from the family council to the family association. Progress reports should include statements about key initiatives underway and how those initiatives are moving the family toward the vision, values, and mission members have agreed upon. Progress reports can also include upcoming activities or events that the family can look forward to. Above all, progress reports are a transparent means of allowing the family council to remain accountable to the association by sharing what the family has agreed to and how it has progressed with those agreements. Policy development is an excellent example to consider. For example, if at its last family association meeting the group agreed to create a policy guiding shareholder use of a family airplane, a progress report submitted six months later would provide an opportunity to demonstrate actions that have been taken to develop the policy.

Sending out agendas well in advance of upcoming family association meetings is highly desirable. Thirty days or more advance notice is recommended, as family members will need to work out final logistics for travel, child care, and the like. Receiving the agenda early strengthens the family's belief that the family council is organized and taking its role seriously. Moreover, sending along articles or sample policies related to topics on the agenda is a way to increase the knowledge base of association members, and they will need time to read and digest the ideas presented. Distributing family council minutes to the association is another excellent way to keep the family informed about the council's activities. Notes should be kept as short as is prudent, with brief summaries of key points discussed and a list of points of agreement or action steps established. When taking notes, it is not necessary to identify who said what when trying to capture discussion summaries. For example, rather than say, "Pat and Karen would like the family to consider a prenuptial agreement policy that would be applicable to all new marriages," it is preferable to simply state, "We discussed the possibility of implementing a prenuptial agreement policy that would be applicable to all new marriages." This latter approach does not single out the presenters and thus allows the entire family council to own the topic. Furthermore, a simple statement identifying any next steps will let the reader know what is happening next, such as, "We agreed to have our attorney present a summary of prenuptial agreement pros and cons at our next family association meeting so we can learn more about the issue prior to initiating any policy discussions." While sharing notes fosters trust, some families prefer not to share family council meeting notes with the broader association. Reasons cited for not doing so include fears that information will be misinterpreted or cause excess work for family council members when they have to explain complex topics; there is also concern that the spirit of the discussions can be presented only orally. Families with these concerns prefer periodic progress reports to sharing notes. Of course, the family council still is responsible for making sure that notes will be taken for the family council meeting to provide a record of the discussions and for distributing them in a timely manner (usually within 20 to 30 days).

While family councils have a responsibility to provide information, family association members have an equally important responsibility to receive that information graciously. It takes a lot of work to coordinate and execute effective communication, and family association members who ignore information or respond emotionally to new information with accusations or complaints are not being productive. When receiving information, family association members have a responsibility to study the information and then to identify confusing areas that need further elaboration. Receiving information graciously means the recipient recognizes the hard work of the family, sends questions to the appropriate family council leader, and prepares to share questions or concerns during the family association discussion in a calm manner. Heightened emotions lead to poor decision making.

Emails, family newsletters, and websites are other common communication forms used by family councils to foster an environment of trust and information sharing. E-mail updates are easy and may include information related to shareholder matters (i.e., dividend reports or upcoming deadlines for tax filing) or family matters (such as announcements of family parties or invitations to a family trip). E-mail should not be used to raise controversial issues or ask loaded questions of the broader family because e-mail is an ineffective means to work through tough or nuanced issues. Family newsletters typically include stories about what individual family members are doing, family members' accomplishments, birthday announcements, pictures, and information about company events family members are invited to attend. These newsletters are usually written in a manner that is fun to read. Family websites range from fun sites (sharing pictures and casual communications) to the very sophisticated (access to all family policies, a platform for family voting, confidential investment or company performance information, family contact information, and so forth). Personal security and information privacy needs should be considered when engaging in these types of family communications.

Active family councils commonly send groups of family members to meetings, workshops, or seminars that enhance the family's knowledge base. These events would include trips to meet with other enterprising families and share insights and attending programs on working in or governing family enterprises, family foundations, or family offices. They might even include competency-based programs, such as courses on financial management for non financial managers, effective wealth management, or effective communication. With any of these activities, it is important that the attendees pass on the information to the broader family, and the family council has the responsibility to make sure that this happens. Requiring summary reports from those attending (especially when the family funded the activity) or having attendees give an oral presentation at the next family association meeting are common approaches. This not only creates a forum to share important information, it reinforces the belief that the family can expand its knowledge while pursuing broader family goals.

Communication between the Family Council and the Board

A second major communication avenue shown in figure 13.1 runs between the family council and the board. Even if your family has a shareholder representative or owners' council in place, there will be times when it is useful for information to be shared between the family council and the board. The family should have a clear policy about how these communications will be managed, but most families will only allow communications between the family council chair and the board chair or between those assigned by the chairs to manage communication. These clear lines assure that both family and board will be speaking with one voice to each other, avoiding time-consuming chaos and distrust that would result if many individual family members or directors were holding side discussions.

These communications commonly update the board chair on the family's philosophies relating to the business or request information from the board about ways the enterprise is fulfilling the vision, mission, and values set forth by the family. Family council chairs may also need to clarify information (sometimes misinformation) that they pick up through the rumor mill, or they may need to ask about the board's progress toward a family initiative. For example, if the family made the decision to hold an annual board evaluation for the first time ever, the family council chair might ask for a progress update from the board chair on the board performance evaluation.

Similarly, board chairs at times need a conduit to the family, and the family council chair represents this conduit. Board chairs may request the family's input on a variety of issues from executive stock ownership plans, changing the nature of the business, changing corporate types, to relocating headquarters and matters of policy. Board chairs may also assign tasks to the family, such as requesting that the family clarify its liquidity needs or that the family give prompt feedback about a staff reduction plan in its hometown operations.

Some family council chairs will sit in on board meetings or even serve on the board in accordance with a structural agreement within the family (see chapter 12 for more on this topic); they represent the voice of the family and gain important information about board initiatives that can be communicated to the family. Similarly, board chairs often meet with the broader family during family association meetings to provide an update on the company and discuss key initiatives or concerns.

Communication between the Family Council and Management

In an enterprising family, it is imperative that the family avoid intrusion into management and minimize communications that can be interpreted as directives to the CEO and other members of management. Figure 13.1 presents the obvious solution, which is to limit communication to a direct link from the family council to the CEO. More specifically, the family council chair and the CEO maintain an open line to communicate necessary information for proper connection between the two bodies.

There are numerous communications that might occur between the family council chair and the CEO. In addition to sending quarterly company updates to the family, the CEO may wish to present a "state of the business" report at an upcoming family association meeting, and the family council chair would work with the CEO to identify the most useful information to present. The family council chair could alert the CEO to the family's feelings on a variety of matters and encourage greater coverage of those areas. Similarly, the family council chair may encourage the CEO to avoid certain topics that the family is not yet ready to address. The family council chair can also communicate the family's appreciation of management's efforts and work with the CEO to find effective ways to communicate this appreciation to the management group. The CEO will not typically give the family assignments as the board chair would, but the CEO may wish to share management's perspective on some aspect of the enterprise and will work with the family council chair on how and in what forum to best present the matter so as to maximize learning. Lastly, the family council chair may wish to coordinate with the CEO the utilization of company resources, such as the family's need to communicate with the CFO on tax matters or with the VP of Human Resources on a family internship program.

Just as important as knowing what to communicate is to know what not to communicate. The family council chair should not communicate any directives that have not been first vetted with the entire family council or even the family association if the matter is of great importance.

The family council chair should also verify that no family members are directing management either deliberately or accidentally through interference. Interference happens, for example, when a family member stops by the firm's office for a visit and remarks to one of the staff, "We should really get a new refrigerator in the room." The staff member hearing of the suggestion may interpret this as a direct request and act accordingly. All family members must be diligent to avoid this type of communication, and the family council chair should work with the CEO to monitor this dynamic. In addition, the CEO should be sure not to direct the family through the family council chair. Directives to the family will emanate from the board chair to the family council chair, unless the CEO and chair roles are held by the same person.

Communication between the Family Council and Outside Advisors

The family will periodically need to communicate with outside advisors of the business, foundation, or family office. Lack of coordination and oversight will lead to high advisor bills and missed opportunities to share information applicable to the entire family. The family council should have a clear policy or practice identified for how the broader family will relate to outside advisors. The most common advisors used are from the accounting and legal professions, and the family council must clearly identify the boundaries between the family and these advisors. The family council chair typically serves as the primary conduit between the family and the outside advisor when the family needs to speak to the advisor. An example illustrates effective communications with an advisor.

> Rob and Janet— members of a small family consisting of twelve members—wanted to complete their estate planning and needed a business valuation to model their plan. They contacted their business's accountant to discuss the matter and obtain the relevant information. The accountant had previously spoken to the family council chair, who directed that all communications between family shareholders and the accountant would need to be approved by the family council. The accountant informed Rob and Janet about the expectations and asked for permission to speak with the family council chair, Amber. They granted permission, and the accountant called Amber to discuss the matter.

During the discussion, it became clear that Rob's and Janet's need was likely shared by other family members, and a more formal valuation would be needed to provide evidence that the valuation was accurate. Amber then spoke to Rob and Janet about the broader family's need, and they agreed to Amber's suggestion that they bring their company accountant in to discuss valuations and their impact on estate planning. Amber then secured the support of the family council and planned for the education session. When the meeting finally occurred the following month, it was discovered that senior generation members Mark and Mary Jo were also in need of updated information to evaluate their estate plans. It had been years since the family had visited the issue of estate planning, and changes in the business and the legal environment required an update.

Note that Rob and Janet were just trying to get an answer to a legitimate question. Had the accountant spent time educating them on the issue of valuation or taken any action to determine valuation, Mark and Mary Jo may have missed the opportunity to learn and get information they needed. Moreover, if the accountant had contacted the company CEO and suggested a valuation, the CEO might have been surprised and resentful of a family member going behind his back and causing accounting fees to accumulate. Instead, the accountant directed Rob and Janet to the family council chair, whose legitimate authority to bring in a family resource lead to a better outcome for the family.

A common family council approach to working with advisors is to clarify what services will be available to family members from family advisors and approve those services with the family association. Family association members are then free to reach out to the advisor within the guidelines set by the family. The family council then monitors the relationship to make sure the family's needs are being met and the fee arrangements are reasonable. On this latter point the family may request that professional fees for work for individual family members are itemized separately from general billing to the family enterprise to allow appropriate monitoring.

Communication Skills in the Family

Whether in a family association, family council, family committee, or family task force meeting, families do well to make sure that the quality of their interactions enhances productive communication rather than detract from it. The time and energy needed to establish these bodies and pursue the family's agenda is substantial, and nothing sours the journey more than confusing or hostile communication or outright failure to communicate. Here are some ways to make the journey more enjoyable.

Family members may not know how to present an idea to the group. What often happens is that a family discussion is taking place and someone gets emotionally triggered by an idea or interaction, then predictably escalates the situation by shouting something like, "Why are we doing that?" This negative energy can spread to other family members who become confused or triggered by the belligerent comment. As a result, the group may soon lose focus; instead of discussing ideas, it will be responding to emotions. This is not productive. Family members do well, either as individuals or in a family forum, to master the principles of emotional self-management. Not only will the individuals feel better about family meetings, but the group will benefit from a more rational discussion. Training in communication or counseling can help foster this greater awareness, as can readings on emotional intelligence and effective interpersonal communication. These are skills that need to be practiced over time.

Even when family group members are well in control of their emotions, making a presentation to the group may cause anxiety, or family members may simply not know how to give an effective presentation. Family council meetings or family association meetings can be an effective forum for teaching these skills. For example, Jeff and DeDe were the co-chairs of their family's education committee and identified a family need to foster group presentation skills. They searched for someone who could work with the association and found Dale, who was an expert at teaching public speaking skills. Later that year, Dale joined the family in Scottsdale to lead a half-day workshop on public speaking and presenting ideas before the group. Nearly the entire family was there, and family members learned what they could do to be more effective as presenters and what they were doing that was ineffective. Everyone had the chance to practice to reinforce the group's learning. Especially in family groups that struggle to hold effective communications, training in presentation skills is a primary way to improve the quality of meetings.

A second needed skill that may not come naturally is responsiveness. Family members may receive information but simply not know how to respond to, or just ignore, prompts for feedback or group input. The resulting silence reduces the connectivity; the communication sender experiences a loss of connection with those not responding and may even perceive the lack of response as passive-aggressive behavior. Working on the family's behalf is challenging in its own right, and failure to respond to those working for the family is evidence of irresponsibility and indifference regarding effective communication. In contrast, responding to each email or call to which a response is recommended creates a pattern that benefits the entire family. Family members who consistently do not respond to requests signal their disrespect for the family's goals and the entire communication process. At the very least, every communication requesting input deserves a quick reply such as, "looks good" or "nothing to add" or "thanks." This message lets the sender know that the effort to communicate has been respected, and it communicates that the recipient is taking on responsibility for himself or herself. Very few people cannot respond within a day or two with modern technology's toys. Some families even agree to a time period in which everyone must respond.

Another communication skill involves managing personal conflict in and outside of meetings. There will be times when an interpersonal conflict emerges outside of the family governance process and involves only a few individuals—maybe just two. For them, being around each other may be difficult and cause feelings of discomfort, anxiety, fear, or anger. It is important that interpersonal conflicts between a few family members not creep into the family process, unless the conflict directly relates to issues that the broader family is addressing at the meeting. If a person cannot control his or her emotions when in the presence of another, it may be more productive that he or she not attend the meeting. This applies only rarely as most thorny family conflicts can be subordinated to the needs of the broader family.

After Edward and his sister Vickie had a blowup over alcohol-induced comments Edward had made regarding Vickie's lifestyle choices, their relationship had soured. For now, both spouses were staying out of the conflict, but both Edward and Vickie could feel the tension. On the day before a multiday family meeting during which they would be in the same room, each ruminated about the other, fearing there would be another major blowup in front of their aunts, uncles, and cousins. The embarrassment of doing so would be terrible, but both imagined it happening. Getting to sleep was a challenge for both of them that night.

The next day, while there was awkwardness when they greeted each other, neither brought up the incident but engaged in the family meeting discussions. With the passage of time came a renewed desire to reestablish contact, and a few weeks later Edward apologized for his actions, as both siblings had done many times before when they had hurt each other.

Fearing an interpersonal conflict at a family meeting is natural if there is unfinished business between two or more family members. However, usually the presence of the extended family is enough to keep emotions in check and allow for a productive meeting. In some families, the parties involved in an interpersonal conflict are encouraged to meet prior to the family meeting so as to get the issue out on the table and begin putting the matter behind them or at least make plans to work on it. This helps defuse emotions and keeps them out of the larger family meeting. Of course, if the conflict is related to the broader family process, time may have to be set aside in the family meeting to acknowledge the issues that are impeding the group's process. But if the conflict is not a group matter, those involved must leave it behind at the door.

Conclusion

When it comes to communication, the saying "An ounce of prevention is worth a pound of cure" is true in many ways. By ensuring a smooth flow of communication between all parts of the family governance process, time-consuming and energy-draining meetings to resolve misperceptions and distrust are minimized. Knowledgeable shareholders are better able to support management and board direction and can enhance decision making that supports the enterprise. By taking time to establish effective communication channels, expectations, and skills, families are better positioned to take on tough challenges as they emerge.

14

The Journey Forward

The changing global business landscape has created tremendous disruption in many traditional industries and launched new wealth-creating opportunities that could hardly have been imagined a few years ago. At the time of this writing, it appears that continued changes in financial markets, geopolitical stability, and technology will require that businesses innovate to cope with and capitalize on these changes. Businesses that were once only local now find themselves competing with global competitors and must find ways to deliver new products and services to maintain their market position. Others find that new technologies offer an opportunity to serve the needs of those on the other side of the planet, not just those in a local, regional, or national community. It will take courage to take on the business challenges the future will present.

The concept of family also continues to shift as changing social mores lead to different definitions of lifelong relationship partners; changing birth rates and immigration practices cause old family traditions to wane and new ones to emerge, and exposure to different cultures is made easy through travel and communication technologies, bringing new thinking to the concept of what constitutes a family. These macro changes make managing ever growing families more complex; new opportunities are accompanied by new stressors that many families simply have no experience managing. It will take courage to take on the family challenges the future will present.

The challenges found in managing family and business dynamics has always been part of human existence. Holy Scripture is filled with stories of family governance challenges. For example, a good king leads his people to prosperity, but then the kingdom falls on hardship when a son fails to hold the throne effectively. Or two siblings may be in conflict over an inheritance and how well they represent the family's honor. In other stories, an entire population and way of life is threatened due to the rise of foreign powers. Indeed, the challenges today's enterprising families encounter are nothing new, nor is the power of the family to manage the challenges they face. Families consistently exhibit the human characteristic of adaptation and endurance, and enterprising families are well positioned to lead the world through these challenges.

We wrote this book with the intent of sharing how purposeful families can organize themselves to deal with the challenges they encounter. Rather than present a model to fit everyone, a task we consider unproductive, we have set about to describe the many facets of family organization, building on the concepts of an integrated family governance process that families can adapt to fit their purposes. While business owners have a long history of experience with effective boards of directors,[1] its family counterpart—the family council—has become popular only in recent years. It will no doubt continue to evolve as families change and new technologies and skill development render old ways of doing things obsolete. It may be that new family organizational structures will also emerge that better aid enterprising families.

As enterprising families continue to become more aware of their organizational needs, new professional services will emerge to meet these needs. Even today, families can access education to address strategic and financial acumen, career direction, wealth and retirement planning, communication and conflict resolution, emotional self-management, decision making, security, and many other topics. The future will no doubt include many services to help bridge generational gaps comfortably with technology providing the means of maintaining family connections.

And yet, even the wealthiest of families are urged to exercise caution when using these services. Learning still starts at home, and the discovery of a family's very reason for existence or carrying on an enterprising tradition cannot be outsourced. At its core, each family has a mandate to discover (or rediscover) its purposes and organize around them. While hired advisors can carry out a family's directives, the family will always own the responsibility for the self-discovery needed to sustain passion and a common purpose among all members. The failure to do so will necessarily lead to erosion of the bonds that connect family members to each other.

Families that have deeply explored their primary purposes for existence often gain enough confidence to more openly share themselves with others who can help them reach family goals. Enterprise founders are often notorious for keeping important information hidden from others in an effort to maintain control and a competitive advantage. This includes information that the family needs to develop its own capacities. When families implement more democratic processes of family governance, such as those described it this book, the act of sharing enhances the family's ability to go outside the family's limits for the sake of accomplishing something greater than each individual's financial gain. Partnering with management to expand the company's footprint and using the family's foundation to achieve community-enhancing goals are just two examples of how a family learning to trust others (outside the family) can expand its influence on the world.

The past few years has seen an increase in support systems for enterprising families, allowing business families to meet with others sharing common challenges and hopes. A growing number of television shows feature enterprising families, making it more acceptable to identify the difficulties experienced when working or owning assets together. This trend is likely to continue as connections between people sharing common interests are made more possible through technology and more families have the confidence to reach out to others in the hope of learning something about themselves. Of course, the learning is almost always a two-way street. Astute families will not try to duplicate another family's organizational processes, but will use the knowledge to integrate new concepts into their current functioning, customizing solutions to their unique situation.

Enterprising families can flourish together as long as they can agree on common purposes and believe that staying together offers the best opportunity to achieve those purposes. Growing families will find that outliers may wish to pursue different purposes or believe that they are better off breaking away from the enterprising family. Respectful and dignified separations are a natural outgrowth of the democratic philosophies we espouse in these chapters. Mature, unified families realize that it is passion that keeps them connected and energized, not force and shame. In fact, when the family is unified around common purposes and wishes to be together, the work of family organization is made much easier than the alternative. Paradoxically, families that consider departure from the family acceptable often find less internal turmoil and greater commitment to making family organization work. This assumes that a compelling and binding purpose is pursued by those remaining.

In today's self-centered world the organized enterprising family offers opportunities to develop personal and leadership skills and capacities that may be difficult to acquire in the outside world. An organized family creates a forum for each of its members to accomplish something he or she could likely not accomplish alone; it offers members a chance to do great things with those most closely related to them in secure relationships despite even the most difficult relationship challenges. Organized families are regenerative; that is, younger members grow up to learn from and eventually replace senior members. This biological imperative, however, has consistently given way to more timeless family purposes, such as carrying on the founders' values long after they have passed away. We challenge each family to connect to its most unifying purposes and to use family organization as the tool that will result in the family's greatest impact on the world.

Appendix 1: Definitions

What is a family council and how does it differ from a family assembly or a family meeting? This is a good question and we will try to provide distinctions that will give practical direction. As a quick answer, we like the distinction we heard from a third-generation family member when his children asked him this question:

> "Well, I don't really know for everyone. But for us, the family council is five members who make the rules and the decisions affecting our relationship to our family business. The family assembly is everyone getting together to stay informed and decide if the ones making those decisions on the family council are going to continue doing it or will be thrown out and replaced, and a family meeting is what we used when we were smaller to do everything we now do in both."

Generally, family meetings can be divided into the following categories:

Family business meeting. When a family first begins to organize itself to share information and make decisions or plans, it uses a family meeting. There is specific attention to who will attend and why; for example, the first family meeting might include the parents and their one teenage child and three adult children to review the results of the parents' estate plan, or it could include the parents and their adult children and spouses to review the insurance programs coving family members and to listen to a family business advisor explain the family firm's compensation best practices. For small business families in the first and second generation, one or two family business meetings a year are sufficient to integrate new spouses into the family business, develop a learning culture with regard to business and family and owner interactions, and to develop group communication and decision making skills the families can rely on if they are confronted by serious matters that would otherwise threaten family relationships.

Family council. A family council is more formal than family business meetings, but the two share similarities in purpose and effect on the family and business. A family council is typically a representative group working on behalf of a larger family; much like a board of directors, a family council works for and represents a larger group of shareholders. Family council formality typically means a written charter that explains the extent and limitations of its purpose, initial goals, selection and terms of members, leadership of the group, and the relationship between the broader family and the family council as well as that between the family council and the board of directors and business management. There may be standing committees of the family council (they continue to exist, e.g., family philanthropy or next generation education) or ad hoc committees (they come together for a purpose, then dissolve, e.g., family employment policy committee). Many business families have family councils that are not representative but include the entire family until the family becomes too large (i.e., somewhere between twenty and thirty adults) for everyone to be on the family council; then the family forms a representative family council.

Family Assembly. This is a large family gathering for the purpose of getting everyone together for business and family reasons. Spouses and even young children are usually in attendance. A family assembly may have few restrictions regarding who participates; in fact, the purpose of many assemblies is to be all-inclusive so as to promote continuity and unity of the family. A family assembly is a forum for their family council to report its progress. Planned programs and activities teach values and culture to a growing family to continue the positive influence their values have had on the business and teach this even to the youngest children who might meet separately to be coached in an investment game or club and/or philanthropy or other age-appropriate activities.

Family association. A family association has a defined membership and is more exclusive than a family assembly. It might be limited to all direct descendants of the founder of the business, or it could be restricted to only those family descendants who continue to be shareholders. Still, it is often defined as including all adult family members, their spouses, and their children above the age of 16 (minimum ages can range from 13 to 18). The family association membership distinction might be defined as such in order to separate out the shareholder branches of a family, whose travel and meeting expenses are paid by the business, from the branches of the family that no longer have ownership. Members of the family association can vote and make decisions, and often this group elects members of the family council.

Owners council. An owners council differs from a family council in that it typically includes the senior family members who control the majority of the stock or are appointed to represent a large family shareholder group. A common purpose for maintaining an owners council is to communicate and coordinate estate plans so that the business is not hindered by conflicting structures; In addition, an owners council helps family members be on the same page with each other when representing themselves to the board and to design a board if one has not yet been formed or if their board will change with the generational transition. Owners councils may in some cases facilitate the cross-purchase of shares in order to maintain a desired balance of ownership among branches and to respond to individuals' liquidity needs. Few family firms need an owners council, but when there are a few senior members who must deal with ownership coordination separate from the affairs of a family council, it is a valuable function that permits active involvement of several family members. By defining the scope of an owners council as limited to ownership matters and the scope of a family council as limited to family relationships and family/business interaction issues, coordinated progress can be achieved in both arenas.

Owners councils can also be like committees. In one family firm, the senior generation of brothers and sisters began late in life to plan ownership transition. This became urgent to them all when one of the five siblings became critically ill. An owners council was formed so that they might catch up quickly with decisions about how their children should own the company, how the family would influence the business appropriately, and how the family could reassure that senior management that having multiple shareholders would not lead to micromanaging. By not using a family council for this purpose, the junior generation was able to proceed with education and similar continuity matters important to its preparation for eventual control and influence. Thus the senior generation focused on control issues and the junior generation concentrated on building teamwork.

Family Reunion. A family reunion is just that. We include the definition here to differentiate it from family assembly and family association. A family reunion has no business purpose, but serves only to reunite the family, strengthen relationships, and introduce remote or new family members to each other. Reunions strengthen large and scattered families through personal connection. A business family may hold a family association meeting and a family assembly back-to-back with a family reunion. A family council may focus one of its meetings on planning a family association meeting and a family reunion together even though many of the individuals attending the family reunion have not been stockholders for many years. The logic here is that a large part of the family will be together, so why not get everyone together and strengthen family bonds and forge a stronger connection between the shareholder family members and the larger family, all of whom are descendants of the business founder. Families may reason that values and family heritage will be strengthened among those who are in the shareholder group and that a strong family shareholder group is a greater asset to the company.

Executive council or executive committee. Another kind of family business structure, which shares a purpose with a family council, is a regular meeting consisting of just the family members who work in the business. It is problematic that the name, executive committee, is also used by many companies to refer to the senior management team's meetings with the CEO. For a family company, the family may or may not be in the senior management team. Executive committees typically include two generations and their purpose is to educate the younger generation and facilitate communication between the two generations. In many cases, these committees can act like a shareholder meeting if the shareholders all work in the business. As an illustration, one executive committee consists of the chairman and CEO and her younger brother, the president, and their eight sons and daughters who all work in a plastics manufacturing business in Eastern Canada. The two siblings consider the monthly meetings a forum for teaching their children how to run the business, and they share important decisions with them. The CFO and the director of sales are not family members and are not considered members of the executive committee, but they have recently become active participants in a portion of the meetings when business strategy is discussed. A separate senior management group also meets monthly; it includes the CFO and sales director and three members of the younger generation who occupy senior management positions. In another instance, four brothers meet weekly in an executive committee.

The weekly meetings allow the brothers to participate in key decisions, remain informed, communicate, and coordinate with each other regarding relevant business and owner matters and to generally support their "sibling partnership." Their weekly meetings last about one hour and are followed by a meeting with the members of the senior management team.

Shareholder meeting. With the existence of appropriate family business structures such as family councils, family meetings, and family assemblies, a shareholder meeting is free to be just that, a meeting of all the owners. Shareholder meetings, usually occurring once a year, include only the family members who own shares; they elect the board, review the past year's business performance, and conduct other business consistent with the corporate bylaws. For example, they may approve major shifts in the business capital structure, approve significant acquisitions or divestitures, and make adjustments to shareholder agreements.

Appendix 2: Family Council Charter Example

Origin

"At our family business retreat on November 7, 20XX, it was decided that a family council will be formed involving all family members above the age of 18. The purpose of the council will be to educate and facilitate communication between family members and to provide a forum for constructive discussion, problem solving, and decision making regarding the family as it relates to Smith Company as well as regarding the business as it relates to the family."

Purpose of the Family Business Council

Two immediate, short-term purposes for the council are to provide a forum for:

1. Managing the transition from John and Mary Smith's generation to the next and
2. Building teamwork among the next generation of owners of Smith Company.

In addition to these initial purposes, we will strive to accomplish other objectives.

1. We want a forum for constructive discussion to deal with the challenges that confront us as a family in business together. Our intention is to deal with challenges directly and the family council will be the forum.

2. We expect the council, as an informal body, to afford regular contact among family members and to be used to nurture relationships among members of the extended family and among members of the next generation of owners.

3. The council will provide a place for general communication between family members involved in the business. It is a place for questions to get answered and for us all to learn what everyone thinks about issues that affect us all. Our intention is to encourage and to make it okay for family members to bring up issues so we can address them properly.

4. As we go forward, we will need to learn. The council will provide an opportunity for individuals with special expertise affecting our family relations, investments, or the business to address us and help us learn.

5. The council will be a place for decision making. We will benefit from having a forum where all members have a voice in decisions that affect them. Our council will provide that opportunity.

6. And finally, for decisions that impact the business directly, the council will serve as the family's voice and provide this input directly to the board of directors. Therefore, regarding issues on which the board needs guidance from its shareholders, the council will serve as a forum for family decision making and consensus on the direction that is provided to the board. The family council will not limit direct communication between any shareholder and the corporation; instead, it will serve as an additional conduit for communication between the family and its legal representatives in the corporation, the board of directors.

Organization of the Family Business Council

Structure of Meetings. Meetings will be held off-site, away from the business. A business setting without interruptions will be selected and arranged for by the host (the one who organizes a particular meeting). Each council meeting will have two phases. The first phase will be a meeting of the next generation of shareholders. The second phase two will include all shareholders and other family members. In general, the first phase of the meeting will be for the business of the next generation, and the second will be for the business of the family as a whole.

Meetings. For the first year, meetings will be held monthly. Thereafter, meetings will be held as needed, but at least quarterly.

Membership. All stockholding direct descendants and relatives of John and Mary Smith, their spouses, and their children above the age of 18 are members of the family council.

Appendix 3: Family Council Assessment Form

Anonymous Questionnaire

Date

Dear Family Members:

I look forward to working with the family and family council. One very important step is to conduct a process of family council assessment and planning, which will take place on April 15. In preparation for our meeting, I've enclosed a questionnaire, and I ask that you complete and return it by Wednesday, April 9. You may mail it or fax your responses using the contact information below:

Steve McClure, Ph.D.

The Family Business Consulting Group

702 W Idaho St, Ste. 1100

Boise, ID 83702

208–342–7775 (phone)

866– 265–4945 (private fax)

mcclure@efamilybusienss.com (e-mail)

Instructions: For each statement, please place an "X" on the rating scale that corresponds to your own view. For comments, please answer honestly and as completely as possible. Your answers will be anonymous; that is, they will not be individually released. A summary of all responses and comments will be provided to each of you as a resource for our meeting on April 15.

Your answers do not have to be long or elegant; usually the first thing that comes to mind is the right answer.

Your thoughtful consideration of the following statements will help me plan the specific steps of our meeting. Thank you very much for taking the time to prepare in this way.

1. The family council is properly configured to help the family achieve its vision.

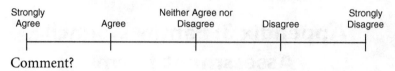

Comment?

2. The family council generally has the appropriate skills to address the opportunities and challenges currently encountered by the family.

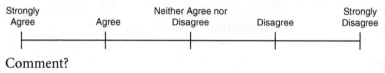

Comment?

3. The family council has a good understanding of the family's expectations.

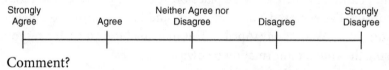

Comment?

4. The family council devotes appropriate time and attention to the long-term needs of the family and to monitoring the effectiveness of the efforts to meet them.

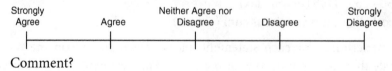

Comment?

5. The family council openly challenges the family, shareholders, and the board when appropriate.

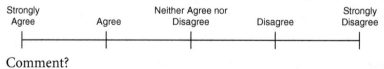

Comment?

6. The family council deals candidly and openly with conflict.

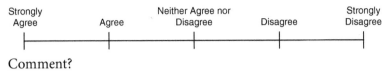

Comment?

7. The family council has a healthy balance of power between members and the full family it represents.

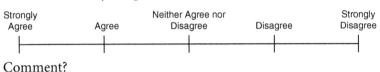

Comment?

8. The family council deliberates issues effectively and reaches resolution on key decisions.

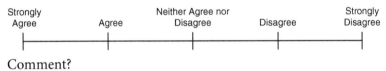

Comment?

9. The family council regularly and properly assesses and provides feedback to the family council chair.

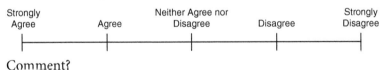

Comment?

10. The family is provided an appropriate opportunity to place items on the agenda in advance of family council meetings.

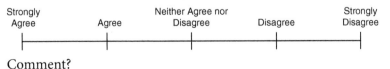

Comment?

11. The family council has an effective committee structure.

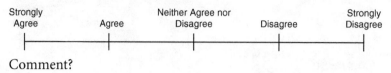

Comment?

12. The frequency and duration of family council meetings is appropriate.

Comment?

13. The full family council receives the appropriate type, amount, and detail of information needed to fulfill its responsibilities in governing the company.

Comment?

14. The family council has ample opportunity to develop as an effective work group.

Comment?

15. The family council is appropriately involved in the matters that fall within its scope.

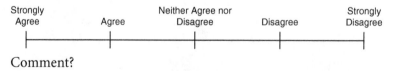

Comment?

16. The company makes available all information needed for the family council to fulfill its function.

Comment?

17. Management is open to provide all information needed for matters related to the effectiveness of the family council.

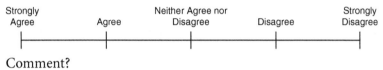

Comment?

18. The family council is appropriately involved in all matters within its scope.

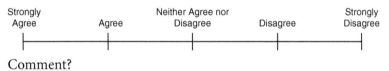

Comment?

19. Communication among the members of the family council and the family it represents is effective.

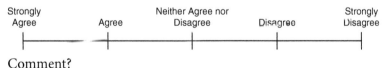

Comment?

Note format change below: The remaining items ask a specific question in addition to your level of agreement or disagreement with the statement or ask a question without the use of the rating scale.

20. Participation on the family council is a rewarding experience for me.

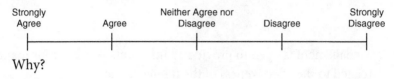

Why?

The family council meaningfully contributes to the success of the company and the family.

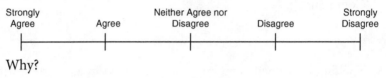

Why?

21. How would you change the meeting format?

22. Is there anything else you would like to say about the family council's effectiveness?

Appendix 4: Decision Making on Family Business Matters

Decisions, decisions—how do business families make them? To begin with, decisions can be divided into four different categories according to the respective roles of an owner, board member, employee (or manager), and family member in an organized setting such as a family council.

Among **owners** at stockholder meetings, decisions such as electing directors are generally made by casting votes according to one's ownership percentage; a simple majority (51 percent or more) carries the decision. **Boards** typically operate on the principle of one vote per person, regardless of how many shares individual directors own. A simple majority is usually required for a decision on most board matters, but good family business boards utilize a consensus style and only seldom call for a vote. For **management** teams, consensus decisions are often utilized to gain broad acceptance and valuable support when it comes time to implement the decision, an important feature when, for example, one department must give up its funding to support another's strategic initiative. Decision-making authority is often very explicitly defined in business management, so that everyone knows when s/he can make an independent decision and when, for example, the CEO must involve the board.

As our associates Craig Aronoff and John Ward have written, family business matters on which a family has primary decision responsibility include the following:

- Family values/mission/vision
- Communication in the family

- Family education
- Family relations
- Aiding troubled family members
- Resolving family conflicts
- Philanthropy
- Family/business relations
- Family employment policy
- Vacation home economics and use policy

These matters must be decided by families, often in family meetings, family assemblies, family councils, or their subcommittees. How do families who take on these issues make good decisions?

Centralized Leader

When faced with tough issues, many families default to a senior generation or senior family member. Parents, for example, are the leaders of a first-generation family and have natural decision-making authority. This makes decision making very clear and efficient. Sometimes, in second-generation businesses, the family decision-making authority will reside with an older brother or sister and be passed down to successively younger siblings as an older one relinquishes control of the business voluntarily or for health reasons. Decisions on family matters related to the business may be made by the one who controls the business.

As the family ages and grows, family leaders may respond by allowing family decision making to evolve. Faced with growing interest and pressure for involvement, a leader may opt for an approach that retains centralized decision making (the last word), but only after listening to the views of all other family members. Thus, in considering all opinions, the leader's decision may be regarded as more satisfying to all concerned, even to those who might disagree with it. A key factor, of course, is the level of trust and respect commanded by the leader; the more trust and respect, the more others will feel that the decision has been made with consideration of input from others.

While centralized decision making may serve some families, it rarely lasts beyond a generation or two. In many second-generation business families, and even more so for the later generations, groups make the decisions. One person making or controlling decisions becomes unfulfilling in that it does not allow all members of the family to feel they have a voice and may even contribute to apathy and reduced commitment to the family business. On the positive side, opening up decision making to a broader group

- makes it more likely that all positions will get a fair hearing;
- helps form the teamwork skills that are required for maintaining unity;
- helps maintain boundaries, in that family members with a voice in family matters will be less likely to get involved inappropriately in management and board decisions; and
- increases the likelihood of all family members feeling that their input is valued and utilized, and this potentially solidifies their commitment to the family business.

Voting

Families who make group decisions may adopt a rule of one vote per person. As with any decision-making method, voting eligibility must be defined, and it varies by the forum and each family's own rules for "who will have a voice." For example, a small family may have a family council that consists of all family members age 16 or older. Some families give the vote only to bloodline family members and exclude spouses while others include spouses. Larger, extended families may elect representatives to a more formal family council.

It is healthy for families to engage in voting on family matters. Voting can bring decisions to quicker resolution, and as long as everybody understands what the voting rules are, the group generally will be able to support the outcome. However, everyone needs to understand in advance what it takes to decide. A full discussion of all viewpoints followed by a vote with a simple majority rule is a common practice. Families who vote find that they are able to quickly move through agenda items. However, they may not achieve the same commitment that would be gained by those who seek consensus decisions.

Some families require a supermajority vote (e.g., two-thirds, 70 percent, or 80 percent) for key decisions. Their theory is that a simple majority may result in splitting the group in two. Members likely feel more support for the decision when the vote comes from more agreement at the time of the vote. However, we have seen families that use a simple majority to make decisions work quite well and that feel very good about their accomplishments.

Consensus

We know families that have successfully used consensus decision making for years. Consensus offers the opportunity for more successful implementation due to the broad support generated through the way the decision is made. However, some families define consensus as "100 percent of the group must agree on a decision" (unanimity), and we have seen these families at times struggle greatly as consensus decision making increases real conflict when the group tries to sway outliers to the group decision. Consensus decision making also takes time as a group tries to formulate the questions under consideration so that a decision can be made by the whole group. The group can easily get distracted and members get frustrates unless they have an excellent group process and negotiation skills, the assistance of a good facilitator, or both.

Most families realize that unanimity is not realistic and can cause too much pain in their families. One person can stop a good decision or frustrate the group to the point where families abandon family meetings. So if it is not unanimity, what is a good definition of consensus that allows progress and a fair hearing for minority viewpoints?

One method of defining consensus is a majority vote with an individual veto feature. This method allows each person to cast a vote in one of four ways. The person can support a decision by voting for it, oppose a decision by voting against it, abstain from a decision (for example, if the family member feels he or she does not have enough information or that the decision would perhaps in some way benefit him or her and the person wishes to allow the rest of the group to make the call), or object to the decision.

If the only possible votes are For, Against, or Abstain, then the majority will decide, and the family assumes that a consensus decision has been made. This is because a Against is understood to convey, "It's not my first choice, but I can live with it." However, if there is even one

Object vote, the proposal is defeated (no consensus). The reason only one Object vote is needed to defeat the decision is that everyone understands that the Object vote means, "I cannot live with this decision." In the case of one or more objections, some families follow these steps:

1. *Modify the proposal right away and vote again.* It is important to note that casting an Object vote obligates an individual to lead the process to finding an alternative that can be approved. The individual(s) who objects can explain further the concerns about the proposal, then he or she must offer an alternative (or someone else may, or the entire family group may seek to find an acceptable alternative) that considers all views, and another vote can then be taken right away.

2. *Discussion and development of an alternative proposal at another date.* Discussion takes the form of seeking alternatives and exploring the interests that are being served and not being served by the proposal. Again, the one with the Object vote leads the process. The objection may not be resolved during the current meeting and may continue until the next scheduled meeting or until an agreed upon deadline. Everyone must agree by the deadline.

3. *Impasse.* If as a result of an honest effort on the part of all to resolve the impasse, there is no change in positions and no acceptable solution is found, the objection remains intact, and the proposal does not go through.

4. *Breaking a deadlock.* This is not part of all policies, but some families insist on a procedure that keeps them from getting stuck or controlled by an "unreasonable minority." They may adopt mediation or arbitration procedures or require a supermajority that includes representatives from all family branches, for example, to move beyond an objection.

We like this method because it clearly defines consensus, allows individuals more choices than voting for or against (people are more complex than that, and they want their specific views to be heard by their relatives), and makes good use of the efficiencies of voting. Individuals must understand that they should use Object votes only in rare circumstances, and the practices of many families provide evidence that such a vote is indeed cast only rarely. Discussion among family members usually reveals early on who would Object, and a consensus alternative is then sought rather than an early vote. Other variations on the method include the following:

- Requiring a cooling-off period of 30, 60, or 90 days in order to allow further study and explore an issue or get more data. Sometimes back channels and further research will help all members overcome whatever objection there was to the original proposal or will allow the proposal to be modified so that it will be palatable to all.
- The family may commit to writing the arguments on both sides of the decision and allow a third party (such as a council of advisors or board of directors) to weigh in and render an opinion. This allows an outside group to share objective feedback as to what it considers best for the family and business.
- A task force can be assigned to study the issue and attempt to draft a new proposal that will take into consideration the needs of all parties.

Another variation is credited to the Quakers. An individual who originally Objected, after listening to the discussion, may choose to "stand aside." Standing aside means that an individual is subordinating his or her interests in favor of those of the family group. An individual is indicating that it is best for the family group to proceed and actively removes himself or herself from blocking a decision. A decision to "stand aside" can be viewed as an additional kind of vote, short of Objecting, but stronger than an Against vote, and sometimes this is just the point someone needs to make before allowing the group to come to consensus and move on.

Families have adopted many different procedures for decision making and rather than recommend one for all, we support families coming together and discussing how decisions will be made. The healthiest situation is one in which the entire family agrees ahead of time, unanimously, before a procedure is needed, as to how decisions will be made and then sticks to the decision-making procedure to which all members have agreed.[1]

Family Meeting/Assembly/Council
Decision-Making Methods

Making & Implementing Decisions

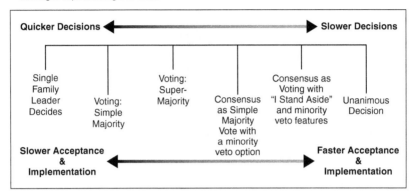

© Article used with permission from The Family Business Consulting Group, Inc.

Appendix 5: Examples of Shared Expectations

- Agendas should be received in time for review.
- All of our views are valued.
- All topics are fair game.
- Always be sober during meetings.
- Arrive on time.
- Ask for time-outs when needed.
- Assign a facilitator.
- Attack ideas, not people.
- Button pushing is unacceptable.
- Do not bring up old issues to spite others.
- Do not cut others off when they are speaking.
- Take responsibility for respectfully speaking what is on your mind.
- Calls or interruptions during the meeting are for emergencies only.
- End on time.
- If it is important, write it down.
- Items for agenda received well in advance of the meeting.
- Listen to what others are saying.
- No heavy artillery or dropping bombs.
- No one should be forced to participate against his or her will.
- No smoking in the meeting room.
- Call for breaks when emotions spike.
- No yelling.
- Say what needs to be said.
- Stick to the topic being discussed.
- Take needed breaks.

- Build on ideas, but don't beat a dead horse.
- We commit to agreements made during meetings.
- We will not set up subgroups or make secret agreements.
- What is said here stays here.
- Young children and infants should be left outside the meeting room.
- Meeting notes will be kept.
- Meetings will be held regularly, not just to manage crises.
- New topics will be discussed only after the agenda is finished.

Appendix 6: Family Advisor Candidate Rating Form

First complete individual ratings, then share and discuss with all members of the search committee.

1. If they encounter a challenge, they have the courage, sensitivity, and skill to engage us to make needed and difficult changes.

2. They will seek to understand our unique goals and values rather than impose a standard approach.

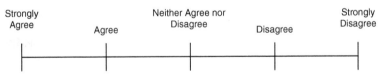

3. The consultants have the expertise and experience relating to both family and business, and they have a good balance between the two.

4. During the meeting, the consultants offered me enough of an opportunity to ask the questions I wanted to ask.

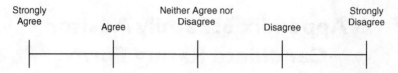

5. During the meeting the consultants clearly demonstrated that they accepted and respected my views.

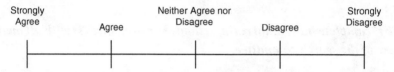

6. From the consultants' explanations in the meeting, I am able to clearly understand what they have to offer, and this fits well with my expectations.

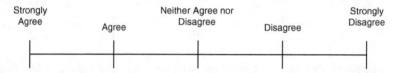

7. The consultants made it clear that they are willing to tailor their approach to our situation and goals

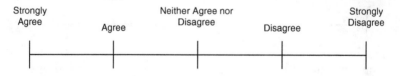

8. The consultants will change their approach when or if we require this.

9. I believe the consultants will be good listeners.

10. I believe the consultants will fit culturally with our family.

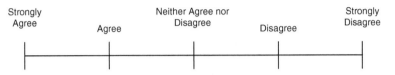

11. During the meeting, the consultants demonstrated wisdom; that is, I felt they provided thoughtful answers to questions based on their experience.

12. I trust the consultants' integrity.

Notes

1 Family Organization and Governance for Sustaining the Family Business: A Field Manual

1. Sullivan family's action plans written at the family's first family business retreat.
2. J. Astrachan and T. Kolenko, "A Neglected Factor Explaining Family Business Success: Human Resource Practices," *Family Business Review* 7, no. 3 (1994): 251–262.
3. Barry Levinson, *Avalon* (Tristar Pictures, 1990).
4. Michael Blake and Kevin Costner, *Dancing with Wolves* (Orion Pictures, 1990).

2 Reasons for Starting or Resisting a Family Council

1. See Gail Sheehy, *New Passages: Mapping Your Life Across Time* (New York: Random House, 1995), 135.

3 Stages of Family Businesses and Types of Family Councils

1. Craig E. Aronoff and John L. Ward, *Family Meetings: How to Build a Stronger Family and a Stronger Business* (New York: Palgrave Macmillan, 2011), 38–39.
2. Craig E. Aronoff, *Letting Go: Preparing Yourself to Relinquish Control of the Family Business* (New York: Palgrave Macmillan, 2003). Craig E. Aronoff, Joseph H. Astrachan, Drew S. Mendoza, and John L. Ward, *Making Sibling Teams Work: The Next Generation* (New York: Palgrave Macmillan, 1997). Craig E. Aronoff, Stephen L. McClure, and John L. Ward, *Family Business Succession: The Final Test of Greatness*, 2d ed. (New York: Palgrave

Macmillan, 2003). Craig E. Aronoff and John L. Ward, *From Siblings to Cousins: Prospering in the Third Generation and Beyond* (New York: Palgrave Macmillan, 2007). Craig E. Aronoff and John L. Ward, *Family Business Governance: Maximizing Family and Business Potential* (New York: Palgrave Macmillan, 1996). Craig E. Aronoff and John L. Ward, *Preparing Successors for Leadership: Another Kind of Hero* (New York: Palgrave Macmillan, 1992).

4 How to Start and Organize a Family Council

1. A. L. Delbecq and A. H. VandeVen, "A Group Process Model for Problem Identification and Program Planning," *Journal Of Applied Behavioral Science* 7 (July/August 1971): 466–91 and A. L. Delbecq, A. H. VandeVen, and D. H. Gustafson, *Group Techniques for Program Planners* (Glenview, Illinois: Scott Foresman, 1975).
2. Anything can be used for individuals to indicate their preferences, including each person marking the flip chart with check marks. The self-adhesive colored dots allow instant recognition of the items with the highest priority.
3. The origin of SWOT analysis is ascribed to Albert Humphrey who developed the technique at Stanford Research Institute from 1960 to 1970. Other participants on the research team were Marion Dosher, Dr. Otis Benepe, Robert Stewart, and Birger Lie.
4. We are unable to track down the original source. One of the authors first learned of using this acronym for meeting ground rules at a University Associates facilitator training program in the late 1970s. The above-mentioned ground rules were adapted to fit family meetings.
5. Craig E. Aronoff and John L. Ward, *Family Meetings: How to Build a Stronger Family and a Stronger Business*, 2d ed. (New York: Palgrave Macmillan, 2002).

5 Running the Family Council

1. John L. Ward, Untitled (unpublished archives of the Family Business Consulting Group, Chicago, 2007).
2. This age cutoff varies greatly and can range from 10 to 18 years. The rationale for an age cutoff is that exposure to the rest of the family at a formative age is important for understanding and appreciating the family's values.

6 Committees of the Family Council

1. Joline Godfrey, *Raising Financially Fit Kids* (Berkeley: Ten Speed Press, 2003).
2. Daniela Montemerlo and John L. Ward, *The Family Constitution: Agreements to Secure and Perpetuate Your Family and Your Business* (New York: Palgrave Macmillan, 2011).

7 The Family Assembly and the Family Association

1. From this point on, we will use the term family assembly to refer to the entire family, family association to refer to the decision-making body of the family, and family council to refer to the executive function of the family.
2. See appendix 4, "Decision Making on Family Business Matters," by Chris Eckrich and Steve McClure, article reprint from The Family Business Advisor, FBCG Publications, Chicago, IL.
3. See Craig Aronoff and John Ward, *Family Meetings: How to Build a Stronger Family and a Stronger Business* (New York: Palgrave McMillan, 2011).

8 Special Family Governance Structures: Owners Councils and Executive Committees

1. Craig Aronoff, "What Do 'Owners' Councils' Do?" in *The Family Business Advisor* (Marietta: Family Enterprise Publishers, 2000).
2. Interrelationships between owner and family governance structures will be covered in detail in chapter 12.

9 Family Leadership

1. Craig Aronoff and John Ward, *Preparing Successors for Leadership: Another Kind of Hero* (New York: Palgrave Macmillan, 2010) and Craig Aronoff and Otis Baskin, *Effective Leadership in the Family Business* (New York: Palgrave Macmillan, 2010).

12 Connecting the Family Council with the Board and the Business

1. A natural evolution for family firms involves an organized family beginning to have a voice in directing corporate donations. This is a transition stage for many. Family councils begin to collaborate with management so

that the philanthropic values of the family can be integrated with the commercial interests of the business. Later, a separation may occur and the business may continue its charitable goals while the family pursues its own philanthropic interests.

2. Christopher J. Eckrich and Stephen L. McClure, *Working for a Family Business: A Non-Family Employee's Guide to Success* (New York: Palgrave Macmillan, 2010).

3. Alden G. Lank and John L. Ward, "Governing the Business-Owning Family," FBN Newsletter FBN Newsletter, 26 (May 2000).

14   The Journey Forward

1. Jennifer M. Pendergast, John L. Ward, and Stephanie Brun de Pontet, *Building a Successful Family Business Board* (New York: Palgrave Macmillan, 2011).

Appendix 4   Decision Making on Family Business Matters

1. For an excellent discussion of the arenas into which various types of decisions will fit in a family business, we recommend the book *Family Business Governance: Maximizing Family and Business Potential* by Craig Aronoff and John Ward (Marietta: Palgrave Macmillan, 2011).

Index

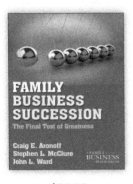

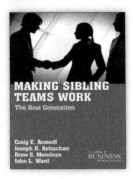

$23.00	$23.00	$23.00
978-0-230-11100-4	978-0-230-11106-6	978-0-230-11108-0

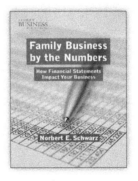

$50.00	$45.00
978-0-230-11121-9	978-0-230-11123-3

"Each Family Business Leadership publication is packed cover-to-cover with expert guidance, solid information and ideas that work."

—Alan Campbell, CFO, Campbell Motel Properties, Inc., Brea, CA

"While each volume contains helpful 'solutions' to the issues it covers, it is the guidance on how to tackle the process of addressing the different issues, and the emphasis on the benefits which can stem from the process itself, which make the Family Business publications of unique value to everyone involved in a family business—not just the owners."

—David Grant, Director (retired), William Grant & Sons Ltd. (distillers of Glenfiddich and other fine Scotch whiskeys)

CPSIA information can be obtained
at www.ICGtesting.com
Printed in the USA
LVHW082011120123
737032LV00001B/1